FLIGHT CALLS

Other Books from Bright Leaf

House Stories
The Meanings of Home in a New England Town
BETH LUEY

Bricklayer Bill
The Untold Story of the Workingman's Boston Marathon
PATRICK L. KENNEDY AND LAWRENCE W. KENNEDY

Concrete Changes
Architecture, Politics, and the Design of Boston City Hall
BRIAN M. SIRMAN

Williamstown and Williams College
Explorations in Local History
DUSTIN GRIFFIN

Massachusetts Treasures
A Guide to Marvelous, Must-See Museums
CHUCK D'IMPERIO

Boston's Twentieth-Century Bicycling Renaissance
Cultural Change on Two Wheels
LORENZ J. FINISON

Went to the Devil
A Yankee Whaler in the Slave Trade
ANTHONY J. CONNORS

At Home
Historic Houses of Eastern Massachusetts
BETH LUEY

Black Lives, Native Lands, White Worlds
A History of Slavery in New England
JARED ROSS HARDESTY

At Home
Historic Houses of Central and Western Massachusetts
BETH LUEY

FLIGHT CALLS

Exploring Massachusetts through Birds

John R. Nelson

BRIGHT LEAF
Amherst and Boston
An imprint of University of Massachusetts Press

Flight Calls has been supported by the Regional Books Fund, established by donors in 2019 to support the University of Massachusetts Press's Bright Leaf imprint.

Bright Leaf, an imprint of the University of Massachusetts Press, publishes accessible and entertaining books about New England. Highlighting the history, culture, diversity, and environment of the region, Bright Leaf offers readers the tools and inspiration to explore its landmarks and traditions, famous personalities, and distinctive flora and fauna.

Printed in the United States of America

ISBN 978-1-62534-470-0 (paper); 469-4 (hardcover)

Designed by Sally Nichols
Illustrations by Jacqueline Noelle Cote
Set in Perpetua and Adobe Garamond
Printed and bound by Integrated Books International, Inc.

Cover design by Sally Nichols
Cover painting by John J. Audubon, details from *Whip-poor-will,* c. 1830, from, *The Birds of America: Plate LXXXII* (series). Courtesy National Gallery of Art, Washington.

Library of Congress Cataloging-in-Publication Data
A catalog record for this book is available from the Library of Congress

British Library Cataloguing-in-Publication Data
A catalog record for this book is available from the British Library

For Mary, hummingbird of my heart

One touch of nature makes the whole world kin.
—William Shakespeare, *Troilus and Cressida*

Contents

Acknowledgments

I'm grateful to many individuals and organizations who brought me into the world of birding. I first learned about birds and found birding friends through the guidance of friendly, knowledgeable volunteer trip leaders from the Brookline Bird Club. Through the lecture series of the Brookline Bird Club (BBC) and Essex County Ornithological Club (ECOC), I discovered an abiding interest in ornithology and bird conservation. I published my first bird stories in the New England journal *Bird Observer*, whose editors, all volunteers, have encouraged me to keep writing about my birding experiences. Trying to do my part to carry on the traditions of bird study, cultivation of new birders, and conservation, I now serve as a director for all these fine organizations.

Through the ECOC and the Massachusetts Audubon Society, I gave my first lectures on birding. Leaders of Mass Audubon, like Chris Leahy, Wayne Petersen and his late wife, Betty Petersen, Joan Walsh, and Carol Decker have made me feel welcome and useful in the birding community. I've been a long-standing member of Mass Audubon, the Trustees of Reservations, and the Essex County Greenbelt Association, all dedicated to preservation of wildlife habitats, nature education, and conservation of our natural resources. I also appreciate the dedicated efforts of bird clubs across the state, which bring birders together, carry on the traditions, and together form the Association of Massachusetts Bird Clubs.

I've seen and learned about the birds of our country and the world through the expert help of guides from some excellent birding tour companies, like Field Guides and Rockjumper.

Guides such as Megan Crewe and Dave Stejskal have become friends as well as mentors and my models for how to guide fellow birders when I lead local field trips for the BBC and ECOC.

My friends Jim Berry and Chris Leahy both provided invaluable critiques of chapters in this book. Author of many fine articles about breeding birds, Jim led the Essex County team during Mass Audubon's second Breeding Bird Atlas, and he coordinates the annual Cape Ann Christmas Bird Count. He's been a mentor and a dependable source of information for questions about the birds of Essex County and beyond. Chris, author of many excellent books on subjects ranging from North American birds to Massachusetts natural history, has just retired from a distinguished career as a Mass Audubon ornithologist but carries on as a conservation advocate and international tour leader. He's a man with the rare combination of acute judgment as a literary critic and breadth and depth of scientific and historical knowledge. His frank criticisms of some of my drafts inspired me to set my standard higher—the best service that any critic can provide a writer. Chris and Jim both helped me to correct some errors in my drafts. Any remaining errors—and I'm sure there are some—are my own.

Editors are the often unsung collaborators of writers, and I've come to value the expertise, dedication, and support of editors who worked with me on the original versions of various chapters in this book, among them Marsha Salett from *Bird Observer*, Matt Mendenhall from *BirdWatching*, Jim Hicks from the *Massachusetts Review*, Robert Fogarty from the *Antioch Review*, Rod Smith from *Shenandoah*, and Christina Thompson from *Harvard Review*. I'm especially grateful to Brian Halley, my editor at the University of Massachusetts Press, for his belief in this book, his encouragement along the way, and sound editorial judgment. Thanks also to production editor Rachael DeShano and copyeditor Sarah C. Smith. Without their work this book would not exist.

Despite some false starts, frustrations, and literary misadventures, I've kept writing over the years with the encouragement of family members, like my nieces Mary Kalin and Kelley Newton, and friends like Geoffrey Harpham, Mike Frantz, and Anita Splendore. Thanks to them for their support.

My strongest source of support has always been my wife Mary—my best birding partner, my delightful companion in explorations from Cape Ann to Mongolia, the love of my life. I've been lucky in love.

Some chapters in this book are revised and expanded versions of essays originally published in the following journals:

Bird Observer: "Birding a Patch," "Birding on Two Wheels," "On a Street with No Name," "Twitcher's Temptation," "Rarity Envy," "For Birds and People," "The Birding John Nelsons," "Convalescence," "Further Adventures in Four-Legged Birding," "Geezer Birding" (Reprinted by permission of *Bird Observer*. All rights reserved.)

BirdWatching: "Whip-poor-will Synchronicity" (BirdWatching Magazine/Madavor Media LLC)

Antioch Review: "Birds of the Promised Land"

Bird Watcher's Digest: "Watching Gulls with Emerson on Cape Tragabigzanda" (Used with permission.)

New England Review: "Mr. Forbush and Mr. White"

Harvard Review: "Death and the Rose-Breasted Grosbeak"

Shenandoah: "Our Birds"

Massachusetts Review: "Territories"

AUTHOR'S NOTE

To make the names of birds stand out, the formal species names of birds (e.g., Magnolia Warbler), but not of other animals or plants, are capitalized in this book.

FLIGHT CALLS

Chapter 1

FLIGHT CALLS

An Introduction

I'd seen this bird before, many times, but not like this. Naked eye, I could detect the diagnostic field marks: bluish overall, white wing bars, lime patch on the back, yellow throat above a smeared black and rufous breastband, white eye arcs. Binoculars brought me so close I could barely focus. The bird's eyes darted, its whole being quivered as it sang—a fast, thin, ascending buzz.

Loud, girly voices were coming our way. Clomp-clomp shook the boardwalk. A young woman appeared: platform shoes, shorts matching the bird's lime, a bare midriff, puffy white blouse, eyes startled by cosmetics, hair titmouse tufted. This wasn't one of the usual birdwatching suspects at Plum Island. She saw me and stopped. "What you looking at?"

"A bird. A Northern Parula." I pointed. "It's just over your head."

She looked up. "Oh, right there close! So pretty. What did you say it was?"

"A parula. It's a type of warbler."

"A wobbla," she echoed. You'd think that after half a century I'd be used to the local accents. How far back were people around here talking this way? On his midnight ride, did Paul Revere announce himself as Pall Ravea?

She watched the parula flit about. I held out my binoculars. "Here, take a look."

"Gee, thanks." She dimpled when she smiled.

I showed her how to work the focus knob. "Don't try to search with the binoculars. Find the bird first, keep your eyes on it, then raise the binoculars to your eyes." I pantomimed the technique.

"Gotcha." She was a quick study. She got on the parula and steadied the binoculars. "Jeez, you can see everything! It's got like a necklace but all smudgy." She looked behind her. "Tina! Get over here. Check out this wobbla."

Clomping approached. The young woman scanned the nearby trees. "Hey, you got any more of these wobblas around?"

"Sure. There's a redstart just over there. And I hear a Chestnut-Sided singing. That's a beautiful warbler."

"Well, guy, what are we waiting for? They might fly away, right?"

Anybody can become a birder. If this young woman seemed an unlikely candidate, it's because my imagination can be biased and shortsighted. Demographics support a profile—more white than brown or black, more old than not, more prosperous than poor, about equally male and female—but demographics aren't destiny. I know butcher and baker birders, cops, nurses, Muslims, Young Republicans, sopranos, farmers, ship captains, metalheads, ministers, great-grandmothers, fourth-graders, Namibians, alcoholics, and astrophysicists. Some birders can't see, hear, or walk. Some, like me, came late to the game. Others seem born to bird, as people are born for music or math. In Peru our group was helped by a young local, with threadbare pants and crappy binoculars, who was still learning conversational English but could call out the exact English name of every bird he spotted. And he spotted every bird around. Birds had called to him. Our guide put him in touch with Birders' Exchange, a program that collects donated optical equipment and distributes it to young guides, conservationists, and educators in Latin America and the Caribbean. The birds are here for everyone.

Raised in a suburb of Chicago, I wasn't nurtured to direct attention to nature. I can't remember anyone from my childhood who cared about birds. My first love was sports. I liked running after balls and catching them. I was born to fetch. I wanted to be Cubs shortstop Ernie Banks, not Henry David Thoreau. When I outed myself as a birder at a high school reunion, one old chum asked, "Are you or are you not gay?" He eyed me as if I'd just offered proof of, if not gayness, then midlife crisis, declining virility, or incipient senility. How else to explain why I'd joined the nerdy ranks of Mr. Peepers and Miss Jane Hathaway from the *Beverly Hillbillies*? Better not, I thought, share my excitement over the Brown Creeper I'd just seen in the yard where I grew up or the Yellow-Bellied Sapsucker lakeside in Chicago. During the reunion I discovered that any mention of birds was a surefire conversation killer. Birders are sometimes accused, with some truth, of not wanting to talk about anything but birds. Some classmates asked: "Do you keep a list?" I was tempted to respond: "Of course I keep a list. I'm not the Rain Man. How else will I remember which birds I've seen?" Instead I smiled and said "yes" and, if prompted, listed my lists and explained why I keep them—to remember but also to educate myself about the ranges and distributions of birds, document breeding birds in my neighborhood, and target new birds in my searches.

I turned to birding only after a midlife run of orthopedic insults ended my amateur careers in basketball, touch football, and tennis. At Monteverde in Costa Rica, just after my first hip replacement, my wife, Mary, and I saw some tourists with bird books and whimsically decided to try a bird walk. We were aghast when told we'd have to meet the guide at six in the morning and stay out till noon, but we showed up. Our guide, a soft-voiced, quiet-stepping young Costa Rican, told us he usually led groups of experienced birders, not beginners like us, but three weeks earlier he'd lost his nephew, his protégé, twelve years old, and he wanted to go easy on his first day back. His eyes held sadness the whole morning in the cloud forest, but he was an encouraging teacher and terrific birdsong mimic. We felt his love for birds. I remember just a few species he showed us, hummingbirds, motmots, loud, clumsy-looking guans, and long-tailed, iridescent green and red Resplendent Quetzals. In a Mayan myth, the quetzals' breasts turn bloodred when they drop into battlefields to mourn fallen soldiers. Only later did I grasp how lucky we were to see these birds.

Back home I started cycling for exercise—a sorry substitute for competitive sports—and brought along my cheap binoculars in case I came across something. Mostly I stopped for big, startling birds—Little Blue Herons, Glossy Ibises—but I also noticed bold, busy little swallows and phoebes. Lots of large white birds hang out around Cape Ann, where we live, and I was embarrassed to realize they either weren't all seagulls or were various kinds of gulls. One day I rode by a wetland, more puddle than pond, and there, lined up like pageant contestants, were a Green Heron, Glossy Ibis, Great Blue Heron, and Black-Crowned Night-Heron. I watched them for a while—surely a sight unprecedented—and then pedaled home as fast as I could to tell Mary. The birds were still there when she drove us back to the wetland. Mary looked at the birds, then at me, and said, "You're a goner now."

My birding career has followed a typical trajectory. I wanted to see new birds, any new birds. Then I wanted to see more new birds—lovely, strange, subtle, or plain—and see them better. Friendly trip leaders from the Brookline Bird Club took me to places where I could find them and helped me know what I was looking at. To find birds on my own and know what they were, I studied bird books and listened to birdsong tapes.

Meanwhile, something was happening to me. So intent was I on not missing a bird, I'd slipped into the habit of absorption. The amorphous world had grown more precise. Ornithologist Richard Prum says in *The Evolution of Beauty* (2017) that "bird-watching might be among the very first functions of mind," since, like face recognition, it trains our brains to "transform a stream of natural history perceptions into encounters with identifiable individuals." In pre–birding days trips with Mary, birds had sometimes caught our attention: White Storks commanding a Spanish bell tower, a dizzy Bananaquit sampling liquors at a Caribbean beachside bar, a shearwater of some sort skimming the waves and keeping time with our catamaran between Crete and Santorini. But I couldn't remember a single bird from our treks along the Inca Trail or the Cliffs of Moher. What the hell had we been looking at? What weren't we hearing? Now I was alert to signifying movements all around, attuned to sounds, an Eastern Towhee's leaf-shuffling, a chipmunk's chip, an Eastern Wood-Pewee's distant *pee-o-wee*, a Red-Tailed Hawk's scream from the sky. I was growing closer to earth, water, and sky. I'd check a bird's field marks to identify it, then I'd stand back and try to take in the bird, its purposeful movements, its attitude toward other birds, its routine. "If a sparrow comes before my window," wrote John Keats in a letter to his friend Benjamin Bailey, "I take part in its existence and pick about the gravel." I'd become as concentrated as a still-hunting Green Heron. In *Speak, Memory* (1966)

Vladimir Nabokov describes his passion for butterflies: "And the highest enjoyment of timelessness—in a landscape selected at random—is when I stand among rare butterflies and their food plants. This is ecstasy, and behind the ecstasy is something else, which is hard to explain. It is like a momentary vacuum into which rushes all that I love."

Nabokov calls his butterfly hunting "an ardent and arduous quest." I am, I suppose, on my own quest, though the word sounds too epic for an activity that won't accomplish much beyond personal gratification. But there's no denying the ardor. In search of birds I've gone further and further afield, first to birdy spots around Massachusetts—Mount Auburn Cemetery for spring warblers, South Beach for shorebirds and terns, Mount Wachusett for migrating raptors—next cross-country to the Rio Grande and saguaro deserts, then beyond to whole new families of birds in Belize, Brazil, Botswana, Bhutan, and Borneo.

Mary and I are lucky to have the means to travel with good optical equipment, and I'm lucky to have an adventurous wife willing to go on birding vacations. She's more photographer than birder, but like many "non-birding partners" she's a fine spotter who, annoyingly, has gotten great looks at some wonderful species I've missed. Together we've watched remarkable birds—the Secretarybird, quilled, leggy, snake-stomping, striding across the Serengeti like a mythical cross between stork and eagle, or the impossible Grayish Miner, a rock-colored little creature that somehow finds food and drink in the Atacama Desert, a land without rainfall, even a sprig of vegetation, or any visible bugs or other birds, nothing but rock. The miner seemed to live in a realm of its own, but other birds were connecting the world to home. The Peregrine Falcons soaring in Greek mountains and the Australian outback are the same species that winter at the city hall towers in Gloucester. The thrushes and warblers we found in Central America might be the migrant birds feeding in our yard. They'll return to Massachusetts each spring only if they find places to thrive during winters in tropical America. Bird conservation knows no boundaries.

Certain birds seemed so at home in their habitats that they came to embody the lands where they live. Visions of the forests of Tikal are inseparable from Orange-Breasted Falcons, totem-like at their nest atop a steep pyramid we'd climbed to see them as the sun set lavender over Mayan temples. My memories of the Rio Negro in Amazonia come with a soundtrack of shrieks from Screaming Pihas—sheer volume as an agent of sexual selection. In Massachusetts a woodland without Ovenbird song would seem profoundly wrong, while a freshwater marsh would sound off-kilter, an orchestra missing its woodwinds, without the trills of Marsh Wrens. Birds ranging from Secretarybirds to Ovenbirds rouse curiosity about the evolutionary history of all birds and their great migratory journeys across the earth.

Birding travel teaches that exoticism—applied to birds, places, or people—is all about perspective. In Thailand I showed up one morning in a shirt featuring a Sulphur-Bellied Flycatcher, a streaky, cardinal-sized bird from the deserts of Mexico and Arizona. Our guide stared at me for some time before he asked, "How can this bird be a flycatcher?" I might've asked the same question about his Verditer Flycatcher, a stunning copper-sulfate songbird, from an entirely different family, common in Asia and hardly more exotic to its human neighbors than Thai people find themselves exotic. Baltimore Orioles and Northern Cardinals seem fabulously foreign to visitors who've never seen any birds from their families, but they're our backyard neighbors in Massachusetts. The birds themselves are just going about their business. And it's been at home that I've become engrossed by bird business, not just glimpsed bird beauty.

Evolutionary biologist Ernst Mayr once said that of all sciences, ornithology most readily allows amateurs to contribute through patient observation, scrupulous record-keeping, and "imaginative posing of problems." A turning point for me was the second Massachusetts Breeding Bird Atlas, a five-year project (2007 through 2011) directed by Joan Walsh from Mass Audubon to determine which species were breeding across our state. By foot and bicycle I surveyed two atlas blocks—my neighborhood in West Gloucester and another sector in Danvers, Middleton, and Topsfield—and I came to know the ways of birds I'd often taken for granted. Finding proof of breeding was a new kind of quest, rewarded by an intent Great Crested Flycatcher gathering nesting material in our yard or a food-bearing Downy Woodpecker disappearing into a cavity. One day I heard a whistling above me, familiar but feeble, and found a Broad-Winged Hawk family. Two adults watched keenly as their single offspring tested its wings in short, wobbly flights, calling repeatedly and glancing toward its parents, like a child on a first bike ride without training wheels. These birds were placing me, deepening roots. I'm a merely competent birder, more avid than skilled, but I know my bird neighbors.

The more time I spend with birds, the more they've become sources of stimulation, not just visual treats or searches rewarded. They've catalyzed the childlike curiosity, one of the great blessings of being human, that becomes dormant in so many of us. Thoreau, in his journals, wondered at the strange harmony between birdsong and the human ear that harkens to it. Birds are just one of many possible entrees into nature's wonders. For Nabokov it was butterflies; for Edward O. Wilson, ants; for Rachel Carson, the life of the New England seashore; for Thoreau, the whole natural history of our state. In his journal in 1820, Ralph Waldo Emerson marveled at the "occult relation" between humans and our fellow inhabitants of the world: "I feel the centipede in me—cayman, carp, eagle, fox. I am moved by strange sympathies." Each realm of nature is a world onto itself: the more you explore, the more intricate, intriguing, and boundless it becomes. Each realm leads to all the others.

The questions I ask when I'm birding aren't original; they're questions that were pondered by Aesop and Plutarch and people long before them. What made that siskin choose that branch in that pine as a nesting site? How are birds' territorial fights related to humans' territorial wars? What can birds teach us? Some questions may be unanswerable. Some have been answered only to raise other challenging questions. Studies of Snowball, a YouTube sensation dancing cockatoo (and Backstreet Boys fan), have enabled scientists to link the capacity for vocal imitation to the rare-in-animals ability to keep time to music, but they're still figuring out what this link reveals about the development of avian brain systems for learning song as well as the evolution of human language. Prum's *The Evolution of Beauty*, a study of the elaborate mating displays of tropical birds like manakins, suggests that birds, and perhaps people as well, choose beauty in mates for its own sake, not just because it signifies good genes.

Beyond birds themselves, I'm fascinated by what people make of birds—the ways various species have been envied, spiritualized, imitated, and reviled in human myths and literature and painstakingly studied by both professionals and amateurs. The explorations in this book are not mine alone but those of many others who've been captivated by birds in Massachusetts over centuries: Native Americans, explorers like Samuel Champlain and John Smith, poets from Emily Dickinson to Mary Oliver, pioneering ornithologists like Edward Howe Forbush, and friends like Chris Leahy and Wayne Petersen from Mass

Audubon who have carried on a long, distinguished state tradition of bird study and conservation. These companions in my explorations have helped me to locate birds within our state's natural and cultural history.

I often bird alone, but birding can be a social activity, whether on local field trips or international guided tours. Like anyone else, birders can be greedy, dense, or drudging, but by and large they're welcoming folks, good spirited, hardy, receptive to whatever they come across—bird, weasel, dragonfly—and generous in sharing their knowledge and enthusiasm. Since birders come together mainly to find birds, friendships can be casual and intermittent, but I've become good friends with some bird comrades, connected by inquisitiveness, a love of wild beauty, and concern over how to preserve what's left of the natural world. Birds summon feelings for all those I love, whether they care much about birds or not.

Collectively, birders constitute a loose community that encompasses anyone, anywhere, who pays regular attention to birds. Modern birders in clubs, and in organizations like Mass Audubon and the Trustees of Reservations, continue a heritage that's been crucial for conservation, scientific understanding of bird populations, and nurturing in people a sense of belonging in and caring for the natural world. Our birding community must spread nature-mindfulness as widely as possible to the next generations. We need to reach out where we haven't reached out. Anybody can be touched by birds, but "anybody can become a birder" is true only to the extent that children and adults, in cities and suburbs, in North America and beyond, have mentors and models to show them that looking at birds outside of zoos is a plausible, pleasurable, and perfectly natural thing to do. Our hope lies in human curiosity.

Since people bird for pleasure, birding is more suited to comedy than tragedy, and some stories in this book were written mostly for laughs. A civilian told me that birders' humor tends to be tame and nerdy, and there's truth in that, since in-group humor is often self-reflexive and repetitious, as in calling non-birders "civilians." If, on a tour abroad, you come across a Paltry Tyrannulet or Drab Hemispingus, I guarantee you that someone in your group—perhaps you—will pity the bird for its unfortunate naming. If you're watching your first Warbling Vireo, someone will quip that it's a species without field marks. I've used the line myself. But wit will surface. The recently discovered Predicted Antwren was so-named because ornithologists had predicted that an antwren of the genus *Herpsilochmus* was living in appropriate habitat near the Rio Madeira in Brazil.

Most birding humor comes at the expense of birders: their blunders, their often exaggerated competitiveness, and the absurd lengths to which birdquests will drive them as they slosh through mosquito-infested bogs or freeze their asses off on winter sea-watches in hopes of spotting this or that species. Try explaining to your non-birding friends why, along with sixty other birders on Plum Island, you stood for hours in the cold and dark praying that, just once, you could hear the *ki-ki-doo* call of a far-off Black Rail, a mousy little creature you knew for certain you wouldn't see. Poking fun at birders' fixation on bird identification goes back to Robert William Wood's 1909 *How to Tell the Birds from the Flowers*, a "manual of florinthology" that teaches readers how to distinguish a crow from a crocus.

Even when birds are the apparent butts of jokes, it's their resemblance to people that usually provokes laughter. The strutting, booming, dandified mating performances of prairie-chickens and grouse seem designed as parodies of human vanity. Sometimes the bird-human likeness strikes disturbingly close to home. Scientists have found that male Wild Turkeys are so desperate to mate that they'll mount wooden models of females, even after the tails, feet, and wings of the models have been systematically removed, so that nothing remains but a fake head on a stick. No doubt these are silly turkeys—and, some say, silly scientists to think up such experiments—but are these birds so different from the millions of human males who masturbate to images of women, even "women" who are literally cartoons?

But the world of birds does have a dark side. Many species in Massachusetts, North America, and the world are declining, endangered, or heading toward extinction. The most severe, pervasive harm comes from destruction and deterioration of the habitats birds need to survive. If you care about birds and want them to stick around, for their sake or yours or your descendants', there's no excuse not to be a committed conservationist. Many species can be preserved only through cohesive, urgent effort. Liking birds is not proof of virtue. What birders might want from birds should not be confused with what birds need.

The title of this book refers literally to the calls birds make as they fly. These calls have definite meanings. On cold, gray days, when insects are hard to find, Cliff Swallows make an odd call that means "Come here, I've got bugs." Learning the flight calls to identify unseen birds is crucial to the burgeoning study of migration at night, when most songbirds migrate, silhouetted as they pass the moon. But for me "flight calls" also represent the pull of attraction to fellow creatures that beckon with sounds not intended for me and compel me to watch as they wing through the air in wild, expressive arcs. Spanish photographer Xavi Bou uses chronophotography to capture birds' flight patterns over time—their contrails in the sky, some like spirals or double helixes, some evoking flowing strands of hair or writhing serpents. Deaf poet David Wright pictures birds' flights as "eye music" (a phrase from Wordsworth), audible even when the birds are silent, each flier "calling" with a distinctive rhythm and grace, its own wing print in space, "from the nonchalant melancholy of seagulls to the staccato flitting of tits."

In *The Peregrine* (1967) British writer James Baker, a late-blooming birder like me, imagines himself a falcon swooping over hills and fields. He remembers "galloping over spring green turf, as a child; over the neglected, fallen farm-land of pre-war years; through the wild hedges and the glorious wastes of flowering weeds flaming with hawks and finches." Yet, as much as he identifies with Peregrines, Baker knows he must always stand apart: "I came late to the love of birds. For years I saw them only as a tremor at the edge of vision. They know suffering and joy in simple states not possible for us. Their lives quicken and warm to a pulse our hearts can never reach. They race to oblivion. They are old before we have finished growing." Like Baker, I know I'll never swoop with a Peregrine's pulse, but I hope I'll never lose the joyous rush of watching a Peregrine plummet from sky to earth. Birds have helped me find and nourish the untamed child within who will never be satisfied by staying merely busy, yielding to easy habit, and keeping the world at bay—a restless, seeking child who needs to get out, gallop or hobble across a field, and explore his earthly home.

Chapter 2

BIRDING A PATCH

British birders talk about a local "patch," an area regularly explored to check which birds are there and what they're up to. In his 1789 classic *The Natural History and Antiquities of Selborne*, Gilbert White, a parson and amateur naturalist, recommended the "economy" of restricting wildlife study to a small district to discover nature's fullness through its details and contribute to knowledge about broad issues like bird migration and territoriality. Thoreau says in "Walking" that an area twenty miles in diameter is enough to occupy a lifetime of close exploration on foot. For the second Breeding Bird Atlas, I covered a block in Gloucester bordered by the Atlantic Ocean, the Annisquam River, Essex Bay, a salt marsh creek, and several highways. This is the heart of my patch.

A few miles from our house, the ocean flows between two long stretches of sand into Essex Bay. From the end of Coffin's Beach in Gloucester, you can see coastline reaching north to New Hampshire, the sandbars off Crane Beach in Ipswich across the bay, and, dominating the horizon, the drumlin of Hog Island planted with spruce. The bay narrows into the tidal Essex River by the isolated community of Conomo Point in Essex. Clamdiggers in rubber boots work squishy mudflats at low tide. Kayakers paddle into ocean currents. Sailboats nap in the bay's calm waters. Seals stick their noses out of the water. Horseback riders sometimes lope along past the Crane dunes.

The residential neighborhood along the ocean and bay is private, but much of the marsh and bayfront is conserved by the Essex County Greenbelt Association, for which I volunteer as a property monitor. In spring I patrol the thickets around Farm Creek to see if the breeding songbirds I found during the atlas, like Brown Thrasher and Common Yellowthroat, still hold territories in the same spots. From out in the marsh, where Ospreys nest on a platform, comes a Willet's piercing cry, an onomatopoeic call familiar to any Atlantic coast salt marsh. Large, sturdy shorebirds, Willets look plain gray at rest but flash startling black and white wing stripes when they take off. Since the atlas several Piping Plover pairs have nested along the bay, an encouraging sign. They skitter in spurts across sand swirled with garnet grains to feed along the shoreline. Sanderlings on the beaches dare the surf to tag them as they feed where waves have retreated. Screeching Least Terns stream by offshore, hover, and dive. Our continent's smallest terns, they're white with bright yellow bill and legs, long winged and swift-like in flight. The terns and plovers, both endangered species, breed in colonies on Crane Beach.

October is the time for the spectacle of waterfowl gathering and migrating along the coast. Double-Crested Cormorants, breeders on offshore islands, may congregate in the many thousands in the bay. Dark, sleek experts in underwater pursuit, cormorants have long been envied for their fishing skills and sometimes attacked by fishermen as fish-catching competitors. Their relatives, Great Cormorants, winter along New England shores. In Asia fishermen capture them and, tying lines around their throats to prevent swallowing, enlist them to catch fish. Cormorants have been called "ravens of the sea" for their predatory voraciousness. In Milton's *Paradise Lost* Satan sits "like a cormorant" on the Tree of Life as he watches Adam and Eve and devises death. Cormorants can hunt even in dark, turgid waters by listening to the sounds of fish as they dive.

In late October the bay is taken over by hundreds or thousands of the three scoter species, variations on a duck theme in black with diagnostic distinctions: the male White-Winged's wing patch and white comma below the eye, the Surf Scoter's bulbous bill and white patches on head and neck, the bright yellow knob at the base of the Black Scoter's bill. Further out, to and past the limits of vision, are migrating Northern Gannets, cliff-nesters from the North Atlantic, big, majestic white birds with long, black-tipped, pointed wings and spiked faces. They're aerodynamic wonders, finely coordinated as they swoop and plunge headlong for fish without breaking their necks when they hit the water.

Each December I census birds for the one-day Christmas Bird Count, administered by National Audubon Society throughout the Western Hemisphere to collect data on populations in a season when few species migrate. Participants try to count large flocks as accurately as possible and avoid duplicating birds counted in adjacent sectors in a count circle. The aim is to tally all birds seen or heard in a locality and then move on, but in fall and winter I'll come to the bay regularly to linger with the seabirds. Brant, called "burnt geese" for their charcoal necks and backs, hug the shore in serene processions. Prowling the beaches are Great Black-Backed Gulls, known as "burgomasters" and "coffin-bearers" for their domination of smaller gulls and sometimes fatal attacks on small ducks. Sturdy-looking Common Loons in winter plumage roam the bay—one always returns to a favored spot in the river mouth. Common Eiders, often in the hundreds, raft in and out of the bay, dive for shellfish, and gather on sandbars to rest and preen. The adult male is an unlikely beauty of a duck with a wedge for a face, a bright lime nape, and buffy blush on its breast. Adult females are a rich, subtly lined cinnamon. Social birds, eiders murmur and coo like parties of continually surprised Mourning Doves. They're joined each fall by a small, restless, noisy group of Long-Tailed Ducks. The chattiness of these birds has inspired a long list of nicknames: old wife, hound, Old Molly, Uncle Huldy, scolder, quandy, and a sobriquet still used by old-timers, oldsquaw, perhaps the only bird name that's simultaneously racist, sexist, and ageist. The ducks don't care which words we use. No human label can capture their calicoed beauty, their long-tailed grace, and their energy in flight.

Every patch has its history. During periods of glacial advance, no ducks or gannets were migrating off Coffin's Beach, no shorebirds foraged on sandbars, no warblers in heathlands. The sea level was several hundred feet lower, and the shore on which I stand with my spotting scope was miles east. Cape Ann was not a peninsula but a cluster of hills above an icy coastal plain. Once the ice melted, the sea level gradually rose, the shoreline retreated west, and ocean currents carried sand landward to form the barrier spits of Coffin's Beach and Castle Neck across the bay.

People long before me thought of this place as their patch. Shell heaps with artifacts have been found at the west end of Coffin's Beach. Stone tools and projectile points discovered at the large Bull Brook site in Ipswich date from around 11,000 years ago, the earliest evidence of humans living in Massachusetts, around the time wooly mammoths and mastodons disappeared from our lands. The indigenous tribes of New England reached a population of close to 150,000 in the pre-agricultural period between 3000 and 1000 BC. In summer small bands lived in circled campsites by the seashore and tidal rivers to fish, collect birds' eggs, and catch birds with nets. In winter they found sheltered sites to live off stores of nuts and berries and hunt for beaver, deer, seals, and walruses. In his 1634 *New England's Prospect*, William Wood described men going out to sea "fowling"—hunting birds—in birchbark and dugout canoes.

Between 1616 and 1619, just before Europeans settled New England, most of the aboriginal people died from an epidemic of smallpox or some combination of diseases perhaps started by contact with trappers. The epidemic then spread from southern Maine to Cape Cod. Historian Ted Steinberg calls the death toll "one of the most dramatic population reductions in the history of the world." Puritan leader John Winthrop saw it as an opportunity granted by God: "For the natives, they are neere all dead of small Poxe, so as the Lord hathe cleared our title to what we possess." By the end of King Philip's War in 1676, almost all Native Americans of New England had died from disease or wars or had fled. A few Abenaki-speaking Pawtuckets remained on Cape Ann until about 1690.

After the Pawtucket, or Agawam, people were gone, this side of the bay reverted to near wilderness, uninhabited except for Peter Coffin's isolated sheep farm. Early in the Revolutionary War, as legend has it, fifty mutton-seeking British soldiers tried to land a barge at his pasture, and Coffin and a handful of men scared them off with a crackling of musketry. Robert Freeman, Coffin's slave, saved his master's life and was rewarded with his freedom. The area remained nearly deserted until 1890, when brothers Edward and James Hawks built castles of granite hauled by barge from a local quarry and then dragged up the beach on sleds by teams of oxen. Even now, especially in winter, when a birder might be alone on the long arc of sand, Coffin's Beach has the same wide tranquility, the same airy glow hued mauve at sunset, that Fitz Henry Lane captured in paintings of the beach in the 1860s.

A boulder cluster separates Coffin's Beach from public Wingaersheek Beach at the mouth of the Annisquam River. The ocean here remains shallow for some distance out, the low tide line a stroll from the eroded dunes behind the beach. It's a place to watch the unceasing cycle of the sea's encroachment and retreat from land. A sandbar where currents crisscross is actually the summit of what local historian Joe Garland calls an "underwater mountain of sand that shifts restlessly and endlessly where the currents of the bay meet the pliant land and make the treacherous shoals, the beaches, the entrance to Squam River." The Annisquam is a tidal inlet, technically not a river, but a dredged canal and a drawbridge by Gloucester Harbor allow boaters to cross Cape Ann from Ipswich Bay to the harbor instead of circumnavigating the peninsula. More Pawtucket artifacts have been found in the Riverdale and Annisquam neighborhoods across the river: bone fishing hooks, a stone plummet used to weight fishing lines, and the Annisquam Head—a stone carving of a woman with a baby strapped to her back.

When the last glacier melted, sediment filled the valleys between Cape Ann's granite outcrops, and rising sea level eventually brought in ocean water and created salt-tolerant grasslands. The Annisquam branches off into the Jones River, a tidal creek meandering past small islands. From Long Wharf, overlooking a mudflat called Maude Gibbons—on our cape, clam flats get named—I scope the flats and marsh for egrets, herons, and shorebirds. Built to export granite from a nearby quarry, the wharf was used at night for rum-running during Prohibition. Across the marsh is Pearce Island, where farmers cut and stacked salt hay. Lane's painting "Looking up 'Squam River from 'Done Fudging'" shows the spot where, transporting hay, farmers stopped using wooden poles to "fudge" their boats along and let the tides work for them.

Wingaersheek Beach is crowded in summer, but in winter, when it's often deserted except for dogwalkers, Mary and I look for Dunlin and Purple Sandpipers huddled standing-room-only on beachside rocks. The droopy-billed Dunlin look dullish without the rufous back and big black belly patch of breeding plumage. The rock-loving yellow-legged Purple Sandpipers hint at purplish only at close range in good light.

Arctic breeders, these are our winter shorebirds here, along with occasional Sanderlings, after other shorebirds have migrated south. Whenever we come upon a roving band of bright-faced Horned Larks on the beach, we feel transported to other lands. The Horned Lark, with a Latin name meaning "loving mountains solitude," is one of the world's most widespread, adaptable birds, though the larks on our beaches are probably a different species from the Horned Larks that were sometimes the only birds in sight on our trip across the vast Mongolian plateaus. One day Mary, generally indifferent to gulls but ever observant, casually pointed out a gull with dark red legs and bill—field marks of the locally rare Black-Headed Gull. On another beach walk, our dog Sierra nosed into some reeds and flushed an American Bittern, the only one I've seen here. *Good dog,* I thought, though I felt bad about bothering the bittern.

West Gloucester, on the west side of the Annisquam, was slow to be developed because of steep, rocky hills, bad roads or no roads at all, and marsh infested with greenheads and mosquitoes. It's now been built up, with spacious modern homes neighboring ramshackle cottages, but it still has a feel of wildness. Whip-poor-wills still sing from the woodlands of Greenbelt's Tompson Street Reservation, and at a nearby pond on Bray Street I've spent hours watching birds fly in and out of holes. During the atlas I confirmed breeding by ten species at the pond, including three types of woodpeckers. Occasionally I found a Belted Kingfisher or Green Heron, but I searched in vain for a kingfisher nest, usually a tunnel in the bank of a pond or river, or a heron nest, which could be in any concealed pondside spot. During one Christmas Bird Count I stood baffled by ice cracking erratically all around the pond, until I spotted an adult and baby river otter breaking through ice to surface. I watched them pop up here and there whack-a-mole style until I remembered I should be counting birds.

In summer I check the pond for Little Blue Herons, elusive in Essex County but reliable here in their progressions from birth to maturity: juvenile white, yearlings' blue and white mottled calico, and adult maroon-blue. Photographers come and wait for a heron to land and pose on a long floating log near the road. Newt and Bonnie Fink, gracious owners of a pondside house, have made a bench from a tree trunk to give visitors a comfortable perch from which to pond-watch. I've compared notes with them and their neighbors about the exact source of whip-poor-will songs and past encounters with Ruffed Grouse, now gone from my patch. During the atlas I met other neighbors by knocking on doors rather than sneaking into their yards to track down breeding birds. Some knew about the birds; others were delighted to learn they had a Red-Bellied Woodpecker or Carolina Wren nesting on their land. Mary and I sometimes come to the pond together to watch birds and listen to the bullfrogs. "Love does not consist in gazing at each other," wrote Antoine de Saint-Exupéry in *The Little Prince* (1943), "but in looking outward in the same direction."

Every patch should have its secret places, and Cape Ann abounds with little backroads and dead-ended streets that narrow into wooded trails, open into weedy fields, or wind back toward the ocean. Each spring I check to see if Broad-Winged Hawks are breeding again at Mount Jacob, an old Jewish cemetery hidden away off potholed, cyclist-ruining Fernald Street. Another potholed street leads to Dykes Pasture Road, a wide, shaded dirt trail that parallels long Lily Pond below and turns uphill to a dam and one of Gloucester's reservoirs. The songbirds here have their preferred spots, and in spring I make my way along avian stations of the cross: Wood Thrush, never-shuts-up Red-Eyed Vireo, Winter Wren, and, at a field near the reservoir, Indigo Bunting—blue-black in shade, bright blue in sunlight. The wren is often absent from its station, a rotted trunk in a dark, damp gully, and it's usually heard only, but what a song—tuneful, enthusiastic, too elaborate and sustained for even a mockingbird to imitate. Restless, tail-pumping Spotted Sandpipers breed by a spillway at the dam.

Never out of earshot on Dykes Pasture Road is an Ovenbird, a warbler suggestive of a small thrush and named for its domed, oven-shaped nest. In "The Oven Bird" Robert Frost says that the bird "makes the solid tree trunks sound again." Jamaicans call the bird Betsy Kick-Up. Its penetrating *teacher teacher* song is nicely featured as a motif in the Pilobolus dance company's "Branches," a dramatization of struggles among animals, with various birdsongs and comic imitations of bird displays. Pioneering ornithologist Margaret Morse Nice, raised in Amherst, marveled at how an Ovenbird family "found their way on the incredible journeys to South America and back to these Massachusetts woods." Even late into summer one can hear the Ovenbird's plaintive neighbor, an Eastern Wood-Pewee, whose song so entranced ethologist Wallace Craig that in 1943 he wrote a whole book about it, a "study in bird music," *The Song of the Wood Pewee.*

One spring day Mary and I were stopped by a warbler song I instantly knew—ringing, emphatic, a bright yellow song—but had never heard on Cape Ann. We followed song to singer, a rare Prothonotary—the golden swamp warbler. The name comes from its likeness in color to the saffron cowl on the robe of an English notary or Catholic prelate called a prothonotary. The bird played a bit role in American history when Alger Hiss, a birder and Soviet spy, was convicted of perjury in part because he claimed he'd never met fellow spy Whittaker Chambers, when in fact he'd bragged to Chambers about his sighting of this beautiful bird. I took a proprietary interest in our Prothonotary, tracking its golden movements around the pond and helping others to find it. I hoped the bird would stay and find a partner to breed, but it flew off after a few days.

Each May I join in Mass Audubon's Bird-a-thon, a conservation fundraiser and friendly competition with donations based on the number of species found by a team from a sanctuary that a donor supports. Our team, led by Chris Leahy, covers only the four towns on Cape Ann. The grasslands of Essex, like those at Cogswell's Grant, a Historic New England farm with a folk art museum, are the only places locally with a decent chance to sight one of my targets, Eastern Meadowlark. Bright yellow with a pointed bill, black V on the chest, and long legs, the meadowlark is emblematic of our American prairies, whether whistling from a fence, dropping into grass to hunt insects, or sitting in sunlight with what poet Thomas Merton calls "Zen quietness." Another target is Virginia Rail, a dark freshwater marsh bird that's opposed on principle to being observed but often responds to imitations of its calls. Click some rocks together, and a rail might click back. On one Bird-a-thon a rail strutted out in the open, glanced right and left as if amazed at itself, looked me over, then scooted back into its reeds.

In May grasslands fill with Bobolinks, each male sounding like a whole flock as he gurgles from a shrubby perch and flutters in a mating display. Males are black below, with snazzy white scapulars and fuzzy yellow napes. Bobolinks are often driven from nests by farmers mowing hayfields—a problem being addressed in New England by the Bobolink Project, which uses donated funds to compensate farmers willing to delay their mowing until birds have raised their young. Just as our woods must have Ovenbird songs, so our fields without Bobolinks would be desolate grass.

Before Sierra died I'd take her to Cogswell's Grant, where she could run free. I worried that she might bother the birds, but she was a skittish animal, a rescued Puerto Rican street dog more apt to be victimized by birds than to threaten them. Zooming Barn Swallows taunted her. One Killdeer confounded her when it feigned a broken wing to lure her from its nest and then flew off in good health. We used to walk an adjacent private road that leads to a causeway and small island, and I'd stop to chat with a frail old man who'd given us permission to walk there. A dog lover, he wasn't much interested in birds, but he always asked what I'd seen, and he recalled the day a "nice Southern gentleman" came down his road looking for a Rough-Legged Hawk. The old man died a few years ago, a loss to dogwalkers and wandering birders, for he was willing to share his land with no expectation but friendly talk in return. Now, "no trespassing" signs mark the private road and block the path to the causeway.

Naturally my patch includes our yard, a scratchy bit of grass that parodies a lawn and a small homemade pond in a woodland atop a hill in West Gloucester. During the atlas, without going beyond our deck, I confirmed breeding by nine species. A Purple Finch pair, the male dipped in raspberry, showed their young how to "forage" for seeds at our window feeder. Downy Woodpeckers jostle daily around the suet feeder, often joined by a bigger relative, Hairy Woodpecker. Like many backyard birders, Mary and I waited years for a Pileated Woodpecker to grace our property, until the day I noticed a large, neat oval hole in a tree behind the house, unmistakably the work of a Pileated. The next morning Mary summoned me—"Get down here quick!"—to look at the magnificent bird chiseling at the hole. When we can no longer travel to look for birds in far-off lands, I'll bear it, but my heart sinks at the thought of living day by day without woodpeckers and finches nearby.

In spring we wait for the migrants to come. One morning I woke to a sound I'd never heard on our land, the *coocoocoo* of a Black-Billed Cuckoo. I jumped out of bed and threw on some clothes and my slippers. The cuckoo sang every few minutes, each time more distant. I followed deeper into the trees, then down our steep hill, losing traction on slick boulders and tumbling ass over binoculars. Never did see the bird. That spring a wave of northbound migrants reached Cape Ann and, stalled by the weather, stuck around through the Bird-a-thon. Just after sunrise the oak outside our bedroom held eight types of warblers, two vireo species, two Rose-Breasted Grosbeaks, a Swainson's Thrush, and four Scarlet Tanagers, one an aberrant oriole orange. Glorious: our own migrant trap. By day's end I'd found sixteen warbler species in our yard.

Mary, a fiend for finding raptors in our travels, is our resident hawk-watcher, an avocation that spices her gardening. In Alaska she astonished other tour members by choosing as her top trip bird a Harlan's variety of a Red-Tail, above the rare McKay's Bunting and a Ruff in outlandish breeding plumage. A few years later we met David Sibley while looking for (and, thanks to his help, finding) a Long-Eared Owl at Dunback Meadow in Lexington, and Mary told him her Red-Tail-in-Alaska story. "If it's not the most wonderful bird in North America," she asked, "why would you put it on the cover of your book?" David smiled and nodded. Mary lets me know if a Red-Tail is around.

In our travels I've seen well over five thousand bird species, but often my experience with a given bird was little more than a glimpse and a name checked off on a list. The Bird-a-thon is fun, but it's hit-and-run birding: find a species and race on. It was during the atlas that I learned to look at birds and consider their lives: where they nest, what they eat, what scares them and what doesn't. Songbird intensity still amazes me: they live at a pace that would exhaust the most hyperactive human. Anthropologist Loren Eisely in *The Immense Journey*

(1960) describes birds as reptiles that "have escaped out of the heavy sleep of time." It seems near miraculous that animals this kinetic have the forbearance to sit still in one spot for days on end to incubate eggs.

As I watch birds I ponder their choices. What cues led that towhee to choose that brush patch in our yard? When Baltimore Orioles construct their finely woven nests, do they consider the challenges of parenthood: eggs to keep warm, young to feed, predators to guard against? Do birds ask themselves questions and come up with answers? Humans can afford to ponder; birds must be quick decision makers. But words like "decision" or "strategy" are problematic in describing bird behavior because they connote a humanlike weighing of alternatives. Anthropomorphism is a tricky issue. We're told we shouldn't project human qualities onto birds, but we're still figuring out which qualities in our species are uniquely human, while many human choices hardly qualify as rational "decisions." And birds do spend their lives making choices that can mean life or death for them or their offspring. Biologist Bridget Stutchbury in *The Private Life of Birds* (2010) points out that even the simplest choice—eat or sing—can have consequences: "A male who spends a large amount of time singing to impress females or scare rivals will quickly get very hungry. On the other hand, the male who eats his fill at the expense of singing may lose his territory or find himself living alone and without any young to show for his efforts."

In a groundbreaking 1953 study of bird behavior, *The Herring Gull's World*, Niko Tinbergen observed that birds don't look far into the future or act with "foresight." Stutchbury too cautions us not to think of birds as "human-like in their minute-to-minute decision-making," since the "birds themselves do not understand why they make certain choices." Still, some bird behavior can't be explained, or explained away, by a crude all-purpose term like "instinct." One case featured an ingenious Blue Tit in England that perched one day on a doorstep, tore the foil top off a milk bottle, and drained the rich upper layer of un-homogenized cream. Other tits watched and followed suit, and within a few years, across Europe, Blue Tits were waiting for milkmen to deliver. Scientists debated whether this constitutes "culturally transmitted learning," while some mystified human victims blamed prankster juvenile delinquents. I watched a similar innovation at our suet feeder. One morning when I was slow to restock the suet, I found a Downy Woodpecker sipping sugar water at our hummingbird feeder. Sugar soon became a habit for this bird. If the suet feeder is empty, one other woodpecker might join him, yet for whatever reason the rest of the woodpeckers won't chance it but rather will wait impatiently for the suet to return or go back to grubbing for insects.

Birds' daily behavior leads to broader questions about how they learn and communicate. Donald Kroodsma, a longtime professor at the University of Massachusetts, has spent his career trying to fathom the diversity and plasticity of birdsong: "Why do some learn and others not?" he asks in *The Singing Life of Birds* (2005). "Among those species that learn, why dialects in some and not others? When, where, and from whom does a young bird learn its songs? Why such impressive vocabularies in some species, so diminished in others?" Kroodsma has helped to answer some questions, but we still don't fully understand why most songbirds must learn their songs, while birds in the flycatcher family know their species' songs with no learning process at all. Part of the answer seems to be that learning songs enables more complex songs, preferred by females of some species. Verbal or musical facility may also factor into human sexual selection, though if Mary chose me for my voice, it must have been my writing voice, not my singing voice.

One summer I focused on the Brown-Headed Cowbirds in our yard. Cowbirds are obligate brood parasites. Females always lay their eggs in other species' nests, and cowbird offspring are always brooded and raised not by their biological parents but by surrogates. One morning I watched a male towhee struggle to feed two hungry offspring and a young cowbird under our seed feeder. When not being fed, the young towhees foraged for themselves, while the cowbird just stood there, waiting for the next meal. Its genus name *Molothrus* means "greedy beggar." But how, I wondered, do cowbirds come to know they're cowbirds? If a female has been raised without contact with other cowbirds, how can she recognize a male, much less mate with one? The answer, ornithologists have reasoned, is that young cowbirds, like other birds, must be genetically encoded to recognize their species' song or chatter, though they need to hear males sing on territories in spring for the instinctual recognition response to be triggered.

If you spend time watching birds, it's soon evident that they have their different styles. Each species, says ornithologist Nathan Emery in *Bird Brain* (2017), has its own "fear database," which can be innate or learned. Winter Wrens are solitary, camouflaged, agoraphobic: they'd sooner peck themselves to death than join a flock or hop into the open for a look around. But Black-Capped Chickadees will fly right up to an approaching human. At Mass Audubon's Ipswich River Wildlife Sanctuary, it's a popular pastime to walk a trail, stop, and hold out a hand with sunflower seeds. The different species that arrive display a continuum of boldness to shyness. The chickadees, after calling for you to stop, will land immediately, their tiny toes tickling your palm; then the shyer White-Breasted Nuthatches; then, if you're patient, a Tufted Titmouse that's managed to overcome its deeper wariness.

But, as with our fellow humans, there's also an array of "personalities" *within* a given species—what Jennifer Ackerman in *The Genius of Birds* (2016) calls "the bold and the meek, the curious and the cautious, the calm and the nervous, the fast learners and the slow learners." If the American Goldfinches at our feeder sense a nearby Sharp-Shinned Hawk, there's always one goldfinch, brave or foolhardy, that's last to duck for cover and first to return once danger has passed. On Wingaersheek Road I'll salute a certain towhee that disdains the safer perches that satisfy other towhees and keeps on singing—*drink your teeeeeee*—from an open telephone wire. A nearby Common Yellowthroat sings variations of *witchety wichety wichety* as persistently as a ballpark beer vendor. This must be the bird scientists studied when they discovered that yellowthroat males sing up to two thousand variations of their courting song in a day.

In 1937 Margaret Morse Nice published *Studies in the Life History of the Song Sparrow*, a pioneering study of the lives of individual birds. Nice was a woman who persisted. At Mount Holyoke, where she studied zoology, she was warned it wasn't safe for a girl to walk in the woods without a man, so she bought a revolver and rifle to explore the Holyoke Range alone on foot and by horseback. When she got her master's degree from Clark University, ornithological societies wouldn't accept women, so she worked alone, publishing papers on birds and child psychology. Later, married to an Ohio State professor and raising five daughters, she conducted her unprecedented seven-year study of Song Sparrows. She banded sixty-nine pairs of birds and watched them from birth to death, over several generations. In her popularized version of the study, *The Watcher at the Nest* (1967), Nice names many of the sparrows and brings out their individuality. Xantippe, named after the scolding wife of Socrates, bosses her long-suffering mate. Uno and Una, a pair, achieve a lasting equilibrium only after many small, subtle encounters prove that neither can dominate the other.

Nice makes us realize how perilous life is for birds. Like most songbirds, her sparrows lead "distressingly short lives." Birds inside eggs must struggle just to be born, and many die in infancy. In a successful brood, Nice found, an average of three young might survive, but only about half will reach adulthood, and few sparrows will live past two years. A sparrow preoccupied by food or courtship can easily pay with its life for momentary inattention. Song Sparrows can withstand cold winters and maintain populations in spite of natural predators, but they have little defense against roaming cats or human development that destroys their habitats.

In my patch I continue to seek answers. Will Song Sparrows breed again here? Where do local Turkey Vultures roost when they're not circling our hill? How do breeding birds know that there's still time in a season for a second or third clutch? The numbers from the atlas and Christmas Bird Counts provide valuable information about distribution of birds and population trends. For me the data has personal meaning. How are my neighbors doing? Are our common birds still common? Is my patch still a place where birds can thrive?

Chapter 3

WHIP-POOR-WILL SYNCHRONICITY

It was among the first birdsongs I came to know. Before English settlers named the bird, Native American tribes gave it their own onomatopoetic names. The Cherokee called the bird *waguli*. Poet Amy Clampitt describes its song as the "whipsawing voice of obsession," a sound "repeating itself like the stuck groove of an LP." If the wind was right, Mary and I could hear it in the darkness beyond our deck: rhythmic, propulsive, unflagging. When did these birds ever eat?

Other birders told me we were lucky to hear them. Eastern Whip-poor-wills are disappearing from eastern North American forests because of habitat loss in their breeding range and winter homes and a decline in their supply of insect food. In Massachusetts their distribution is shrinking. The woods in nearby Tompson Street Reservation have become the only place where they still breed regularly on Cape Ann.

One spring I got a notion: that year I'd be the first birder in Essex County to report an arriving whip-poor-will. It was a silly sort of vanity, but all I'd have to do was wait until late April, go out on the deck each night, and listen. But I wasn't the first that year, or the next, or the next. Each spring I was preempted by Avocet and Curlew—Jerry Soucy and Judge Larry Jodrey—two old birders from Rockport who drove into our neighborhood every night until they heard their first whip-poor-wills.

It was hard to begrudge Jerry and Larry. Premier birders as young men, inseparable partners for life, generous mentors

to new generations of birders, including me, they were local legends. Dignified despite their big, hulking frames, they were now plagued by severe arthritis and nastier infirmities and able to bird only by vehicle, with their beloved dog in the back seat. Amazing, what these two car-bound old guys managed to turn up: they were on a first-name, call-me-when-you-come-in basis with every bird on Cape Ann. They seemed like my personal scouts, reporting local species that eluded more mobile birders.

Only once did I ever see Jerry without Larry. On a raw March morning, an impromptu congress of birders gathered in a dense neighborhood in Malden to see an exciting wanderer from the South, a male Painted Bunting at a feeder. Unable to get a vantage point from his car, Jerry stepped out—the only time I ever saw him on foot. Shuffling along, he wore a bulky winter coat and red plaid pajama bottoms—no need for pants if you never leave the car. He'd seen many Painted Buntings, but his face brightened when the bird, with its lush palette of primary colors, showed up. Larry would have loved the bunting too; only sickness or great pain could have kept him away. Three years later Larry and Jerry both died, five months apart. Afterwards, whip-poor-wills continued to come to my patch each spring, but as if responding to a cue, they moved deeper into the woods. We could no longer hear them from our house.

One evening at dusk I was reading William Faulkner's "Barn Burning," a story I'd meant to recommend to Jerry and Larry. I was working on an article about writers we rarely associate with birds—Faulkner, Theodore Dreiser, Eudora Welty—who use birds in surprising, powerful ways in their fiction. I knew the Faulkner story well; I'd taught it to college students and prison inmates. Sarty Snopes, a ten-year-old boy, is torn between his troubled conscience and his loyalty to his father, Abner, a mean-spirited, abusive man, seething with grievance. Abner repeatedly manipulates situations to make himself feel wronged and then retaliates against his enemies by burning down their barns. With each arson he enlists his son to help him and then lie to substantiate his father's alibi. Sarty struggles to keep believing in his father's righteousness and bravery, but one night his belief is strained too far. Abner sets fire to yet another barn, this time with animals inside. In "grief and despair" Sarty warns the owner of the barn, betraying his father, and then runs to the crest of a hill, with a burst of gunshots behind him. He spends the night there, cut off from his family and every other human connection.

I'd reached the story's ending, the whip-poor-will part. The scene still chills me. Sarty, determined to keep moving, instead falls asleep. When he wakes, just before dawn, he hears whip-poor-wills everywhere in the woods below him, "constant and inflectioned and ceaseless." Sarty gets up. Alone but unafraid, as if drawn by the whip-poor-will chorus, he leaves his cruel father and old life behind and heads toward the "dark woods within which the liquid silver of the birds called unceasing—the rapid and urgent beating of the urgent and quiring heart of the late spring night. He did not look back."

I put down the story. Instantly I heard a sound outside the window. No, it couldn't be, but it was—a whip-poor-will in the yard, near our pond, whistling in my ear, on and on. Afraid I'd spook the bird, I eased out onto the deck. I felt the presence of Jerry and Larry. As I moved closer to the sound, I envisioned a boy alone in the night with urgently calling birds. A sense of wonder fought with a premonition of irrevocable loss. Then the whip-poor-will flushed and rose, floated, fluttered erratically as if suspended, just visible in the sky's last light. Somewhere, spirits with bright eyes were watching with me.

Chapter 4

BIRDS OF THE PROMISED LAND

In the sixth century, according to a story written three centuries later, Saint Brendan the Navigator led some Irish monks on a westward voyage to the Promised Land of the Saints. The monks got lost in fog, ran aground, put ashore on an island that turned into a gigantic whale, fought off beasts and fire-breathing dragons, and neared the stinking edge of hell. At several points they found refuge on an island called the Paradise of Birds. Here, a great flock of white birds rhythmically flapped their wings and sang hymns at vespers. One bird, speaking Latin, explained that the birds were Lucifer's fallen angels, put on the island by a merciful God. The bird told Brendan it would take the monks seven years to reach the Promised Land.

Back at sea the monks were rescued by another bird, which killed a flying griffin that had beset their boat. Beside a wide river in a beautiful land, a young man proclaimed that God had prolonged their voyage so they would discover many natural wonders in their quest. He urged them to sail back to Ireland, for it was prophesized that Brendan would soon die, but he promised that the Promised Land would be found by Brendan's descendants, who would need a new home at some time when Christians faced persecution. Brendan never got to his destination, but some modern scholars speculate that, almost five hundred years before the Vikings and nine hundred before Columbus, the monks might have reached the shores of North America. In 1977 a navigator built a replica of their boat and sailed across the Atlantic to Newfoundland to demonstrate that such a voyage was possible.

In 1492 Christopher Columbus, fearing failure and mutiny on his first transatlantic voyage, was heartened by the appearance of small birds around his ships, a sign that land—a continent, in fact—was close. He set his final course by following flocks of birds migrating south in October. In 1630, off Cape Ann, after another long voyage, John Winthrop anticipated landfall when a dove and small songbird perched aboard the *Arbella*, the Puritan fleet's flagship, which carried the charter to establish the Commonwealth of Massachusetts.

Like Columbus and Winthrop, most early European explorers and colonizers who reached the Promised Land—the New World, the New Eden—met the birds of North America as they moved west across the Atlantic and then pressed inland. But the first human inhabitants had come from the far north of Eurasia, spreading south and east across the continent and to the tip of South America in a long, gradual, punctuated dispersion. These aboriginal Americans came to know our continent's birds as prey, vital clues to seasonal changes, and spiritual ancestors and kin. Tribes varied in their knowledge of native birds, but the distinctive birds of each region became powerful inspirations for the distinctive peoples that settled there, such as snipe and herons in Iroquois lands. Each tribe had its own names for birds, often onomatopoetic, like *chuwquareo*, an Algonquin name for Red-Winged Blackbird. In *Spirits of the Air*, a study of birds in southeastern Native American cultures, Shepard Krech notes that Cherokee "collectively distinguished 110 kinds of birds," most corresponding clearly to species recognized by modern ornithologists, like the Ovenbird and Hooded Warbler. One Cherokee village had a name equivalent to "Birdtown"; One clan consisted of "bird people." Some Cherokee had names like Moses Barred Owl or Sally

Screech Owl. The Red-Headed Woodpecker, much admired by Cherokee for its pugnacity, was invoked in war and in ball games that simulated war.

There's no equivalent to Krech's book about the birds of New England tribes, in large part because of the epidemic that decimated tribes in our region before Europeans settled here. What we know comes mostly from reports of explorers and settlers who weren't focused on birds but recorded their contacts with Native Americans along with observations about climate, timber, fish, sheltered harbors, and overall prospects for settlement. In 1606 on Cape Cod, French explorer Samuel Champlain met Nausets who used turkey feathers for arrows and decoration. Thomas Morton in his 1637 *New English Canaan* described Wampanoags who wore hummingbird earrings and traded in "tassels" made from the dead bodies of small raptors, which were dried, stretched, and fashioned into ornaments worn in knotted hair. Captain John Smith listed eighty-six native names for birds from Virginia to New England. Trade in goods, including bird feathers, brought distant tribes together. Some northerners bartered buckskins with southern tribes for the bills of now-extinct Ivory-Billed Woodpeckers, to be used as coronets for warriors.

From the Caribbean to the northern islands of New France, a common refrain among Europeans was amazed exclamation at the abundance of American birds. In Newfoundland in 1534, French explorer Jacques Cartier found island cliffs turned white by legions of nesting gannets, flightless Great Auks wonderfully plentiful, fat, and easy to kill, and waterfowl swarming in such density that "all the ships of France might load a cargo of them without one perceiving that any of them had been removed." Champlain described such bird plentitude that "one could not imagine it, if he had not seen them." He noted the "infinite number" of cormorant eggs taken from islands along with the various birds his men caught and ate during their explorations from New France to Cape Cod. "If this Land be not rich," wrote Morton in Merrymount, now Quincy, "then is the whole world poore." The sense of almost unlimited resources continued as settlers pushed westward, finding great flocks of prairie-chickens in the Ohio Valley and pelicans perched endlessly on snags along the Mississippi.

In the woodlands of what are now Boston and Manhattan, settlers marveled at and even complained about the sheer volume of bird whistling and chattering. Europeans were awed by the bounty they found, and unlike Native Americans, they had grounds for comparison. Well before the American Revolution, English writers at home were lamenting the clearing of forests and the decline of once common birds like cranes, kites, and bustards. Ornithologists can piece together which birds inhabited the forests, fields, and coves of coastal Massachusetts four centuries ago, but we can only imagine the rich soundscape of songs and flight calls now lost to time.

Natural abundance was hardly uniform across New England, and availability of resources did not lead automatically to ability to make use of those resources. *Mourt's Relation*, published in 1622 by early Pilgrim settlers on Cape Cod, describes a land with "excellent black earth," endless woodlands, and "the greatest store of fowl that ever we saw," yet John Smith described Cape Cod as "only a headland of high hills of sand overgrown with shrubby pines, hurts [huckleberry] and such trash." Along much of the coastline, from Cape Cod to Dogtown on Cape Ann, the soil was too sandy, stony, or wet for successful cultivation. Cape Cod historian Henry Kittredge says that it took English settlers several generations to look to the sea for food because their farming struggles consumed virtually all their energy: "They had to be farmers or starve." One early colonist wrote: "We hope meat will last 'till fish comes, and fish will last 'till meat comes." A pioneer heading west in search of more fertile pastures would have to confront the forbidding Berkshire Barrier—the mountains of western Massachusetts.

The birds reported by early settlers were usually game birds. Modern readers may be appalled by accounts of mass killings of wild birds, but birds were more readily available than other food sources. Laborers complained if they were fed Heath Hens more than a few times a week, but the hens were sometimes the only source of protein. The Plymouth Pilgrims fended off starvation during their second winter by eating waterfowl and Wild Turkeys, so common they were later hunted in collective drives involving up to three hundred men. The ultimate emblem of abundance—now the prototype for extinction through human agency—was the Passenger Pigeon. In New England and beyond, observer after observer, over several centuries, described flocks in the millions, darkening the skies as they took hours or days to pass overhead or descending in hordes to eat crops and bring down trees with their weight. The pigeons were at once pests, food, and sources of needed income. In 1643 Plymouth farmers feared famine when a huge flock put down in their fields. By the late seventeenth century it was common practice to trap the pigeons in nets or knock them off the trees with sticks at night, since shooting them for the market was too inefficient.

With survival threatened by starvation, sickness, terrifying storms, and conflicts with natives, it's not surprising that early explorers and colonists left us with few descriptions of pretty birds or glorious American landscapes. They didn't come here to look at birds, and many seemed oblivious to our continent's distinctive wildlife. Columbus compared birdsong in the Bahamas to "April in Andalusia," but descriptions of birds by conquistadors were rare and vague. "We know little of what the Spaniards saw," Peter Matthiessen says, "so intent were they on gold."

Still, explorers and settlers in New England were struck by the beauty and strangeness of some local birds. Near Nauset Harbor, Champlain's crew gawked at impossibly long-billed Black Skimmers sweeping the surface of a marsh. How could birds eat with such beaks? Colonists were amazed by what early naturalist John Lawson called the "Miracle of all our winged Animals," hummingbirds, endemic to the Western Hemisphere and at first mistaken for insects. Ruby-Throated Hummingbirds were soon being shipped to Europe as decorations for women's hats, specimens for collectors, and pets, though the birds rarely lasted more than a few months in captivity.

In his 1977 *A Species of Eternity*, a study of early American naturalists, Joseph Kastner cites one New Englander who wrote of "a thousand different kinds of birds and beasts of the forests which have never been known in shape nor name neither among the Latins nor Greeks nor any other nations of the world." The weirdness of these birds could be theologically unnerving. "The uniqueness of the New World called into question the whole Christian cosmogony," historian Alfred Crosby says in *The Columbian Exchange* (1972). "If God had created all the life forms in one week and one place and they had spread out from there over the whole world, then why were the life forms in the eastern and western hemispheres so different?" Some Dutch pioneers in New York were terrified by a flock of garish, tropical-looking Carolina Parakeets (now extinct) that showed up mysteriously one winter—a sign, they believed, that the end was near.

Yet other species were noticeably missing from settlers' observations. "On the whole," Krech says, "small birds went underreported, unreported, or overgeneralized." Rarely mentioned were whole families of birds: flycatchers, wrens, vireos.

Our New World warblers are now cherished for their subtly patterned beauty and variety, but many warblers appear in Massachusetts only briefly during migrations and are often high in treetops when they sing. Without modern optics they were tough to see, much less identify and admire.

Our knowledge of early bird discoveries in Massachusetts and beyond is also complicated by the vagueness of many descriptions, uncertain identification or definite misidentification of species, and confusing naming of birds. Some reports come to us uncorroborated from questionable observers. In 1583 English sailor David Ingram was stranded with two other men when their slave ship was sunk by a Spanish warship off Veracruz. When they were found by French fur traders near the modern Canadian border, Ingram claimed they'd walked all the way from Mexico, up the entire East coast of North America. He accurately described a Great Auk he'd seen but also insisted he'd found elephants and animals he called "unces," never seen since. John Smith admitted he'd seen many birds "whose names I know not," and he used now archaic vernacular names like "dive-doppers"—probably grebes, since Shakespeare referred to grebes as "dive-dappers." Bartholomew Gosnold, exploring the islands off Cape Cod, mentioned various birds that, as John Hay and Peter Farb say in *The Atlantic Shore* (1966), "are either not designated specifically or else given such fanciful names that we cannot guess what they may have been." In *New England's Prospect*, a catalogue of the region's natural resources, William Wood asserted there were no jays, cuckoos, or sparrows in New England—puzzling, I thought, until my friend Chris Leahy reminded me that there's only one jay and one cuckoo in Europe, neither of which resemble North American jays and cuckoos, and that the English (House) Sparrow had not yet been introduced to our continent.

One source of ongoing confusion was that settlers often named American birds after more or less similar European birds. Thus we have the American Robin, which, while red-breasted, is decidedly larger and not closely related to the Eurasian Robin. The Northern Mockingbird, the first songbird Europeans recorded in North America, was for the next two centuries misleadingly called the Virginia Nightingale, after the Nightingale of Europe from an entirely different family. The term "flycatcher" was applied to both wood warblers and species now called New World flycatchers, a large family endemic to the Western Hemisphere and genetically far removed from the assorted birds, from several different families, that are still called "flycatcher" in the Old World.

Sorting through this confusion were the first American naturalists, self-taught, daring explorers who were excited by the prospect of discoveries, determined to identify birds accurately, and sometimes risked their lives to find new birds but lacked modern optics and scientific training in a time before modern Linnaean taxonomy was even established. In the early eighteenth century, Mark Catesby published his pioneering *Natural History of Carolina, Florida, and the Bahama Islands*, the first comprehensive and illustrated work on the colonies' natural history—a book that, given the challenges, had remarkably few errors and became the basis for the bird list in Thomas Jefferson's *Notes on Virginia.* Wood's earlier account of New England birds, set in rhyme, was both sketchier and more judgmental. Birds, Wood thought, could yield colonists both "profit" and "honest pleasure," but he didn't like "ill-shaped" loons, while cormorants were "greedy" creatures that tasted "rank and filthy"—a judgment shared by other cormorant-eaters. But the gorgeous "humbird" was "for some queen's rich cage more fit, than in the vacant wilderness to sit." John Josselyn in his 1672 *New England's Rarities Discovered* shared Wood's enthusiasm for the region's birds but complained that it was now hard to find a "wild turkie" in Massachusetts. He offered an early warning that, through overhunting, the bounty of birds was thinning.

The Puritans who settled Massachusetts may have written more prolifically than any other immigrants in world history, but they said little about birds or other wildlife. In his 1662 *Day of Doom*, minister Michael Wigglesworth described the bird-rich woodlands surrounding their settlements as nothing but "a waste and howling wilderness" inhabited by "hellish fiends" and brutish devil-worshippers. When Puritan poets like Edward Taylor and Anne Bradstreet wrote about birds, they didn't write about the songbirds outside their doors but the staples of English poetry, the nightingale and skylark, absent from Massachusetts, or strictly literary birds, like birds of paradise, chosen for their potential as spiritual metaphors. Bradstreet, a passenger on the *Arbella*, raised eight children in the New World until her death at age sixty, but, as historian Perry Miller says in *Errand into the Wilderness* (1956), her "flowers are English flowers, the birds, English birds, and the landscape is Lincolnshire."

One exception might have been Jonathan Edwards, a revivalist minister in Northampton now best remembered for his fire-and-brimstone sermon "Sinners in the Hands of an Angry God." As a child he communed alone with God in the woods and was curious to explore God's "amazing works" in the natural world. But, like other devout Puritans, Edwards was seeking the Design of Creation, not thrushes or nuthatches, and the birds in his writings are never birds alone but "shadows" or "images" of "divine things" that exist to demonstrate God's excellence and provide spiritual lessons, or "analogies," for human souls. His birds are generally beautiful and benign, flying like angels while "sweetly praising the creator" with their music, but he also uses traditionally evil birds, like scavenging ravens and wailing, light-shunning owls, to represent the incessant workings of devils on earth: "Ravens that with delight feed on carrion seem to be remarkable types of devils who with delight prey upon the souls of the dead." The symbolism, based on convention, is utterly arbitrary. Ravens will indeed feed on dead flesh as well as anything from toads to tacos to Twinkies, but they might be used just as easily to embody prudence, conjugal loyalty, and a host of other Christian virtues.

In 1692 Puritan leader Cotton Mather wrote *Political Fables*, a series of bestiaries in which Massachusetts Puritans are allegorically portrayed as birds, some catching fish, some eating grains, some scraping for a living with their claws. Increase Mather, Cotton's father, is the eagle in charge, who has secured their settlement in a new land with a promise that infidel birds will be kept away from the "singing of their songs to the praise of their Maker, for which they had sought liberty in the wilderness."

Cotton Mather later wrote, "What is not useful is vicious"—a principle that guided the treatment of actual birds by many colonists. The "vicious" birds were rivals and pests, like the hawks judged guilty as menaces to poultry and game birds, or the "rice birds," Bobolinks, sometimes shot in southern colonies as rice field raiders. Useful birds, on the other hand, were easy to hunt and good to eat. In his 1977 *Natural History in America from Mark Catesby to Rachel Carson*, historian Wayne Hanley notes that the first lists of American wildlife were "little more than suggested menus indicating that settlers would find plenty to eat." John Smith itemized the "supplies" of birds in the air. Thomas Morton boasted of seeing a thousand waterfowl "before the mouth of my gunne" and killing fifty Sanderlings with one shot. Birds, like other natural resources, were commodities. Wood specified the market value of each bird he killed—a partridge worth four pence, a duck, six, a teal, three. If hard-to-shoot, foul-tasting cormorants were bad, then the tasty shorebirds, or "simplicities," were good, though stupid, so simple they could be driven into a heap like sheep. Some birds were valued for medicinal benefits. Since the species is now extinct, the recipe can't be tested, but Josselyn claimed that the Wobble, or Great Auk, could be an effective analgesic if one made a "mummy" of it by killing, salting, drying, roasting, burying, quartering, and then stewing the bird.

I imagine that some settlers must have been enthralled by the sky-earth colors of bluebirds on a misty spring morning or charmed by the berry-sharing of waxwings or felt pangs of homesickness when on a cold, windswept pasture there appeared a lively flock of Snow Buntings, birds that are also winter visitors in England and Holland. For some individuals the sounds of birds must have evoked intimate memories—maybe an oriole that had sung sweetly above two young lovers or an owl that had whinnied in darkness during a woman's long trial of labor. We'll never know. In fact we know little about what birds meant to ordinary colonists, though we can draw some inferences from Keith Thomas's *Man and the Natural World* (1983), a study of English attitudes toward nature during the time of American colonization. The view of birds that emerges in Thomas is a mix of utility, competition, superstition, moral judgment, gratuitous cruelty, and fond familiarity. Quail are salacious, choughs thievish and incendiary, and woodpeckers and swallows unclean because they feed on bugs, while robins are loved because they love people in return. Children routinely rob nests and torture small birds, but powerful superstitions warn that to rob a wren or swallow nest is to risk death. Even small songbirds are hunted for food, yet some vernacular names—Tom Tit, Jenny Wren, Philip Sparrow—suggest affection as well as familiarity. By the late seventeenth century, Thomas says, there was a thriving London market for pet birds, "some caught at home by professional bird-catchers, others exotics imported from the tropics."

To get a more personal sense of what birds meant to immigrants in the Northeast, we have to cross into eastern New York, where, around the time of the American Revolution, Hector St. John de Crevecoeur wrote *Letters from an American Farmer* and *Sketches of the Eighteenth Century America*. Living at "the edge of a great wilderness," de Crevecoeur was a "cultivator of the earth," nature's collaborator, proud of his role in settling "this fair country." As a farmer he had a love-hate relationship with birds. He killed crows and blackbirds, his corn's "greatest enemies," by using poisoned corn and then hanging dead birds to terrorize their companions. Yet, admiring his enemies' wiliness and temerity, he asks, "But after all the efforts of our selfishness, are they not the children of the great Creator as well as we?" He esteems Eastern Kingbirds, or "bee martins," for their skill on the wing and fierce defense of territory against "tyrant" hawks, yet he feels obliged to shoot "these little kings of the air" for eating too many of his bees. Killing some birds while condemning the killing of others, de Crevecoeur prefigured John James Audubon and other Americans who both hunted birds and worked to preserve them. He shot great numbers of Passenger Pigeons, using tamed pigeons to "allure" them, yet he was outraged by the "barbarous" hunters who murdered the "harmless" Northern Bobwhites he fed during harsh winters. Appreciating the birds on his patch, he also anticipated today's backyard birder. He delighted in the "passion" of hummingbirds, stopped to listen to "delicious" thrush songs, marveled at the artistry of nest-building, commended birds for their self-reliance, and wondered at the "sublimity of knowledge" that enabled songbirds to migrate great distances and return to his farm each spring.

After the Revolution the great nineteenth-century wandering naturalists, like Alexander Wilson and Audubon, would travel thousands of miles on foot, on horseback, and by boat to discover and catalogue new birds and other fauna and flora in the immense American wilderness. In 1822 Harvard College hired Thomas Nuttall as a natural history lecturer and curator of its botanical garden. Nuttall had discovered and collected specimens of new birds and plants from the northern Great Lakes to Arkansas Territory, and he would later explore the Pacific Northwest, California, and the Sandwich Islands (now Hawaii). He was a popular teacher, guiding his students on rambles through nearby woods, but Harvard was then a backwater in the study of biology, and Nuttall grew restive, later describing his Harvard period as a time of vegetating with the vegetation. In his last years there, he devoted himself to writing his two-volume *A Manual of the Ornithology of the United States and Canada*, published in 1832 and 1834 and generally considered the first field guide to North American birds. "They play around us like fairy spirits," he wrote, "elude approach in an element which defies our pursuit, dart like meteors in the sunshine of summer, glide before us as beings of fancy." Nuttall concluded with an outraged cry to stop the mass shooting of birds: "Public economy and utility, then, no less than humanity, plead for the protection of the feathered race; and the wanton destruction of birds, so useful, beautiful, and amusing, if not treated as such by law, ought to be considered a crime by every moral, feeling, and reflecting mind."

By Nuttall's time at Harvard, the prospect of owning land had brought generations of immigrants to the Northeast. "There is room for everybody in America," de Crevecoeur had written, and the great expansion continued across the Promised Land to the Pacific coast. Abraham Lincoln once said that of the three factors that make a nation—territory, people, laws—only territory is durable, and by the end of the nineteenth century, all the vast, "empty" territories on early maps of our country were finally occupied. "The movement of so many people," proclaimed Frederick Jackson Turner in his 1893 *The Frontier in American History*, "the mad pace of settlement—chopping, clearing, buying and quickly selling out—had there ever been anything like this in the whole history of the Western world?" Throughout our country, the whole idea of territory was redefined. Natural boundaries like mountains and rivers, the acoustic spaces claimed by birds, and the boundaries set by Native American tribes were all subsumed by conceptions of territory based on geometrical surveying of land, fragmentations of space into fixed private properties, nationalistic claims to sovereignty, and multitudes of borders—between neighbor and neighbor, city and city, free states and slave states, Indian reservations and land not yet settled and still contested. The political power behind border definition and control is nicely illustrated by the scheme of "gerrymandering," a term that originated in Essex County. The borders have changed since the days of Eldridge Gerry, our fifth vice president, but the land itself has been demarcated to such an extent that we can barely move through space without some awareness of manufactured boundaries, landmarks, and objective-looking maps. This book focuses on an artificial territory—a state with straight lines on three sides—that means nothing to the birds we see in Massachusetts.

As humans gained territory, birds lost it, often through deforestation. Some contemporary writers such as James Fenimore Cooper were angered by the indiscriminate clearing of the land. Natty Bumppo, his hero in *The Leatherstocking Saga*, is literally a voice crying in the wilderness as he rails against axes scourging the earth and seeks refuge in woodlands, where he can be alone with "the occasional and lazy tap of a woodpecker, the discordant cry of some gaudy jay." In her 1850 *Rural Hours*, Cooper's daughter, Susan Fenimore Cooper, calls the wasteful felling of forests a sign of "careless indifference" to God's gifts that betrays "a reckless spirit of evil." In his 1849 *A Week on the Concord and Merrimack Rivers*, Thoreau predicted that when the fish hawk (Osprey) returns in spring, "he will circle in vain to find his accustomed perch, and the hen-hawk [probably Red-Shouldered Hawk] will mourn for the pines lofty enough to protect her brood." Thoreau mourned the loss of "nobler animals" in Massachusetts like bears, beavers, deer, and Wild Turkeys: "Is it not a maimed and imperfect nature that I am conversant with? As if I were to study a tribe of Indians that had lost its warriors."

Modern writers often look back at this human takeover of the natural world as wasteful overexploitation of the environment. In his 2001 *The Eternal Frontier*, an ecological history of North America, Tim Flannery says, "The very essence of the frontier experience lies in the extent of its resources, and when resources are boundless, why conserve them or even use them efficiently? The principal goal is to exploit them as quickly as possible, then move on." William Cronon concludes *Changes in the Land* (1993), a historical study of New England ecology, by saying: "The people of plenty were a people of waste." But when Americans were still moving across the continent and clearing forests for farming and industry, the voices of protest were few. I remember learning about "manifest destiny" in school and thinking it made intuitive sense, even if some capitalists might cynically exploit the concept to rationalize their greed. A land mass naturally bordered by oceans, vast areas unoccupied, people needing land to live on—it seemed inevitable that Americans would settle the continent from coast to coast. Emerson loved to walk among the birds in uninhabited Concord woodlands, but he believed that America's spiritual expansion must go hand in hand with the physical tasks of surveying, farming, and building on the continent's immense tracts of land. Thoreau was disturbed to see forests impoverished, but Walden was one of many Massachusetts woodlots providing fuel for homeowners, and he worked in part as a surveyor, helping to divide woodlands into parcels of private property.

The point is not to bash Emerson and Thoreau—we all still live with such contradictions. I'd like to think that if I'd settled in Gloucester four centuries ago, or two, I would've been considerate and frugal in cutting down trees and shooting birds. I also would have been a righteous abolitionist, a fighter for women's equality, and an enlightened humanist waiting for Darwin to tell the world the truth about our species' animal ancestry. The year 1890 is often cited as marking the closing of the American frontier. It's no coincidence that in the next few decades, American wilderness was first set aside in national parks, bird conservation movements were first organized and gained widespread support, and birding clubs were formed to bring city people out into the natural world. People were beginning to realize that there were no more Promised Lands to move on to.

Birds and humans have had a complex history together since the first European settlement of what is now Massachusetts. If Champlain and Smith were transported to our coastlines now, they'd surely be stunned by the transformations—wilderness turned into metropolises, unmapped spaces now a maze of boundaries, Great Auks gone. But they could still find Black Skimmers on Cape Cod and dive-doppers off Cape Ann. Our history includes the story of wonderful discoveries of new birds and growing knowledge of the birds we live among. Another story is about abundance found, abundance diminished, and sometimes desperate efforts to preserve what remains. It's now unusual to find a bird book that doesn't end with a call for conservation, and this book is no exception. There's no refuge for us in a Paradise of Birds. The Promised Land has been found and settled. We've left our mark everywhere, but the land still holds promise.

Chapter 5

WATCHING GULLS WITH EMERSON ON CAPE TRAGABIGZANDA

One June morning my wife, a self-described beach bum, strolled in to tell me she'd just seen some swallows flying into holes in the Wingaersheek dunes. "Bank Swallows?" she wondered.

"Sure sounds like it." Other swallows did not nest in dunes.

"Is that good?"

"Sure would be. Thanks, honey."

Swallows in holes: some spouses might not find this exciting news, but I was in the midst of the atlas, trying to confirm breeding by as many species as possible. Bank Swallows nested in the Crane dunes across Essex Bay. I'd seen some hawking insects above the marsh in my atlas block. But to my knowledge they didn't breed anywhere in Gloucester. In fact, I couldn't recall any record of Bank Swallows nesting on Cape Ann.

I drove to the beach. There, swooping over humans digging in the sand, twelve Bank Swallows commuted to and from burrows in the sandy banks. One close bird emitted shrill, agitated cries. Two chased each other as if playing you're-it. But at least three were clearly feeding mouths inside the burrows. I noted the date and place—Bank Swallows, breeding confirmed—and posted a report to tell other birders about the Wingaersheek swallows.

The next day Chris Leahy, a Gloucester man well versed in the arts as well as birds, sent me an e-mail with a link to an art website. In 1873, when Winslow Homer summered in Gloucester, he'd painted the watercolor "How Many Eggs?" Two barefoot boys, with swallows in the air around them, hunt for eggs in a dune. The next year Homer published a wood engraving with four egg-thieving boys, "Raid on a Sand-Swallow Colony—How Many Eggs?" The scene might be Crane, not Wingaersheek, but it didn't matter. Swallows in sand, local boys up to mischief generations ago, Winslow Homer and my wife in a line of breeding bird observers: this is why I love Cape Ann. Here you can go birding with history.

Birding can lose you in the moment, released from the anxiety or aimlessness of time-consciousness, but there's another dimension—a sense of connection to those who came before us and knew the same birds in the same places. Some were Native Americans, some groundbreaking ornithologists like Edward Howe Forbush. Others were writers and artists, both locals and visitors, inspired by our landscapes and seascapes to express what those scapes and their birds meant to them. Through the gulls, owls, and warblers of Cape Ann, I've found the cultural history of this place I call home.

With ocean, offshore islands, beaches, rivers, salt marsh, brushy fields, rocky headlands, and expansive woodlands, Cape Ann offers fine birding in all seasons, but it's especially known among birders as a prime destination in the Northeast for winter seabirds. A winter birding tour of our cape can also be a way to explore its cultural history. When I lead trips for the Brookline Bird Club and Essex County Ornithological Club, our route begins at Stacy Boulevard, a long, arcing, harborside promenade. We meet at the icon of Gloucester's proud fishing history, the bronze Man at the Wheel, sculpted in 1923 by Leonard Kraske, with the names of fishermen who died at sea and an inscription from a psalm: "They that go down to the sea in ships, that do business in great waters: These see the works of the Lord, and his wonders in the deep." Rudyard Kipling's 1897 *Captains Courageous*, set in Gloucester, dramatizes the dangers of life at sea in our waters. From the boulevard we look across Gloucester's outer harbor to Ten Pound Island in the foreground and Dog Bar Breakwater further out. From the breakwater we can see the Boston skyline thirty miles distant.

The harbor offers vistas that have long enthralled painters. In 1880 Homer spent his second Gloucester summer living on Ten Pound Island, looking back at the city from inside a scene he'd painted: a sailboat glides past the island's lighthouse on a sea rippled with prismatic reflections. In a soft, summery Frederick Childe Hassam painting, women read in rocking chairs overlooking the island. Fitz Henry Lane, Cape Ann's foremost marine artist, returned time and again to paint harbor scenes from fresh perspectives, in meditative moods, in all seasons: boats large and small passing the island, with men onshore launching a dory; schooners emergent in fog, icebound, or full-sailed under high skies; a sailboat under a full moon on a navy blue night. Lane has been called the taxonomist of the Gloucester coast. His paintings of Norman's Woe and Rafe's Chasm show the rocky, treacherous shorelines that await fishermen just out of the harbor.

On winter birding trips we search mostly for seabirds: ducks, loons, grebes, gulls. It's my job as trip leader to count the birds we find, but this isn't the Christmas Bird Count. If someone is struggling to differentiate species—say, Greater Scaup versus Lesser Scaup—or is beguiled by a particular bird, we'll take a leisurely look. It's always fun to watch the Common Buffleheads, compact, buoyant ducks, black and white with a big white patch on the back of a black head. Their name means "buffalo-headed." In the right light, the black head turns iridescent purplish green. They're also called "spirit ducks" for their sprightliness, quick plunges, bursts of flight, and gregarious bobbing on the ocean. As with many duck species in which males and females don't look much alike, the drabber females puzzled early naturalists. Mark Catesby called them Little Brown Ducks.

Jodrey State Fish Pier, in the inner harbor, is Gull City. Here we scan the water, pilings, and warehouse rooftops for uncommon "white-winged" gulls like Glaucous and Iceland among hundreds of Herring Gulls. John Kieran, surely the only member of the Baseball Hall of Fame (as a sportswriter) with a bird sanctuary (in Rockport) named after him, described one "dignified" gull standing aboard a floating ice cake like "a ferryboat captain in command of his gallant craft." Poet Anne Sexton watched a world of gulls "swinging over Gloucester to the top of the sky" or letting the fog slip through their fingertips. Charles Olson, living in the Fort neighborhood at the entrance to the inner harbor, met gulls all over town, hungry, tough, bold birds that talked to him and flew into his breast. In one poem his gulls are "bummaging," a word that perfectly captures their brazen panhandling while playing on Olson's name for the working city he loved, Ragged Arse Gloucester. During his famous gull study Niko Tinbergen was fascinated by the birds' "wonderful adaptations" and "astonishing limitations." He thought it wonderful to "see a gull take a shellfish up into the air and drop it in order to crush it," yet he was astonished by one clueless gull that dropped a shell into soft mud, over and over. Birds, he decided, might be smart, but they could behave stupidly when the "correct" stimulus occurred in the "wrong" situation.

Like many birders, I was slow to warm up to gull study—too much plumage variation, not enough color, some distasteful feeding habits—but the world has some great gulls, like our

Glaucous, frosted pale, robust, an Arctic neighbor to polar bears in its breeding season. Seventeen species have been found on Cape Ann, and some have enticed rarity-seeking birders from far-off places. In 2008 at the fish pier, David Sibley sighted the first Slaty-Backed Gull ever recorded in Massachusetts. When I got the word, the gull wasn't visible from the pier, so I tried a snowy knoll above the inner harbor, where Lane had lived in a gray seven-gabled stone house, once a jail called the Old Stone Jug. The pink-legged Slaty-Backed stood atop a warehouse below. Beside me, a Herring Gull landed wryly on the sculpted stone head of Lane painting a harbor scene.

Herring and Great Black-Backed Gulls are opportunists, and their populations exploded around Cape Ann in part because of the dumping of fish waste and disposal of human-generated trash in our waters and landfills. When they started nesting on offshore islands in the 1920s, they took over areas held by nesting terns. The gulls were present year-round, while the terns wintered in the tropics and returned only in May, after the gulls had claimed territory. To some people these usurpers symbolize the degraded world we now inhabit, but we can't blame the gulls. Humans offered them an opportunity, and the gulls naturally took advantage.

The fish pier provides a view of the Victorian cupolas and copper domes of the City Hall clock tower. Since 2007 a pair of Peregrine Falcons have wintered on the tower, commanding our city like sentinels. By the mid-twentieth century Peregrine Falcons had nearly disappeared from the eastern United States as pesticide buildup reduced calcium in their eggshells, so that few eggs hatched and populations were decimated. But through successful efforts to restrict DDT use, the falcons have recovered, and, adaptable birds, many have found homes in our cities, roosting on towers, church steeples, and the ledges of skyscrapers like the Boston Custom House.

Downtown was part of Edward Hopper's patch, not the lonesome Hopper of "Nighthawks" and "Automat" but a brighter Hopper who summered here in the 1920s and painted watercolors of sunny sailboats in the harbor and rambling Victorian houses with mansard roofs. Above the inner harbor, on Portuguese Hill, stands the blue-domed Church of Our Lady of Good Voyage, built in 1914 by fishermen from the Azores and designed after an Azorean church, with one of the oldest sets of carillon bells in the country. Olson feared that Gloucester would one day forget its maritime heritage—the great migrations of its peoples and a tradition of self-reliance—and become like the rest of the nation, smaller in spirit, tamer, fallen from grace.

From the fish pier we wind through East Gloucester, all pasture land until the railroad's arrival in 1847 helped make Gloucester the country's busiest fishing port, its harbor trafficked with wind ships. At Niles Beach we scope for Horned and Red-Necked Grebes among the scoters and other ducks in the harbor. The grebes, from an ancient family of aquatic carnivores, are long-necked divers, smaller than loons and here only in winter on open water. The family name *Podicipedidae* means "rump-footed." Feet positioned at the extreme end of their bodies make it hard for grebes to stand, walk, or take off from land. In the traditional Koyukon culture of Alaska, where Red-Necked Grebes breed, only old people eat the grebes, since young people would become as clumsy as a grebe on land if they ate them.

Eastern Point is a peninsula, described by Garland in *Eastern Point* (1971) as an "arm of wild-grown ledge that makes the Bay of Gloucester." Mansions with vast lawns overlook the harbor. You know you're among the rich when the houses are named, like the lovely stone Villa Latomia, or Quarry House, built around 1915 with stucco balconies and a harbor-facing belfry.

The woodlands here, though dwindling through development, still attract migrating songbirds in spring and fall, but in winter we head for the lighthouse and coast guard station at the southern tip. If you stand in just the right spot here, you might see Mother Ann, a jumble of surf-battered rocks supposedly resembling a sleeping woman. Purple Sandpipers often crowd on rocks at the end of the long granite breakwater. One day from the breakwater I spotted a close Common Murre, more likely outside than inside the harbor. It's one of six northern-breeding alcids, or auks, that can be seen off our coasts in winter. People sometimes think they're northern equivalents of penguins, but they can fly and are genetically distant from the penguin family.

Before we leave Eastern Point we check Niles Pond, once saltwater but a spring-fed freshwater pond since the mid-nineteenth century, when farmer Thomas Niles built a dike to separate the pond from Brace Cove. Niles owned the entire peninsula and tried his damnedest to keep it to himself, fighting battles in court with locals long accustomed to free roaming of the area. Most residents now are friendly enough, and the public has access to the pond and a Mass Audubon sanctuary by the lighthouse, but the neighborhood association worries about outsiders disrupting their privately maintained enclave. A few times I've been accosted by some territorial squire. During a Christmas Bird Count one indignant homeowner complained to police about two bearded, unkempt young men "in hoodies" prowling his street with binoculars.

At the pond we look again for unusual gulls. Standing on ice here, the Slaty-Backed was easily identified by its diagnostic dark pink legs. Open water may bring ducks like Red-Breasted Mergansers and Ring-Necked Ducks, or American Coots, all black with stout white bills, not ducks but related to rails. Coots cluck, grunt, and mutter as they drift along the edges, sometimes joined by Pied-Billed Grebes, small, dark pond-feeders with little chicken-like faces. Frustrated hunters used to call these grebes "water witches" and "hell divers" because they'd submerge instantly at the flash of a fowling gun. In the reeds an overwintering Great Blue Heron might stand erect as a marine.

Across the dike, the beach at Brace Cove was built up by a long, gradual erosion of the cove's soft bottom, forming a sand bar, then a barrier reef, then a dune. Shorebirds feed along the wrack line during migrations, while blubbery harbor seals sprawl in the sun on offshore rocks. False Point, the northern headland, was once so notorious for shipwrecks that the Massachusetts Humane Society maintained a boathouse here as a rescue station. Yet the cove is also the scene of a stunningly serene Lane painting. Generations of *plein air* painters have been drawn here by the quality of light.

Eastern Point is where T. S. Eliot spent his summers from 1895 to 1909, the last of these in a house his father built by the moors above Niles Beach. "What seas what shores what grey rocks and what islands," Eliot wrote in the poem "Marina," "what water, lapping the bow and scent of pine and the woodthrush singing through the fog." In Gloucester Eliot learned to sail, dig for crabs, and look for birds. When he turned fourteen his parents gave him Frank Chapman's *Handbook of Birds of Eastern North America*, and birds appear in his poems throughout his career. Some are Eurasian, like a Common Kingfisher in "Burnt Norton" "at the still point of the turning world," but often they're birds of his childhood, like the Hermit Thrush that sings from pines in "The Waste Land." An early poem published in the *Harvard Advocate* celebrates a "great white bird" slipping from an alder, a Snowy Owl, a species still found in winter on our cape's islands and rocky coasts.

Some of Eliot's most famous poems, like "The Waste Land," are his bleakest, but especially in later works, he had a lighter side, evident in "Cape Ann," a poem devoted to birds. The last of five *Landscapes* from 1933 to 1934, "Cape Ann" expresses Eliot's simple joy in the "delectable" birds of his boyhood: the "quick quick quick" sparrows singing at dawn and dusk; the Blackburnian Warbler, "the shy one"; the Purple Martin, "the dancing arrow"; the Yellow Warbler singing "sweet sweet sweet"; and the Common Nighthawk, or "bullbat," flying through silence. At poem's end Eliot bids us to resign this land to its "true owner, the tough one"—the gull.

Eliot's "Ash Wednesday" is narrated by an old man who has given up hope and imagines himself an "aged eagle whose wings are no longer wings to fly." But "East Coker," published ten years later, in 1940, concludes with an urging to keep moving, to strive—where does not matter—to the end. "Old men ought to be explorers," he writes. We should seek a "deeper communion" with the cries of waves and winds, with "the vast waters of the petrel and the porpoise." It is advice I try to follow. And Eliot's legacy in Gloucester continues: the family house just off Eastern Point has recently been converted to a writers' retreat.

Our next stop is Bass Rocks, on the Back Shore, with a view of the twin lighthouses on Thacher Island. The shoreline here is heaped with boulders, some time-painted with dark bands. Purple Sandpipers congregate on seaweed-covered rocks below the Elks Club, former headquarters of the Cape Ann Winter Birding Weekend. A Bass Rocks specialty is a drake King Eider, scarce in our state, an Arctic breeder with a head like a carnival mask: powder blue crown, bright yellow facial shield, and a deep orange bill above a softly rouged breast. Since the eider is much in demand, I'm proud of my record of finding the bird but frustrated when it won't cooperate. Another of our targets is the Black Guillemot, a small, high-riding, gull-like alcid, dark in breeding season but pale in winter with a white oval flank patch. In "Guillemots" poet Marianne Moore pictures the shore-hugging birds "merged with the wilting apex of the tide, without colliding with the rock." In "Noss" poet Brendan Galvin describes guillemots on remote breeding grounds in the Shetland Islands, shuffling for position in "formal stag lines ledged on the cliff walls" of a barren island "where humans have thrived even less than trees."

Sometimes, as I scope for seabirds from the Back Shore, I'll fall into a reverie. The vantage shifts and I find myself at sea, without binoculars and straining to pick out signs of human life—and safe harbor—in a wilderness of rock and forest. I've been transported to 1614, teeter-tottering with the waves aboard a merchant ship with Captain John Smith. Smith is most associated with Jamestown, but he was the first European to map and name our cape, after a Turkish princess called Charatza Tragabigzanda, and the first Englishman to list the birds of New England. His name for our cape didn't stick—too barbarous, thought King Charles I, who renamed it after his mother—but the Back Shore still has a little street called Tragabigzanda Road.

What we know about Smith's voyage to Cape Ann we know from Smith, who was sometimes mocked in England as a braggart and liar. In his 1616 *A Description of New England* Smith was trying to recruit colonists by correcting the impression that our region was "nothing but a miserable desert," and some of his descriptions suggest he'd found a lush tropical paradise—the northern Promised Land—with New England winters conveniently omitted. And there's something suspect in Smith's tales of being saved from death or enslavement by a series of love-struck brown-skinned women—the "beauteous Lady Tragabigzanda," the "charitable Lady Callamata" from the steppes of central Asia, and "blessed Pocahontas" in Virginia—all overcome by his courage and charms and offering "rescue and protection in my greatest dangers." One wag called Smith the "white Othello." Yet Charles Olson defended him as a "truther-teller." "Why I sing John Smith is this," Olson wrote, "that the geographic, the sudden land of the place, is in there, not described, not local, not represented. . . . I can feel now the way his boat bent along the same coasts I know."

Romance aside, Smith predicted accurately that Cape Ann could support a profitable fishing industry, and other explorers' accounts support his reports of myriad birds as well as abundant timber. On shore Smith found many "partridges," probably Heath Hens, a prairie-chicken subspecies once abundant but extinct now for almost a century. When Smith's bird reports are questionable, it's because of his limited knowledge and sometimes hard-to-decipher terminology. His "cranes" were probably herons, still commonly mislabeled "cranes." His "sheldrakes" were likely mergansers. Another name he uses is "gripe," an ancient Anglo-Saxon word, related to "griffon," that has been applied loosely over centuries to various fierce-looking raptors, including hawks, fish eagles like our Bald Eagle, and so-called sea falcons.

Just north of Bass Rocks, across a tidal channel, is popular Good Harbor Beach, part of a barrier spit that's backed by an eroding dune ridge. Just offshore is shrubby Salt Island, an "erosional remnant" that marks the former coastline. If the King Eider has eluded us, we've sometimes found it near the north end of Salt Island, hidden from birders at Bass Rocks. Horned Larks, the occasional Lapland Longspur, and Snow Buntings may roam the beach and parking lot, camouflaged on patches of sand beside dirty mounds of snow. Late fall is the time when rare vagrants, often lost juvenile birds, most often show up in Massachusetts, and I've seen both Lark Bunting and Mountain Bluebird, birds of the West, seeking shelter from the wind behind the dunes.

Heading north, we pass necks and coves, pebbly and sandy beaches, and the wharfs and galleries of Rockport to reach a shoreline of granite outcrops jutting into the Atlantic. Halibut Point, Andrews Point, and Cathedral Ledge all offer seabirding vantages. At these headlands, our cape's northernmost point, ages of storms have sculpted cliffs and gorges and stripped the land to rock. The faults of Cape Ann have probably not moved for millions of years, but in more recent geological history, the advances and retreats of glacial ice have scoured and beveled the coastline.

At Halibut Point, jointly owned by the state and the Trustees of Reservations, we explore woodlands and heathlands home to hardy plants like bayberry, huckleberry, and pasture rose that can tolerate salt air and acid soil. On very lucky days we've found rarities like the Northern Shrike, a carnivorous songbird that preys on smaller songbirds. We loop around wide, steep, smooth-walled Babson Farms Quarry, one of many Rockport quarries from the nineteenth century, when fine-grained granite, more than four hundred million years old, was shipped by sloops to build jails, the Customs House tower and Longfellow Bridge in Boston, and paving stones in cities from New York to Havana. Our sea-watching promontory offers a long view north up the coastline to the speck of Mount Agamenticus in southern Maine. Below the overlook are the tide-created gradations of the intertidal zone: mossy seaweed, tide pools, barnacle-encrusted rocks, and kelp.

The seabirds here are as rugged as the plants. Surfing dangerously close to the rocky shore are Harlequin Ducks. Further out are scoters, grebes, and loons, like the Red-Throated Loon, slender and elongated in flight, with bill upturned, and the rare Pacific Loon, often confused with the slightly bulkier Common Loon. We hope for scarce Common and Thick-Billed Murres, up-again, down-again divers that may surface far from where they dove or somehow manage to fly off unseen while we're waiting for them to bob up again. The most common alcids, and the closest living relatives of the Great Auk, are the Razorbills—strange black and white creatures with crunched necks, blunt bills, and long, pointed tails. If we see a Razorbill soar, we know we're hallucinating, for they invariably fly close to the surface, their elliptical bodies often in long, winding flight lines just below the horizon.

In his 2002 *Eye of the Albatross*, Carl Safina says of seabirds: "These birds live all their lives out in open weather. They know no sense of cover. Not only do they take no shelter, but they're exposed to some of the harshest extremes of heat, cold, water, and wind the world can hurl. These are sturdy beings." Winter storms may blow thousands of seabirds past Halibut Point or nearby Andrews Point. For decades now, Rick Heil has come to Andrews Point regularly for long sea-watches, using a scope mount from inside his car. Rick is well known locally for his identification skills and discoveries of rarities, and during some storms he's counted amazing numbers and diversity of passing birds. I've never mastered his method. Instead I'll stand exposed at the point with rigor mortis fingers, wind rattling my tripod and rain pelting my scope lens as I try to identify distant seabirds in flight. At least I'll get astonishing looks at gannets, no longer way out at sea but now swooping overhead with the wind. A November 2012 storm brought waves of Dovekies, or Little Auks, which flock in the thousands around islands in the far North but are hard to find in Massachusetts. Before I froze I counted about four hundred as they blew past the point like a flock of intent footballs. Rick stuck around to record 3,470.

Cathedral Ledge, our last stop, is among the best places in the Northeast to get close looks at Harlequin Ducks, fantastical beauties named for a clownishly dressed character in commedia dell'arte and once called the Lords and Ladies of the

Sea. On slow birding days I count on the Harlequins to put satisfied smiles on birders' faces at morning's end. Behind the ledge stands the Ralph Waldo Emerson Inn, named after its most famous guest. Emerson came to Cape Ann for both business and pleasure. Between 1845 and 1864 he lectured fourteen times at the Gloucester Lyceum on topics ranging from "The Natural History of the Intellect" to "The Uses and Obligations of Wealth." He was admired for his wisdom, though some local ministers thought his ideas dangerously radical and un-Christian, while one Gloucester reporter called him an "unmitigated bore." Emerson often had an abstracted air that both amused and annoyed his friends. Oliver Wendell Holmes described him at a lecture podium like "a cat picking her footsteps in wet weather." Henry Wadsworth Longfellow refused to go on one Agassiz Club camping trip if Emerson brought his gun along because "somebody will be shot."

Emerson's Cape Ann visits illustrate the artistic cross-pollination that flourished here in the mid-nineteenth century. Emerson met Fitz Henry Lane through the lyceum, where Lane was a director, and the Lane gallery at the Cape Ann Museum now features a quotation from Emerson: "Currents of the universal being circulate through me." We don't know if Lane was consciously influenced by Emerson, but many art scholars view Lane's "luminist" seascapes as the visual equivalent of the search for spiritual light—divinity revealed in the natural world—in Emerson's Transcendentalist essays.

On Cape Ann Emerson found his love for the ocean, that "noble friendly power." In his journal of 1856 he imagines the sea talking to him. "Why so late and slow to come to me? Am I not here always, the proper summer home? Is not my voice thy needful music; my breath, thy healthful climate in the heats; my touch, thy cure?" Emerson was apparently introduced to Cape Ann by Thoreau, who took him for long hikes along the Rockport coast, with stops for tea in the coves. He described Thoreau as a "woodgod," the perfect companion for a nature walk, a man who'd been taught directly by sparrows. In his funeral oration Emerson said of Thoreau, "He knew the country like a fox or a bird, and passed through it freely by paths of his own." Emerson envied Thoreau's ability to commune with nature: "He knew how to sit immovable, a part of the rock he rested on, until the bird, the reptile, the fish, which had retired from him, should come back and resume its habits, nay, moved by curiosity, should come to him and watch him." Emerson also realized that, by contrast, his own nature writings were too impatient with close observation, too quick to leave behind birds or lichens and leap into spiritualized abstractions: "In reading him, I find the same thought, the same spirit that is in me, but he takes it a step beyond, and illustrates by excellent images that which I should have conveyed in a sleepy generality." Yet he felt that Thoreau was too antisocial, too lacking in ambition, and ultimately too obsessed with the minutiae of birds and plants. "Instead of engineering for all of America," Emerson said of his friend, "he was the captain of the huckleberry party."

Emerson and Thoreau didn't exactly "bird" together, since Emerson wasn't much interested in details of bird identification, while Thoreau was too interested in everything. Emerson describes him showing up for one walk: "There came Henry with music book under his arm, to press flowers in; with telescope in his pocket, to see the birds, and microscope to count stamens; with a diary, jack-knife, and twine; in stout shoes, and strong grey trousers, ready to brave the shrub-oaks and smilax, and to climb the tree for a hawk's nest." Yet Emerson fondly recalled the birds Thoreau found on their hikes, like the Rose-Breasted Grosbeaks whose brilliant color "made the rash gazer wipe his eye" and whose song Thoreau compared to a "tanager who has got rid of his hoarseness." Amused by Thoreau's fixation on a mysterious "night-warbler" (probably an Ovenbird) that he'd failed to identify for twelve years, Emerson warned him to "beware of finding and booking it, lest life should have nothing more to show" and the "charm of the mysterious bird disappear in the light of mere identity."

In his poem "Bacchus," Emerson hopes to learn how to "rightly spell" the "bird-language," but he believed that humans are "analogists," and, like Jonathan Edwards, what he wanted from nature was "an image of the human Mind," a path to the divinity within. "Every natural fact is trivial," he wrote, "until it becomes symbolical or moral." Still, he had his favorite birds: the "geographer" eagle; the magnificently soaring Osprey; and the mockingbird with its "healing song"—now heard daily outside the Emerson Inn, though mockingbirds weren't in Massachusetts during his time and it's hard to determine where he saw them. Emerson celebrated the "perfect virtues" of birds and asked them to "teach his awkward race courage and probity and grace!" In "The Titmouse" he praises our state bird, the Black-Capped Chickadee, for its gymnastic ability, its friendliness, and its cheerful, courageous heart. Emerson thanks the bird for showing him how to buck up through one rough day during a harsh New England winter:

> Here was this atom in full breath
> Hurling defiance at black death:
> This scrap of valor just for play,
> Fronts the north-wind in waistcoat gray
> As if to shame my weak behavior
> I greeted loud my little savior.

In the chickadee's song he finds an antidote to despair and fear of death. To be brave, he realizes, "we must come down to the titmouse dimension." When his son Waldo died at age five in 1842, Emerson wrote in his journal: "He gave up his little innocent breath like a bird."

The best place to watch seabirds is from the sea, and each year the Cape Ann Chamber of Commerce sponsors a winter birding boat trip with the Seven Seas Whale Watch, captained by Jay Frontiero, a topnotch birder and raconteur of local lore. Joining Jay in the pilot house to spot and identify birds have been Chris Leahy and Wayne Petersen from Mass Audubon and Jim Berry from the ECOC. We usually head for the Stellwagen Bank National Marine Sanctuary, a plateau in the sea, formed by glaciers, where marine life is concentrated in nutrient-rich waters. The bank is a prime spot in the Northeast to find varieties of dolphins and whales—humpback, minke, fin, and the endangered North Atlantic right whale. In winter it's a great place to look for alcids and Black-Legged Kittiwakes, agile tern-like gulls from the North that roam far from shore.

On one trip, instead of heading to Stellwagen, we followed the cape's coastline. Just offshore we chanced upon a diving Atlantic Puffin, a small, clown-faced alcid so irresistible it's hard not to call it "cute." Its genus name means "little brother." The puffin was a life bird for many onboard. I'd seen just one before, off the breakwater. We then passed the islands—now Milk, Thacher, and Straitsmouth—that Smith named the Three Turks' Heads, after three Turks he'd decapitated. As waves roughened, we approached a place where Cape Ann's history comes together: the Dry Salvages, a cluster of guano-dripped rocks now lit at night by a flashing green beacon after a long history of shipwrecks. It was Champlain who named the Salvages—derived from the French *sauvages*, meaning "wild" or "savage"—and we can envision Smith skirting these rocks as he scouted the shoreline. Lane and Homer both painted scenes of storm-tossed boats in these waters. From the veranda of his inn, Emerson could have seen gulls fly over the distant breaking surf. But it was Eliot who made the Dry Salvages famous, in the third of his *Four Quartets.*

"The Dry Salvages" is a wartime poem, written in late 1940 when Eliot lived in London under attack by air raids, but he knew these rocks from his childhood, and the poem is immersed in our cape's seafaring tradition. Where Emerson heard the ocean's voice as "needful music," Eliot hears a multitude of voices, both caressing and menacing, the "howl" and "yelp" of the sea itself, the "whine" of rigging on ships, the "wailing warning" of treacherous rocks, the cries of gulls as a ship rounds homewards. The "losses," "wastage," and "drifting wreckage" in the poem, both metaphorical and literal, include the wrecks of fishing boats and "the torn seine, the shattered lobsterpot, the broken oar" coughed up by the sea onto our coastline. The poem asks us to pray for those "whose bodies will suffer the trial and judgement of the sea," the fishermen who must "fare forward" despite the danger, and the "women who have seen their sons or husbands setting forth, and not returning." The gulls glide through a seascape where hope fights against fear and resignation, where we learn only through suffering that "time the destroyer" is also "time the preserver."

When I talk about winter seabirding, civilians and even other birders might ask, "How do you stand the weather?" The answer is simple. Wear your warmest mittens, long johns, wool socks and hat, and, if you must, heated ear muffs, though they'll muffle bird vocalizations. Or if it's that bad out, stay indoors. It'll warm up. New Englanders like to boast about toughing out nor'easters, but if you'd rather not suffer windblast and iced-over spectacles just to glimpse a few gulls through a winter haze, we won't call you a wimp. Well, maybe we will. Actually, once we're out there, frigidity usually enhances the camaraderie and humor of a birding group, though on some frozen days I've driven to the Man at the Wheel praying that no one will be there. One morning I waited until five minutes past the meeting time and was about to high-five myself and go when a van pulled up. Six guys spilled out, all armed with optics, but thanks to a merciful deity, they weren't seeking me to lead them. They were a church club from out of state. We chatted, shared some recent reports, and I went home to fresh coffee and the Patriots game.

On another raw morning, just one person showed up, a boyish local minister and novice birder. I thought I'd happened upon a strange new sect—the Church of Demented Winter Birders—until he explained that most club trips were scheduled for Sundays (not a good time for him) and this was a Saturday. At the fish pier and becalmed Back Shore, I found the Preacher three life birds, including the King Eider. Normally we would have gone to Eastern Point, but I knew the wind would be wicked there, and the Preacher was already so demoralized by the cold that I took pity and opted for Rockport. At Cathedral Ledge he delighted in the Harlequins beneath us, and as we admired some berry-eating Cedar Waxwings, I picked out five darker, bulkier Bohemians, boreal breeders in North America and Europe but rare on Cape Ann. The Preacher didn't know how lucky he was. Game for more birding, I tried to convince him that we birders weren't the crazy ones. What about the winter golfers slicing their little white orbs into headwinds, or the scuba divers dabbling with ducks in bone-chilling surf? The Preacher wasn't buying it.

Soon after I got home, a birding buddy called me. An Ivory Gull was being seen, that very moment, at the breakwater. I gobbled my sandwich and rushed off. Forbush described the gull, or Ice Partridge—its Latin name means "frost-lover"—in its usual habitat in the far North: "Where countless crowding icebergs rear their snowy pinnacles; where dark blue, racing seas, flashing and roaring in the clear sunlight, dash their foaming crests high up the pallid slopes of crashing ice; there we may find the Ivory Gull." Of all the rare birds I craved, this frost-lover, this scavenging follower of polar bears, topped the list, and here was one right across town. Approaching the breakwater, I damn near drove into a thicket when I looked over at a gull hovering like a kingfisher above the ice a hundred feet away. It had to be the whitest creature in creation. I parked, joined a throng of birders, and feasted on the bird for another hour. I was tempted to track down the Preacher and tell him, "If it hadn't been for you, my fine frozen friend, I would've found this rare gull myself." Then I realized that, if not for the Preacher, I wouldn't have gone out birding at all. I don't know whether he's still a birder, but if he is, I hope that one day he sees an Ivory Gull.

Chapter 6

BIRDING ON TWO WHEELS

Your typical birding stroll hardly qualifies as an aerobic workout. The pace is too poky, the breaks in rhythm too frequent, unless you're aiming merely to surpass the cardiovascular output of a dormant Common Poorwill. Birding walks can sometimes be strenuous, like the treks to see a Bristle-Thighed Curlew on Alaskan tundra or a Colima Warbler up the mountains of Big Bend, but most birds can be found without signing on to a death march. True, at age fifty-eight, long after my days on the Harvard track team, I set a personal best for the three-thousand-meter run while hauling a heavy scope in the brutally humid Everglades, but that was only because I was being chased by Uzi-armed mosquitoes through a gauntlet of open-jawed gators and startled vipers. I found my bird—a lone, distant Greater Flamingo blurred by heat shimmer—but after the race back to my car, I vowed never to go down the Snake Bight trail again. Now if I'm tired at the end of a bird walk, it's usually because I've been standing around too long. A friend of mine tried to become a birder, or faked becoming a birder, to win the birder she loved, but after the wedding she gave up the act because her feet needed to go faster.

A more vigorous alternative is bicycle-birding. At fifty, after cartilage had fled my body, I turned to more joint-friendly cycling for exercise. On a ride through a marsh, I saw four big, iridescent, scimitar-billed birds that belonged in Nubia or Paleolithic Cape Ann. I figured out their names, called Mass Audubon's Rare Bird Alert, and checked that Sunday's *Boston Globe* for a report of my finding. Incredibly, someone else had seen sixty of these birds at Coolidge Point in Manchester-by-the-Sea. My four measly Glossy Ibises weren't mentioned. No matter. At a local pond I saw my first Wood Duck in his coat of many colors, a beauty dressed for a wedding, as his Latin name indicates. I saw my first Eastern Phoebe, sallying forth for bugs, as I rode across a low bridge over a swamp, and my first American Oystercatchers—eyes made googly by orange-red rims that matched their long, oyster-opening bills—from a seaside path on Martha's Vineyard.

I bird by bike a few days each week from early April into November. My favorite time is June, when spring migrants have moved on but local breeders are still singing. If I bike-bird spring during migration, I don't make progress. One May day, Mary and I rode around Eastern Point, a popular biking destination since the nineteenth century, when John Webber published his cycling guide *In and around Cape Ann* and riders would pedal to the lighthouse and a fort armed with cannons in 1863 to protect Gloucester schooners from Confederate raiders. That day the trees around the point teemed with warblers, vireos, and grosbeaks. Mary and I lingered with bird after bird, especially a foursome of Bay-Breasted Warblers, a bit heftier and slower than most warblers, the crown, breast, and flanks saturated with bay. If you won't stop to look at birds like these, you're not birding by bicycle. You're pedaling and woolgathering.

Urban nature writer Louis Halle once compared the sensation of cycling in a breeze to what birds must feel in flight. For me the great pleasure is wheeling through a breeze of birdsong. After migration season I might ride twenty-five miles with just a few stops. It's enough to keep moving from Bobolinks bubbling over in a meadow to Red-Bellied Woodpeckers squawking along suburban streets to rows of the *sweet sweet* Yellow Warblers that T. S. Eliot must've seen flashing in the shrubs along Niles Pond. When I do stop it's often because I've heard a song—a Least Flycatcher's abrupt *chebek chebek*—I wouldn't have heard from a car, in a location I wouldn't have thought to bird on foot. One week I found Broad-Winged Hawks whistling in woods in four North Shore towns. On another ride I heard three wren species, House, Winter, Carolina, within a half-mile stretch and found a fourth, Marsh, on a detour with Marsh Wren potential.

It's generally impractical to hop on a bike to chase a rare bird, but I've done a little drive-and-ride rarity-chasing. In August 2004 the first Red-footed Falcon ever in North America was found on Martha's Vineyard. It stuck around, luring birders from around the country, as many as a thousand one day, all speculating on how the falcon had found its way to Massachusetts and where it might go from here. It's expensive to ferry a car to the Vineyard, so my friend Susan Hedman and I drove to Falmouth, boarded the ferry with our bikes, disembarked at Vineyard Haven, and rode across the island to a field by an airport. We joined a transient community of onlookers and a slate-colored falcon with red feet. The bird hunted, hovered, put on a show, and perched wittily on an All Aircraft Must Register sign. We watched, chatted with other birders and delighted civilians, and were interviewed by a local reporter. I don't recall saying anything brilliant: "Wonderful bird. Great to see so many kids here. We came by bicycle. Fun."

Each spring I patrol my patch by bike to listen and count common breeding birds like House and Carolina Wrens, Eastern Towhees, and Baltimore Orioles. One nostalgic route takes me down Western Avenue, the coastal road back when stage coaches carried visitors on the long trip from Boston to Cape Ann. In the Magnolia neighborhood of Gloucester, I pass by Hesperus House, a three-story wooden apartment building. When I lived there, in a lifetime before marriage and birding, it housed a sort of commune with cheap rent, fend-for-yourself meals, and stoned parties that danced out to the beach, but the original Hesperus House, built in 1878, was a grand summer haven for Boston high society. It was named for a ship that, in Longfellow's 1842 "The Wreck of the *Hesperus*," is wrecked at Norman's Woe, where "black evil boulders" in shallow water have ruined many ships, though the actual *Hesperus* ran aground off Maine, years before Longfellow came to Gloucester. Hesperus House was later subsumed by the Oceanside, the biggest summer hotel in New England with 750 rooms and twenty-two cottages. Guests danced or marched to John Philip Sousa's twenty-piece oompah band. At nearby Coolidge Point in Manchester-by-the-Sea, Great and Snowy Egrets, Little Blue Herons, and yes, scores of Glossy Ibises all stream over the beach at dusk to their night roosts on Kettle Island. When I lived down the road, I wrote a mawkish poem about Mute Swan cygnets yanked to their deaths by snapping turtles at the pond near the point. Why wasn't I watching the ibises that feed along the pond's edges? Why didn't Little Blue Herons spark my birding as a young man?

Going further afield, I'll drive somewhere, bird on foot for a while, then work out a loop route to ride. I've cycled Essex County from sailboat-filled Marblehead Harbor to the wide Merrimack River, past cattail marshes, shady woods with touch-me-nots, bogs with sphagnum and carnivorous pitcher plants, wet meadows with Turk's-cap lilies, and fields with black-eyed Susans and butter and eggs. Along Boxford State Forest I might hear a Scarlet Tanager's *chick-burr* rasp or the whistles of a Rose-Breasted Grosbeak—Thoreau's tanager without the hoarseness—or the tinny toy trumpet of a Red-Breasted Nuthatch. Along the gravel road through Ash Street Swamp in West Newbury, I'm ready for a Yellow-Throated Vireo's paused two-note whistle and the *eek! eek!* of female

Wood Ducks splashing off in alarm. One morning I hit the brakes and stood like a crossing guard as a Virginia Rail with three huddled offspring scuttled close across the road. I listen with faint hope for Golden-Winged Warblers along Turkey Hill Road in Newburyport, the last place they nested in the county, in 2002. The warblers are losing their competition with more common Blue-Winged Warblers; they often share habitat, and the two species can sing one another's songs. They interbreed often enough that their hybrid offspring, and the young of paired hybrids, have their own names—Brewster's and Lawrence's Warblers—striking birds distinguished from the originals and each other by facial patterns and plumage variations.

One day I was riding through Topsfield's Bradley-Palmer State Park, listening to a Wood Thrush. Writers have long tried to capture the strain's elusive quality, rising and falling, sweet and melancholy, a suspenseful pause before a held high note at the end. It was the favorite birdsong of Audubon and Thoreau. Up ahead of me, a woman gazed into the trees. Beside her a chihuahua strained for freedom from its leash. When I stopped she told me she was looking for an owl, so I looked too. Her last visit to the park, she said, had been a nightmare. Just after she'd let the dog off its leash, a monster owl had swooped down, snatched the dog, and carried it off, flying low to the ground, failing to gain altitude and finally dropping the chihuahua into a bush. Traumatized, woman and dog walked another few hundred feet before she unleashed the chihuahua again. Same scenario: owl swooping, talons clutching, dog in air yapping, owl struggling, dog dropped, the hunt abandoned. The owl had inflicted only minor wounds, but the woman was still pissed off at it. I managed sympathetic sounds. I like dogs. I looked down at the antsy chihuahua and envisioned dog with owl in the air—twice! I strained to keep a straight face. Should I tell her that a Great Horned Owl was watching us now?

I regularly ride, sometimes dodging dogs or Canada Geese, along a straight, two-mile packed-earth path on a dike along the Wenham Canal through the Great Wenham Swamp. Blue flag irises line the shore; pickerelweeds stand erect in shallow water; water lilies float in deeper water. The canal flows into the Ipswich River, and a little hitch leads to a ride through woodlands and swamp on the Danvers Rail Trail. As the landscape opens, the birds along the canal nicely illustrate species' habitat preferences: Black-and-White and Black-Throated Green Warblers in hemlocks near the parking area, hidden Northern Waterthrushes with their accelerated whistles in a wooded swamp: Red-Winged Blackbirds flashing epaulets and Willow Flycatchers sneezing from perches where the swamp opens up into high grasses and snags, and a few Great Blue Herons at water's edge, lifting off if I get too close. The plain, blank-faced Warbling Vireos, always nesting by water, bring me back to Mexico, where Mary and I saw a Slaty Vireo, a longtime challenge to taxonomists because of the very features—slate set off by rich olive green, bright white eye, and long, rounded tail—that make it so un-vireolike and so improbably pretty. How could vireos have diverged in such directions?

It's always entertaining to watch the noisy Common Grackles stalking along the canal. Like gulls, grackles bring out the metaphors in poets. In "The Voice of the Grackle," Marge Piercy, from Wellfleet, compares their purple satin bodies to "oil slick colors shimmering" and their voices to an "unoiled door hinge creaking" and the "screech of unadjusted brakes." She imagines one slumped at the back of a classroom "making off-color comments in his cracking voice, awkward, half clown, half hero." In "The Grackles" Brendan Galvin, from

Truro, describes their "failed storekeeper's eyes—worry trapped in a bile-yellow ring of anger." In "Grackles" Lisa Williams is struck by their group cohesion: "They were not one body. Yet they seemed held together by some order."

My favorite bike-birding route is the paved stretch of the Plum Island refuge. In early May, Laura de la Flor and Mark Burns lead a Brookline Bird Club cycling trip here. Eastern Kingbirds zit and sputter back and forth across the road, flashing white tail bands. They'll hound any intrusive hawk or crow, bouncing above the invader's back like miniature bronco riders and pounding it with their bills. Brown Thrashers, long tailed, their backs a rich reddish brown, perch on treetops along the road and sing, rasp, and wheeze their repertoires of borrowed two-note phrases. It's hard not to describe thrashers anthropomorphically: I envision a line of guys at a club trying out every possible pickup line. We might pass groups of roving Palm Warblers, early migrants known by their ever-wagging tails. We stop to investigate any mix of birdsong that suggests a migrant pocket. We laugh as we go, sometimes at profusions of birds, sometimes at our foolishness for freezing our faces and fingers on raw, bird-quiet mornings.

Outside Essex County, a ride along the popular Minuteman Bikeway, from Bedford to Cambridge, is a good excuse to arrive at dawn at Great Meadows National Wildlife Sanctuary in Concord. I'll walk alone on the dikes amid stunt-pilot swallows and Great Blue Herons, stationary in the mist, and listen for the calls of freshwater marsh birds hidden in reeds and cattails: Virginia Rails, American Bitterns, Least Bitterns. South of Boston in Hingham is Wompatuck State Park, a great place to bird-bike, especially on the paved loop road closed to motorized vehicles. On one ride I cruised through a never-ending Veery chorus, twenty-two birds in all. Its syrinx allows the Veery to sing two notes at once, like a pair of tremulous spirits, soprano and alto, harmonizing in the ether. The Veery also calls its name: a querulous *veer*. I always listen for the songs of the specialty birds at Wompatuck: the slurred whistle-sputter of stream-loving Louisiana Waterthrushes, the fast insect trills of Worm-Eating Warblers on wooded hillsides. A few Ruffed Grouse have hung on here, drumming deep in the woods.

Cape Cod and the islands offer fine birding bikeways like the Cape Cod Rail Trail, the network of bike paths on Martha's Vineyard, and the many routes described in Kenneth Blackshaw's *Bike Birding Nantucket*. I've yet to cycle around central and western Massachusetts, but the Pioneer Valley Bike Week has featured a birding trip along the Norwottuck Rail Trail from Amherst to Northampton, while the Allen Bird Club has sponsored cycling outings along the Westfield River. Beyond New England Mary and I have explored bike-friendly bird havens like Sanibel Island in Florida, Bentsen–Rio Grande Valley State Park in Texas (now threatened by the border wall), and the Cook Inlet path in Alaska. Birders on bikes often have access to miles of paved bike paths and dirt roads off-limits to cars. At Seney National Wildlife Refuge in Michigan's Upper Peninsula, we looped past breeding-plumaged Sandhill Cranes, a grouse ambling into the woods, and a belching American Bittern that took us twenty minutes to locate in the reeds. Mary, rounding a bend, glimpsed a bear she mistook for me—a sign that, despite vigorous exercise, I could still lose some weight.

Biking can also be a good way to carry out citizen science, or scientist science. During the atlas I could cover a whole block by bike in a day, at a pace slow enough to hear the songs of possible breeding birds: a Blue-Winged Warbler's *bee buzz* in a bushy field, a Chestnut-Sided Warbler's *pleased, pleased, pleased to MEETCHA*. In three separate marshes I heard the whinny of a bird I never expected to find, the unconfiding Sora. One finally emerged from the reeds, scratching in the mud like a lost, tiny chicken with a bright yellow beak. I stopped for any sign of breeding: a Northern Flicker rising from the ground to a hole in a dead tree or an Eastern Bluebird carrying off a fecal sac to keep predators from its nest. I envisioned the birds I couldn't see—unfledged chicks with gaping mouths, all hunger and growth, and birds of the future inside private eggs.

Bob Stymeist, a longtime proponent of urban birding, uses his bike to carry out a regular freshwater waterfowl survey at Fresh Pond in Cambridge as well as an annual breeding bird survey along the Charles River from Waltham to Boston. A cycling census, he cautioned me, is inadvisable in many habitats but well suited for circuits around large ponds and along rivers, especially in city areas. He surveys the breeding birds from late May to mid-June, when song peaks, and he brings a notebook "with the most likely species to be encountered already written in with enough space to stroke-count as I'm hearing or seeing the birds en route." For the many Yellow Warblers and Warbling Vireos he's got hand clickers, one in each pocket. He's also come across "surprise birds," like a wayward Osprey and "a skulking Mourning Warbler still on its journey."

For his book *The Singing Life of Birds*, Donald Kroodsma studied birdsong by bicycle as well as by foot, canoe, and roof-sitting. At Zion Canyon in Utah he rode up mountain switchbacks and recorded the matched counter-singing of Bewick's Wrens to determine whether the wrens learn their songs from their fathers, neighbors, or both. On Martha's Vineyard he strapped recording gear to his body and circled the island to record Black-Capped Chickadee songs. "Extraordinary!" he exclaims. "On this small island of Martha's Vineyard, less than twenty miles across, was more variety than I had known across the entire continent of North America." He suffered an occupational hazard when Vineyard police stopped him for questioning after some citizens mistook his sound gun for a real gun and reported him as a possible terrorist. A few years later Kroodsma and his son, David, cycled cross-country. "It's the ultimate celebration of birdsong," he says, "listening to every chirp in our 4500-mile route across the entire continent."

I've gone bird-traveling by car or plane too often to pose as a righteous exemplar, but one value of bike-birding is its low impact on the environment. In the Rio Grande Valley, Father Tom Cincelli, or "Father Bird," a nature guide and Roman Catholic priest, promotes bike-birding to minimize motorized traffic in prime bird habitats. The annual Great Texas Birding Classic now includes a "human-powered" category, and the Bird-in-Hand group sponsors a regular Amish Country Classic Bike Ride. In 2014 my friend Dorian Anderson set off from Gloucester on his all-bicycle Green Big Year. He found 618 species as he cycled eighteen thousand miles across and around the country to raise money for conservation. I ran into him, all bundled up on his bike, on a frigid New Year's Day at Salisbury Beach, where he pointed out a rare Black-Headed Gull to our BBC group. A week later, when I was leading a club trip, he rode up on his bike and soon found the morning's highlight, a Dovekie crouched on the water underneath a pier in Gloucester Harbor. I'm not ready to follow Dorian cross-country, but I've been covering most of my patch by bike or on foot for the Bird-a-thon.

I ride a hybrid bike, more efficient than a mountain bike on paved roads yet sturdier than a racing bike if a dirt path looks promising. A cautionary note: if, while birding by bike, you see or hear an intriguing bird, stop pedaling, dismount, and secure your bicycle well off the road before trying to see the bird with your binoculars. I've learned this lesson the hard way.

Chapter 7

ON A STREET WITH NO NAME

A Rant

When I bike I'm always on the lookout for birds, but I'm also watching for history: street signs that tell stories. Along with the humdrum street names in our state, the Mains, Middles, Gardens, are more evocative names that draw me into the past. The story is geological at High Popples Road, a short, winding Gloucester street that ends at Bass Rocks, where boulders have been tossed up by the sea and heaped along the shore. A "popple" is a heaving of water over stones: storm surges here send waves crashing over abraded rocks, sometimes swamping Atlantic Road. Drumlin Road in Rockport was named for one of the rounded hills, formed by glacial deposits, that mark eastern Massachusetts from Hog Island in Ipswich to Bunker Hill. A Boxford street is called Bald Pate, a name for a bald hill above a prairie (in a location now neither bald nor prairie) and for the American Wigeon, a dabbling duck with a creamy cap.

Other names recall human history. Wonson Road on Rocky Neck was named for Captain John Wonson, who ferried passengers to East Gloucester in the mid-nineteenth century when the neck, now an art colony, was an island. Near Wonson Cove a plaque marks the spot where Samuel Champlain put ashore in 1605 to get water for his crew and called the place Le Beauport (beautiful port). In the only firsthand European account of Cape Ann's aboriginal settlers, Champlain described

Pawtuckets dancing onshore in what he thought were Portuguese clothes, and he claimed they danced better after he gave them some knives and biscuits. He drew a map depicting habitations and garden plots around Gloucester Harbor, and at his request the natives drew an outline of the coast to the south.

Names like Rocky Pasture Road and dead-ended Labor in Vain Road in Ipswich conjure up the hard times when farmers struggled to cultivate fields strewn with rocks, some of them enormous erratics or "orphan boulders" left behind by moving glaciers. Any number of New England roads might be called Rocky Pasture. After the Civil War most farmers here abandoned their lands, leaving behind stone walls that had marked boundaries, and went west looking for pastures less rocky and labor less vain.

Naturally I watch for streets named after birds, like Hoot Owl Way, a little cul-de-sac in Rockport near a cemetery where I've heard hooting Great Horned Owls. I'm gratified by the enclave of bird-honoring roads on Great Neck in Ipswich—Pintail, Merganser, Nuthatch, Longspur, Kingfisher—all species that can be found here or just across Plum Island Sound. Gulls fly over Gull Lane, a tiny dead-end street just down the hill from us. Ravens have yet to nest on Gloucester's Raven Lane, but they're among the world's most adaptable birds, breeding from the Aral Sea to the Mojave Desert, and they're coming our way. A few years back, a pair bred on a cliff not far from our house, and I'd hear their expressive croaks and pick out their diagnostic wedge-shaped tails as I rode around their neighborhood.

One day in search of birds, I hit the brakes when I passed a sign for Meadowlark Farm Lane. I'd never seen this street before. I was sure it wasn't in my road atlas. I rode to the end, another cul-de-sac, and listened. Not a whisper of birdsong. What had once been farmland and woodland was now a tract of trophy mansions (one priced online at $1.4 million "for the discerning buyer"), each house guarded by a landscaped terrace and sprinkler-fed lawn barren of birds. Sprawl: the bane of birds, trees cleared for new developments, then more roads and shopping plazas, until even the preserved places become stranded islands too puny to provide good bird habitat.

A scowl came over my face, and I thought of my mother. A hard woman, Mother used to tell stories about her no-count brother-in-law, Walter Tanner, a man so lazy that when her sister died at home, her body had to be squeezed out through a window because Walter had never gotten around to fixing the rotted planks and gaping hole on the front porch. Years after Mother died, I went to Wilmer, Alabama, outside Mobile, to meet my southern cousins. My cousin Margie drove me across town to visit cousin Gene and his daughters, who lived side by side in the only houses on a short dirt road. As we turned on to their street, I burst out laughing. "What?" Margie asked. "What's wrong?" Convulsed, I pointed to the green sign on the corner. Surely Mother was glowering in her grave, as I glowered on Meadowlark Farm Lane. My cousins had named the street in memory of their beloved slacker father: Walter Tanner Road.

It's a pet peeve of mine—not the honoring of work-shy relatives but the practice of naming streets or entire developments after birds that have no connection to these places or, worse, have been driven out and supplanted by those very roads and houses. Granted, among the world's problems, this one ranks low, but I can't help feeling irked when I come upon a Woodcock Lane that harbors no woodcocks, an Eagle's Nest Lane where no self-respecting eagle would nest, or a Black Duck Circle that lacks any habitat for waterfowl unless you count a blue plastic swimming pool. Down the road from us is the Village at West Gloucester—"luxury living" if you're fifty-five or older—blasted out of granite and forest on a hillside above the marsh. Its logo features a Great Blue Heron. Its streets include Heron Circle, Plover Lane, Dowitcher Drive, and Curlew Court, but you won't find these birds at the village. Before I moved to Gloucester, developers had wanted to build along a nearby causeway called the Window on the Marsh, where one can gaze across an open expanse of salt marsh toward Ipswich Bay. Had locals not stopped the project, we'd now have streets here named for former bird inhabitants—Killdeer Boulevard, Greater Yellowlegs Avenue.

But it's the meadowlark, Eastern or Western, that seems most favored by builders, business people, and street-dubbers who poach on bird names for their own uses. There's Meadowlark Hills retirement home in Kansas, Meadowlark Country House in California wine country ("the atmosphere is HETERO, GAY, and NATURIST friendly"—well-behaved dogs allowed, but no children), and Meadowlark RV Park in Rhode Island, along with countless streets and businesses in other states. The word itself sounds musical, and for those who live, work, or recreate at these places, "meadowlark" may summon a pastoral vision—country living amid birds and wildflowers in those bygone days before North America had retirement homes and RV parks. I don't object to every appropriation of the name. I've got no beef with Harlem Globetrotter Meadowlark Lemon.

My annoyance extends to streets and developments named after ruined habitats as well as threatened birds. Ride down a road named for woodlands, like Forest Street in Georgetown or its neighbor Tall Trees Way, and it's probably a road that fragments what was once more or less intact forest. In *The Undertaking* (2009) poet/undertaker Thomas Lynch notes that cemetery names are often interchangeable with those of golf courses, a truth that also holds for bucolic-sounding housing tracts. In fact, if you ever have occasion to christen a development, I recommend the following: choose any one item from

Category A (Meadowlark, Mockingbird, Tanager, Cardinal, Bluebird), one from Category B (Grove, Ridge, Valley, Brook, Hollows), and one from Category C (Farms, Estates, Manor, Acres, Court). Put the three together, and you'll do just fine. If you'd prefer a less birdy, more historical flavor, substitute a Native American name for Category A: Pequot Valley Farms, Choctaw Ridge Manor. The Natives need not be native to your particular locality.

Mind you, I'm no purist. You won't find quail or pheasant running on Quail Run Road in North Andover or Pheasant Run Drive in Newburyport (just around a bend from Fox Run Drive and Quail Run Hollow), but pheasants were never native here anyway, and if quail ever ran in these places, they stopped running long before these roads were built. If prospective buyers imagine that owning property there will transform them into fox-and-hounds English gentry, who am I to snipe? I can even sympathize with the golf course owners in Ohio and New York who succumbed to the same urge and called their establishments Bob-o-links.

I'm not opposed to all development, especially on land already degraded as bird habitat, and I do appreciate the dilemma faced by developers. Truth in advertising has its limits. You won't attract buyers by naming your projects No More Meadowlarks Farms or Wood Thrushes Gone Woods. And I can't honestly endorse the alternatives proposed by one J. L. Seagull in an online post: Falling Timbers, Hawkless Ridge, Leveled Hills. Maybe some places should remain nameless.

One day as I biked around Cape Cod after a date with a Yellow-Throated Warbler, I stopped at the corner of a side street. A thought came to me like fate: "Mary and I should move here." There was a newish development down the street, Pine Oaks Valley, a fine place to live, I was sure of it. I'd just seen a For Sale sign put up by a real estate agent with my name.

Maybe my brother-in-name would swing us a good deal. But it was the street sign that got me. Years ago, a former student of mine had sent me a photo of herself posing satirically with a saucy hand-on-hip stance and a goofy grin. She was pointing proudly at this very sign: John Nelson Way. Now that's a nice name for a thoroughfare.

Chapter 8

THE BIRDING JOHN NELSONS

Just past daybreak I walked through the cemetery's granite gate. "Until the day breaks," read an inscription above the portal, "and the shadows flee away." The shadows hadn't fled yet. The sun strained to come out. Towering oaks filtered light through fog into phantasmic umbras on the hillside. The woods smelled dank. On the Strange USA website, Oak Hill Cemetery in Newburyport ranks high among places rumored to be heavily haunted. An unsettling number of the old mossy gravestones are unmarked.

I love birding in cemeteries. In Massachusetts Mount Auburn is *the* cemetery birders must visit, but I've explored graveyards from my patch to Patagonia. In a neighborhood cemetery a Barred Owl asked, "Who cooks for you?" A second owl answered, "Who cooks for *you*?" At Bonaventure Cemetery in Savannah, beneath hanging Spanish moss on a riverine bluff, a Cooper's Hawk sat still as stone on the shoulder of a giant winged woman reaching her hands out toward a skeletal Grim Reaper holding an hourglass. At Père Lachaise at Paris, my first Eurasian Treecreeper crept up above a bronzed artist reclining with a paintbrush and easel near Chopin's grave. We met some other Americans who were indifferent to treecreepers as well as to Chopin, Oscar Wilde, Colette, and Maria Callas, all buried there. They were heading straight for the cemetery's most popular spot, Jim Morrison's shrine.

Most memorable was a cemetery in Punta Arenas at the tip of Patagonia, where rows of cypresses are trimmed into fat round green thumbs and the monuments are like little cottages lined up close together in a cozy village. Most are painted white, but some are orange or magenta, with little garden plots in front of headstones and window boxes with flower displays, tiny toys, and photos of smiling children. Whatever birds I'd hoped to find there, Mary and I saw nothing but Rock Doves and House Sparrows until we heard a shrill, insistent whistle near the Tomb of the Unknown Indian. We investigated. The whistling grew louder but more ventriloquial, now high, now low to the earth. Then it stopped. We looked around—no birds in sight. Then we heard another sound, a voice, importunate, from *below* the ground. "Auxilio!" We jumped out of our skins. We crept toward the edge of a deep, open grave and looked down. A small, dirt-smudged man in overalls looked up. He was holding a shovel and gesticulating toward a ladder in the grass. "Auxilio!" I lowered the ladder, and he climbed out and shook our hands, not wanting to let go. "Muchas gracias."

Warblers and thrushes, not Chilean gravediggers, called from the woods of Oak Hill. The cemetery could be a birdy place. I'd seen my first Black-Billed Cuckoo here, my first Swainson's Thrush. Today warblers and thrushes would have to wait until I found the bird I'd come for. I climbed down a slope into a hollow. Below me a kingfisher rattled across a hidden pond. I found my bird right away, exactly where it had been reported. Flycatching from a snag, it was burlier than an Indigo Bunting, a lovely dark blue with rusty wings and a fat silver beak that shrank the rest of its face.

I watched for a while, then headed upslope toward the thrushes. I hadn't heard another soul, but coming toward me over a ridge was a man who stepped around the slanted, weather-battered tombstones as if afraid he'd disturb the dead. Something about him was terribly familiar, his gait or frame if not his features. A ghost, a doppelganger.

He stopped a few feet from me. "Have you seen the Blue Grosbeak?"

"What? Oh yes, I just saw it." I pointed. "Over there. I'll show you."

We walked side by side down the slope. He had a friendly face, a birder's quiet alertness. The kingfisher rattled. We heard the grosbeak's hoarse, rushed two-note phrasings. The bird was still on its snag.

"Thanks," he said. "I haven't seen one for years." He turned toward me. "By the way, what's your name?"

"John Nelson."

He chuckled. "Oh, it's you." We shook hands. "John Nelson. We finally meet."

"I'm John *R.* Nelson," I said.

"*I'm* John R. Nelson," he answered, like an owl.

"I blame our parents."

I don't much like having such a common name. With no disrespect for my grandfather, Johann Nielsen, I would've been more adventurous if I'd christened myself. And my wife is Mary Nelson. Is there a couple in the country with names more white-bread? Granted, I've sometimes profited from confusion over my identity. In high school I was elected to student council—and made a leap in social standing—on the strength of votes no doubt intended for John C. Nelson, a nice guy from a different town with a different circle of friends. But more often the ordinariness of my name annoys me. Self-googling requires a carefully worded search, and I'm often misidentified in the field, not just as the wrong birding John Nelson but also as the wrong English professor and twice as a chief of police. It's fortunate the other birding John Nelson is an honest fellow, for *Birding* once sent him a check for an article I'd written. One day my friend Jim Berry, a stickler for correct usage, sent me an e-mail: "English professor makes rare error!" I'd allegedly confused "site" and "sight." Not this English professor, I informed Jim.

The next week Bill Drummond, one of my birding mentors, congratulated me on finding a Dovekie off Plum Island during a Christmas Bird Count.

I shook my head. "Wasn't me, Bill. That was the other John Nelson."

"Bummer," Bill answered.

"I suppose." Was there any difference between being a John Nelson who didn't see a Dovekie and being a Bill Drummond who didn't see the bird?

The other John Nelson and I now share grins when we meet in the field and other birders make unoriginal jokes about multiple John Nelson sightings. There's an odd satisfaction when we look at a rare bird together. White-Faced Ibis, seen by both John Nelsons. We continue to be commingled both online and in the field. There's one guy—let's call him Birder X—who posts regularly on MassBird and likes to shoot from the hip. He'll make wisecracks about some birder; he'll be upbraided for his rudeness; he'll apologize, retract the wisecracks, and protest that he was just joking. One day Birder X sent me an indignant message. Why was I on his case? Yes, he'd said impulsive things, but he'd apologized, hadn't he? Hadn't we sorted this whole thing out a year ago? I assured Birder X I had no beef with him; in fact, I had no clue what he was talking about. Maybe the other John Nelson had scolded him, though the other John Nelson doesn't seem like a scolder. A month later my name was mentioned from the podium just before Birder X presented a slide show at a club meeting, so naturally he began his talk with a little joke: Was I the good John Nelson or bad John Nelson? Afterward I approached him, shook his hand, and said with a smile, "Just so you know, I'm the good John Nelson. But the bad John Nelson is also a good John Nelson. Get your John Nelsons straight."

It's one thing when mix-ups create moral confusion, conflating "good" and "bad" John Nelsons. It's more serious when one's reputation as a birder is at stake. In my first year of birding, at Mary's urging, I posted a report of a Great Horned Owl we saw atop a pole along the interstate as we drove to Worcester to visit her mother in a hospital. It seemed unlikely—a Great Horned in broad daylight in the center of a field—but on our ride home at dusk, the owl was still there, swiveling its head to survey its improbable realm. I soon received many messages, kindly or snidely suggesting that my owl was mechanical. They make scare-owls with moving parts? I retracted my report and vowed to restrict future postings to animate birds. If my fellow John Nelson was birding at the time, he must have been mortified. Please, people, he must have thought, don't think that bozo was me.

But my owl problems didn't stop there. During a Bird-a-thon I checked a tree where I'd seen Pileated Woodpeckers excavating a cavity. No Pileateds, but inside the hole were two, no, three little owlish faces. I was thrilled. Any daytime owl is a good owl, and here was a whole screech-owl family. I proudly announced my owls at our team's tabulation meeting and posted my sighting on MassBird. The next day I got a message with photos attached: three adorable, huge-eyed baby owls, not screech-owls but unmistakable Northern Saw-whet Owls, poking their heads out of my Pileated hole. The photographer, Phil Brown, thanked me for finding the birds and graciously omitted the fact that I'd misidentified them. I'd have to post a correction, but I consoled myself: it's really hard to find baby saw-whet owls, even if you don't know what you're looking at. Still, I felt tricked. With me these owls had been coy, hiding in a dark recess. For Phil they'd become flashers, thrusting their cute little faces out into the world as if to proclaim: "We are Northern Saw-whet Owls!" I envisioned the other John Nelson shaking his head at his computer.

Luckily, the situation has never been reversed. The other John Nelson is an excellent bird spotter and dependable reporter. Still, doubts about John Nelson sightings persist. You see, there's a third birding John Nelson in Massachusetts, a man I've never met, and he once reported an Eskimo Curlew, a species generally considered extinct. I remember thinking his report was plausible. This John Nelson had been a Mass Audubon naturalist, and he and his son, an ornithologist, had seen the bird well on Chappaquiddick in suitable habitat. He'd noted its field marks and behavior and explained in detail why the bird wasn't a Whimbrel, the only other likely candidate. But without photographic evidence, no report of such an extreme rarity could ever be officially accepted, and many birders probably dismissed his sighting out of hand. For years I waited for someone to ask me, "So, John Nelson, seen any Eskimo Curlews lately?"

Since I started writing about birds, I've thought about adopting a pseudonym. I'm resigned to being John Nelson among friends, but "John Nelson" is not a brand to spark curiosity in bird book readers. Some sort of birdy name would be best. Jay Nelson? Too ordinary. Robin? Too androgynously British. Raven? Pretentious. Little Blue Nelson? Sounds like a harmonica player from the south side of Chicago. Killdeer? Too *Last of the Mohicans*. Creeper, thrasher? Sociopathic. Woodcock? Pornographic. Wait, there's a Jeremiah Nelson at Oak Hill, an early Massachusetts congressman. Nice biblical ring, catchy. John Nelson and I had passed Jeremiah's gravestone on our way through the cemetery.

"We probably shouldn't both be buried here," he said.

"Right. We'd both need an inscription: 'Not the Other John Nelson.'"

Lately I've been thinking more outside the box. It's a truism that no single birder can see two different birds in two different places at the same time, but what about two birding John Nelsons, or three, or five? Imagine the possibilities if we coordinated our efforts: Malaysian Plover on a Filipino beach, Crab Plover on the Kenya coast, and a pink-legged Magellanic Plover at a sheltered lagoon in Patagonia—three great rarities, seen simultaneously. Or we could search for birds in cemeteries around the world. Think of the potential life list: birds seen by a John Nelson.

If there are other John Nelsons out there birding somewhere, please come forward and identify yourselves.

Chapter 9

TWITCHER'S TEMPTATION

I admit it, I'll chase a bird. Pink-Footed Goose in Newbury? Honey, I'm going birding. Smith's Longspur at a Saugus landfill? A challenge in its muted winter plumage, but better birders would be searching with me. Yellow Rail? Long odds, a marsh skulker, but if I weren't already retired I might blow off work for that bird. Brits call it "twitching." A birder gets a report of a rare bird. The birder feels an urge, a neurological spasm, a twitchy need to see the bird. The birder takes off to chase after it. Call it obsession or a comical addiction to bird-listing—Mary can tell you what to call it—and I'll plead guilty. Sometimes I wish I were like her, a self-proclaimed Alzheimer's birder. In truth, she remembers far more than she lets on, but she keeps no lists, targets no birds, and won't jump in the car to go see a goose. For her *every* bird is a new bird, a life bird, a unique delicacy at nature's feast.

How far will I go to chase a bird? I have no idea. When I started birding I would entertain civilian friends with tales of fanatical birders, like the one who complained about a whale watch on which he'd seen nothing but scores of whales. I'd make pompous pronouncements fixing rational limits on the birding excursions I would undertake. "I'm not going all the way to Plymouth and slogging miles down some beach for some dinky little shorebird." "I'm not driving clear across the state just to see a towhee with dots." Sad to say, it took years before I finally saw a Red-Necked Stint and Spotted Towhee in Massachusetts. What was I thinking? I've since roamed the Commonwealth from South Beach (Elegant Tern, no) to Mount Watatic (Gray

Jay, yes!) in search of new birds for my state list. Now, I need only say, "I'm not—" and Mary collapses in merciless laughter. How far will I go? It depends on whether a Ross's Gull ever comes within five hundred miles of our house.

I'll particularly chase my nemesis bird—that bird, of all birds I've chased, which remains most defiantly unobserved, most intractably unchecked on my list. Nationally, my nemesis is the Chukar. I've hauled Mary from Colorado to California, from barren rocks to barren rocks, to hunt for this bird. I even biked across Gloucester in search of a reported Chukar that couldn't possibly be a wild bird. Mary finally decided that this creature is not merely elusive but apocryphal, no more real than the backward-flying Goofus Bird in Jorge Luis Borges's *Book of Imaginary Beings*. But what about the birders who claim to have witnessed Chukars—two, ten, thirty at a time—sunning themselves on rocks or cavorting along a road? Bullshitters, one and all. I'm reluctant to add David Sibley and other bird guide authors to the list of liars, but . . . maybe they've shared a hallucination. Maybe a detailed depiction of a fabricated bird is their idea of some sick birding fun. Just because Sibley draws it, with all those clever little field marks, doesn't mean a bird exists.

Statewide, my nemesis has evolved as I've spent more time in the field. In fact, you have to bird seriously for some years and accumulate a load of frustration before you can call any bird a "nemesis." For a while the Connecticut Warbler topped my list, until that blessed morn at Cumberland Farms when one, two, three warblers showed themselves for split seconds before sneaking back into the shrubbery. The honor of being my state nemesis instantaneously passed on to the Northern Goshawk. I'd had wonderful looks at goshawks at Yellowstone, even in Thailand. I'd careened off a road in Concord while trying to identify a goshawk-like fly-by before it disappeared into the trees. But I'd yet to fix my binoculars on a certifiable goshawk within Massachusetts borders. I hung out in goshawk neighborhoods, meditated with a goshawk mantra, beseeched the spirit of Goshawk to invite me into its realm. No goshawk.

One evening I saw a MassBird report of two goshawks at Mass Audubon's Wachusett Meadow sanctuary in Princeton. I'd been meaning to visit the sanctuary, and with the prospect of goshawk goading me, I woke at four the next morning to drive there. Technically I wasn't twitching, since goshawks aren't rare or vagrant in our state, but I was twitching in spirit. As I left behind the coastal plains I fell into a familiar road fantasy—the bold adventurer on a quest, heading west and back in time, escaping a style-cramping Puritan village for the promise of discovery in a wilderness. The name "Massachusetts" means "place of great hills" in Algonquin, which may seem like a joke in the Rockies, but we do have mountains here, perhaps once as high as the Himalayas. They're just old and worn out. I knew I was close when, in dawning light, I saw the rounded top of Mount Wachusett. From the edge of the sanctuary, the trail to the spruce-fir summit is only about three miles.

The parking lot was empty when I pulled in. Sheep grazed near a big gray barn. An Eastern Bluebird pair preened on a wooden fence. Beyond a field, dead trees stood like wardens in a vast beaver pond. I checked the map outside the office to get a feel for the layout of the place. A notice was posted next to the map. Goshawks, it said, were nesting in the sanctuary, and to ensure the safety of visitors and breeding success of the birds, the nesting area had been closed to the public. I shook my head. Why was I trying to chase down nesting birds?

A bit disoriented, I wandered down a path across the field toward the pond. Tree Swallows swung by. A Belted Kingfisher, a female by the rusty breastband, rattled her maracas as she took flight and hovered plunge-ready over the water. Some juvenile kingfishers drown before they become adept hunters. Below the kingfisher, painted turtles basked companionably along a log. I heard an excited *keer keer keer* and a Red-Shouldered Hawk materialized overhead—a "good" bird, once fairly common in our state but now scarce. An illustrated sign said that a rare butterfly, Harris's checkerspot, had been seen in the sanctuary. I heard a splash, glimpsed something elongated, sleek dark fur, thick tail, as it slipped into the pond. A mink? It was a beautiful day, calm, brightening.

The trail took me into the soundscape of the woods. "Here I am. Where are you?" recited a Red-Eyed Vireo, called the Preacher, with the briefest of pauses between its repetitive sermons. A technicolor Scarlet Tanager rasped his song. I found him and looked for his yellow bride. Young love, I thought, but romance for tanagers comes with hard requirements. Beauty alone won't cut it. A nesting female needs a resource provider, a mate who can reliably find food and bring it back to the nest. If her mate can't manage, if he's gone too long, she might desert the cause and begin anew elsewhere with a different mate.

At a junction I turned on to another trail, heading vaguely toward the goshawk area. I stopped to examine a gallery of ferns and felt some feathery white flowers on spiky stems. Foamflowers? Wildflower identification would have to wait for another lifetime. I hopped over little streams with mossy rocks and entered neighborhoods of mushrooms in the seeps and shadows of boulder outcrops. Dorothy-like, I skipped along a row of stepping stones across a stretch of mushy ground. I was moving into the heart of the woods. Goshawks are known for both their determination as killers and their ability to navigate through dense forest stands at high speeds without crashing. Scientists at MIT have studied them in flight to write equations that set speed limits for obstacle-avoiding drones.

I reached a sign at another trailhead. I was at the border of goshawk territory: it was the same off-limits notice posted at the office. I looked around, listening. I was at the far end of the sanctuary. I'd seen no one on the trails. Nesting goshawks could be ferociously protective—birders had been strafed and bloodied—but I was willing to sacrifice a few chunks of scalp to see my nemesis. I felt a presence looming, a mounting conviction that if I went down that trail, Goshawk would be there. I'd read about "intensity experiences," moments of ecstatic discovery when, outdoors and alone, people feel the boundaries crumbling and embrace oneness with all the life around them. I was a lone, quiet intruder. How badly could I disturb these birds? If someone saw me, I could swear I'd never seen any sign, I'd just been birding along obliviously. Who could call me a liar? Even if someone did, so what? Would I lose my birding license?

I stood at the trailhead, the gears of rationalization grinding. I'd noticed no changes in the nearby songbirds, no signs of goshawk-induced panic, yet I sensed that goshawks were watching *me,* noting my eye movements, checking my body for any sudden gesture, any quickening of pace, any enemy behavior. As a child I'd wondered what birds see. How does the world look to them? Why, I asked myself now, was I so driven to see this bird or that bird? When I'm on my deathbed, will I care about my state bird list, one more, one less? What was I doing here?

Lists: life lists, state lists, birds seen, birds still to see, the official checklist of North American birds. The definition of North America is political, not ecological. The southern boundary should be Panama, not the Rio Grande. There's an old Mexican saying: "We didn't cross the border. The border crossed us." Most birders uphold standards; they've got to see a species distinctly to put it on a life list. But a few let list-obsessiveness get the better of them. They're as loose as a bartender who glances at a fake ID and serves a fourteen-year-old a beer. Put their sightings on trial before a letter-of-the-law judge, and they'd need to raise Johnnie Cochran from the dead to defend them. Other birders boast of keeping no lists at all, as if the failure to keep records demonstrates freedom from the tyranny of numbers and a more profound aesthetic joy in birds. Much ado about nothing. There's no intrinsic link between watching birds and making lists. Those who fudge and rationalize when listing birds would fudge and rationalize if they weren't birders at all. I like making lists. In grade school I listed Top Forty songs, NFL wide receivers ("ends"), and islands I wanted to see someday. Now I've got lists of must-read magical realist novels, top female rhythm and blues vocalists, and the birds on those islands I wanted to see someday. Lists give the world a semblance of order. We wouldn't have a coherent system for naming and classifying species—a means to organize our knowledge of birds and all other organisms—if Carolus Linnaeus hadn't spent a lot of time making lists. No lists, no biology.

Was I the master of my list, or was my list the master of me? I turned away from the trailhead. I wasn't afraid of getting caught. I'm not inherently law-abiding. If I were, I wouldn't have driven seventy miles per hour down Route 2 to see a bird, and I would've passed up that first joint in college. The reason was simple: if something was bad for birds, it couldn't be good for me. Birds have enemies enough already, feral cats on the loose, cell towers. They don't need another. If every birder gave in so easily to temptation, I wouldn't be one lone intruder. There would be lines of intruders and fewer birds to breed and see.

I loitered for a while at the fringe of the forbidden zone, hoping, expecting that the Bird Gods would reward me for ethical rectitude and send a goshawk my way. But life doesn't work like that, or it shouldn't. A felon shouldn't win the lottery because he's magnanimously decided not to mug anyone again.

From behind me I heard jackhammer knocking. I found the knocker high up, its long body silhouetted, the light catching the red crest that gives the Pileated Woodpecker its name. Between blows to the tree, wood chips flying, it paused to rest its beak or listen for grubs crawling beneath bark.

Guided by birdsong, I headed down another trail. A flute led me to a Hermit Thrush pair, hopping with spring in their steps. They tolerated my presence if I stayed still. How at home they seemed in this play of light and shadow, leaf litter with insects on the forest floor. Above me a Black-Throated Green Warbler sang *zee zee zee zoo zeet*. It seemed so carefree, but it needed sustained vigilance to feed a family while keeping its nest hidden from goshawk eyes. These birds' voices belonged in *these* woods. Mary knew the answer. Open yourself to wonder, and every bird *is* a new bird.

I found myself in a field of wildflowers, asters, violets, others I couldn't identify. The air fluttered with Nabokov's butterflies. I knew a few—spring azure, tiger swallowtail, clouded sulphur—but I didn't see any checkerspots. Butterflies would require yet another lifetime. Then, amid a frog chorus, I was standing on a platform overlooking the pond, the water rippled by a beaver, the great change-agent of this community. Beavers build dams and made ponds. The flooded trees eventually die, and woodpeckers chisel holes in the dead trees. The holes later become nest sites for Wood Ducks and Hooded Mergansers.

The kingfisher hovered. A male joined her on a snag. Dragonflies with spotted wings skimmed the pond and clutched in the air like acrobats. Three male Hooded Mergansers dabbled along the water's edge, their white crests as hydrodynamic as fins. A water snake spiraled through murk and crawled ashore into mud-dwelling vegetation. The snake might be looking for a nest, eggs, or hatchlings to prey on. I had much to learn yet: the animals and plants in this pond were interdependent in so many ways I understood only superficially. I left the sanctuary feeling contented, communed.

How far will I go to chase a bird? I know part of the answer now—not to the point where the chase might harm the bird. A while after my visit to Wachusett Meadow, a goshawk was reported a mile from our house. Twice I came home mud spattered and briar scarred after a fruitless search. Perhaps, I thought, if life is poetic, my first goshawk in the state would be the offspring of the Wachusett Meadow pair, or their offspring's offspring if their breeding was successful. I could wait. The next year I went to Crooked Pond in Boxford in hopes of finding a Winter Wren pouring forth music from its gully or a Louisiana Waterthrush slurring its song above the rush of a stream. I was almost back to my car when I heard a resonant *cack!* Above me were two goshawks, masked, fierce, brawny, bodies that spoke power. Songbirds ducked for cover. The goshawks didn't deign to look at me. They flew *cack*ing from tree to tree for a few minutes and went deeper into the woods.

That doesn't mean I've stopped twitching. Purple Gallinule in Gloucester? Swainson's Hawk at Cumberland Farms? I've tried for the hawk a few times and dipped. A new nemesis. I could circle the farm fields on my bike. Honey, I'm going birding.

Chapter 10

RARITY ENVY

Joni Mitchell sang about a crow's restless soul as I drove by Noquochoke Lake. Bob Marley's "Three Little Birds" and Howling Wolf's "Little Red Rooster" were up next on my Birdy Mix. I passed a sleepy country graveyard at first light and cozy little settlements called "corners." It was fine country here, the roads winding through planted fields and along the Westport River. A rooster crowed along with the Wolfman. Since I'd retired, I'd been exploring Massachusetts—Wachusett Meadow, the Quabbin Reservoir, now the coast of Buzzards Bay. I kept an eye out for Bald Eagles along the river.

Old men fished from the bridge as I crossed the river to a barrier beach, the site of Horseneck Beach State Reservation. To the right the beach ended at the river's mouth, across from a point called the Nubble in the enclave of Acoaxet. Just west was the Rhode Island line. Boat-Tailed Grackle and Eurasian Collared Dove, never seen in our state, had both been found in Connecticut, and sooner or later they'd cross into Rhode Island and then hop into southeastern Massachusetts. A year earlier a rare White Ibis had been found in marshland here, but it moved south after an oil spill in Buzzards Bay.

I turned left and heard the clamor of Laughing Gulls as I passed the reservation. Waves churned against cobbles. I parked at the lot for Mass Audubon Allens Pond sanctuary and grabbed my binoculars. An American Kestrel hovered over the marsh. In "The Windhover," about a Eurasian Kestrel, Gerard Manley Hopkins describes a "dapple-dawn-drawn Falcon, in his riding of the rolling level underneath him steady air, and striding high there, how he rung upon the rein of a wimpling wing in his ecstasy!" Farmers in England called the bird "hoverhawk" and "windfucker." Kestrels fly forward at the same speed as the wind coming at them, a labor-intensive method of hunting used by only a few other birds, like Rough-Legged Hawks and Belted Kingfishers.

I walked east along the beach toward a point called Barneys Joy. Oystercatchers worked the shore. In an ancient nuptial ritual a Common Tern offered its mate a fish. More terns flew by, all Commons, though I tried to turn a few into uncommon Roseate Terns. I couldn't find any Piping Plovers either. Absence of evidence, I reminded myself, is not evidence of absence. The oil spill had come at a bad time for the plovers, already mating and choosing nest locations. Roseate Terns had been struggling for years to find the isolated breeding grounds they need, and their nesting often failed. The Roseate colony at Buzzards Bay was the largest in North America.

It had been the fifth major oil spill in this bay in thirty-five years. About a hundred thousand gallons of fuel oil—black, with molasses consistency—leaked out of a single-hulled barge after it collided with an unknown object. An oil slick drifted and touched more than a hundred miles of coastline. The oil coated animals on the ocean's surface, pancaked beaches with tar, infiltrated marshes, and fringed the sea with a black bathtub ring. A friend of mine, a volunteer for Mass Audubon's Coastal Waterbird Program, helped to rescue birds, wading with a net into frigid waters and chasing ducks among the rocks. It was like a Chinese fire drill, she told me, snatching birds, some alive, some not, and handing them off to someone else. She caught a wobbly Harlequin Duck, dripping oil, but it slipped away and zigzagged up the beach, wings flapping but unable to lift off. She stopped in her tracks. She thought she was looking at a Black Oystercatcher—a West Coast species, never seen in New England—until she realized it must be an American Oystercatcher, its white breast darkened by oil. She caught up with the Harlequin collapsed on the sand. "I'm getting too old for this," she said.

Halfway toward Barneys Joy I found a mangled, rotting Herring Gull. Who knows what killed it? I'd seen signs of the spill—rocks blackened along the shore, sand spattered with greasy little gobs—but it was a glorious morning, the sea dazzling. During summers through college, I'd worked on iron ore ships on the Great Lakes. One day the chief engineer ordered me to clean up the paint locker. Despite the mix of noxious fumes in a cramped room, I liked the job, sorting the useful from the useless, turning disarray into order. Finished, I had a pile of empty containers—paints, thinners, turpentine—so I asked the engineer what I should do with them. "Throw them over the side," he said. "In the water?" I asked. "We're on a boat, aren't we?" I can still see the long train of cans bobbing behind the stern on the waves of Lake Superior, into a gorgeous sunset.

What was the point in stewing over it? I turned back, climbed some sea-worn rocks, and found a path to the pond through shrubby sand-dwelling vegetation, beach rose, seaside goldenrod, patches of bayberry. At marsh's edge, trilling from a tussock, was a dark, flat-headed little bird with a white throat and yellow lores—a Seaside Sparrow, a bird I'd hoped to find here. Breeding only in tidal Spartina marshes, it's one of just a few species endemic to the lower forty-eight states. Further down was its cousin, another marsh specialist, the Saltmarsh Sparrow, its voice thinner and slurred, its face orange and pointy. It dropped, hopped into the open, looked my way, and ran off.

Turkey Vultures tilted with the wind as I turned toward the pond. Joni's restless crows waddled across cowlicks of marsh grass. An Osprey clutching a fish soared past. People once believed that Ospreys could cast spells on fish. How could an Osprey, or a tern feeding its mate, know its fish was oil-laced?

The pond was filled with Mute Swans, one of them "busking"—arching its wings and curving its long white neck to threaten a trespasser. I jumped back when another swan, suddenly close, extended its muscular neck and hissed at me. I glimpsed two chicks in the reeds. I kept my distance and scanned the flats for shorebirds: a few dowitchers, probably Short-Billed in June, and some yellowlegs—Greater, not Lesser, going by overall size, bill length relative to head length, and the bill's slight upturning.

One bird, the same size as the yellowlegs, seemed to have paler, greenish legs. It wasn't a Willet. Could a juvenile yellowlegs have greenish legs? A thought insinuated itself. No, not possible. Common Greenshank? The species had never been found in Massachusetts. A mega-rarity. I had to think, not get ahead of myself. What would the experts do? They'd have cameras. And spotting scopes. They'd know whether juvenile Greater Yellowlegs could have paler legs, and if they didn't know, they wouldn't have left their field guides in the car. There are reasons birders like me don't find rare birds.

I crept closer, fixed my binoculars on the bird, and tried to take a mental photograph, capture each field mark. Oiled birds were out of my mind. Legs, or shanks, definitely pale—if the light could be trusted. Bill slightly upturned. Aside from leg color, how did a greenshank differ from a yellowlegs? The bird seemed to have less extensive streaking than the birds around it, but the distance made it hard to tell. I needed my scope.

The birds all took off, some of them calling. What did a greenshank sound like? I was slow to get on the birds in flight. My bird was lost in the flock. The flock flew farther off. I scanned toward the beach, the shoreline stretching toward Barneys Joy. My bird was gone. In the marsh a crow carried a paper bag in its mouth. Another cawed and yanked at something dark and shaggy. They didn't care about greenshanks.

In my car I flipped through my Sibley guide. The greenshank wasn't illustrated, but in the "Rare Shorebirds" section Sibley described it: "Very similar to Greater Yellowlegs but legs greenish and rump entirely white, creating dowitcher-like white stripe up the back." If my bird had a white rump and white stripe, I hadn't noticed. I turned to the Greater Yellowlegs page: all had bright yellow legs, no stripes up the back. I could post a report: "Possible Common Greenshank at Allens Pond, but a distant look, and observer lacked scope, camera, field guide, and brain." Who would chase that bird?

Rare birds. For some birders, a compulsion to see them drives all plans for birding travel. Websites itemize the world's fifty rarest birds and where to seek them. Movies are made about rarity-searching, books are written, like Vernon Head's *The Rarest Bird in the World*, about the Nechisar Nightjar in Africa. I've known the exhilaration of seeing rare birds: a Gurney's Pitta sifting through leaf litter in a gully in Thailand, long-tailed Indigo Macaws flying like blue spirits through mist over a Bahian field. There was something odd, even perverse, in the pleasure I felt. It wasn't pride in birding skill, since expert guides had led me to these birds. It wasn't schadenfreude—a spiteful glee in knowing that other birders, poor saps, had failed and would fail again to find the bird I was looking at. It was more than the dumb satisfaction of adding a species to my life list before it became extinct. Honestly, I can't explain it. A bird doesn't become more beautiful just because we know it's rare. Its behavior doesn't become more interesting. Maybe the explanation is as simple as a quest fulfilled, or ordinary egocentricity. A bird or rhino or rare butterfly doesn't become real until *we* possess it with our own eyes.

On that greenshank morning I'd been a birder for a while. Retired, I had time to contemplate all sorts of frivolous questions, such as: how could I enhance my reputation as a birder? To find an answer I'd sought guidance from more experienced hands, eavesdropped on birders' gossip, and consulted books that examine status among birders. The answer wasn't complicated. To gain respect, to rise within the unofficial hierarchy of birders, one needed to do just two things: (1) establish credibility as a reliable reporter of bird findings, and (2) find rare birds.

The first goal seemed achievable. Documenting bird sightings is not like trying to verify UFO sightings or reporting on the arcane demographics of gerrymandering. The process is straightforward. Do some homework. Go out in the field. Observe carefully. Be precise and accurate in reporting what you see and hear. If you have doubts about identification, say so, and articulate *why* you have doubts. Resist hyperbole. Don't make up field marks or entire birds. In short, don't lie. If you lack the moral fiber to refrain from lying, be pragmatic. The literature on birding offers many cautionary tales of depraved status-seekers who've tried to gain attention through dubious sightings. Repeatedly reporting rare birds that no one else ever sees will not win your peers' admiration. After a few years I figured I'd met the minimum standards for credibility, but it felt like a modest accomplishment.

The second challenge, finding rare birds on my own, proved tougher. I tried. I annotated my Sibley guide until it disintegrated. I listened to tapes, perused websites, read birding magazines. I learned what was rare, where and when, and what wasn't. I chose role models, rarity-finders extraordinaire, and tried to emulate them. I spent hours along the shores and in the woodlands of Massachusetts. I found some good birds, an American White Pelican here, a Prothonotary Warbler there, but nothing spectacular, nothing truly rare. I began to despair.

But as I walked around Allens Pond, hoping the might-have-been greenshank would come back, I had a revelation.

Many birders were dependable reporters. A more select but still substantial number had discovered rarities. I needed to go in another direction. *I* would stand out, *I* would achieve distinction, by *never* finding a rare bird. I wouldn't resort to deception or malingering. I'd try my damnedest to come upon vagrant birds. But I'd always come up short. Other birders would come to count on me. My reputation for never finding rarities would precede me. Now, years later, I think I've earned the acknowledgment I crave. My record speaks for itself.

A caveat. To be honest, my record is not unblemished. Serendipity has cursed me. I have found a few rare birds, through no fault of my own. First, that Lazuli Bunting I reported from south Texas. The bird, six hundred miles out of its usual range, made the Texas Rare Bird Alert. But that was in my first year of birding, long before the greenshank, when I couldn't tell a bunting from a bullfinch. It was Mary who actually found the bird. She described every field mark. It took me five minutes to get on it. When she asked me what it was, I didn't have the foggiest. I'd studied only those birds I thought we might actually see in Texas. Okay, I figured it out, but what else looks like a Lazuli Bunting? How much blame do I deserve?

Then there was that Black-and-White Warbler, six months before the greenshank, on one of our first international trips. I'd been hoping for a manakin. How was I to know that the warbler had been found only twice on Tobago? Was it my fault that our guide went into a whirling calypso of life-bird celebration? All I'd done was hear the bird's squeaky wheel song and point. It was one of few songs on the island I recognized.

Mrs. Hume's Pheasant, spotted shortly after I vowed never to find rare birds, remains the most garish blotch on my record. I knew that the species was possible in Thailand, but I never expected to see one. I was gazing out of a slowly moving van. The bird was there, in a small opening in the forest. The bird was gone. It took no skill to ID it. The thing was enormous, with a rich reddish chestnut body, big white wing bars, and a silvery tail two feet long. Why didn't the guide find it? In all his trips to Southeast Asia, he'd never seen one, and it was the Thai bird he most wanted to see. Why wasn't it spotted by someone else in our group? There were thirteen of them, some crazed to see this pheasant, and every single one missed it. Herein we see the cosmic but commonplace injustice of birding. Despite his disappointment, our guide, Dave Stejskal, defended me when some disgruntled birders in the other van suggested I'd really seen a not-very-similar Red Junglefowl. "Why would Nelson lie about the pheasant?" he said. "He knows he's ruining his reputation." Luckily these lapses occurred in far-off foreign lands like Thailand and Texas. Within the borders of my home state my record remains virginal.

To what, you may wonder, do I attribute my success at not finding rarities over many years in Massachusetts? A prerequisite is an absence of God-given talent. I look out across the ocean and see water and sky, maybe a boat. The Prodigy beside me sees a speck. Five minutes later I perceive what might be a speck. The Prodigy is calling out field marks. It's a dark juvenile Long-Tailed Jaeger, and it's calling. Aberrants like this guy, with X-ray vision and preternatural hearing, are the Ella Fitzgeralds, the Madame Curies, the Seth Currys of bird-finders. The rest of us are singing-in-the-shower, calculator-dependent double-dribblers. I take no pride in my deficiencies: all praise goes to the Creator. Native inability, though useful, is also overrated among the factors involved in missing rarities. Let's say the Prodigy finds a first-state-record Pacific Golden Plover at Plum Island. Is it because he can see seventeen long-winged angels jitterbugging on the head of a pin at eight hundred yards? No. He knows that the species might show up there. He knows its field marks, its habits. He studies every bird that resembles it.

A far more important factor is ignorance. But how, you ask, can I claim ignorance after I've studied so hard, ravaged my Sibley, led field trips, participated in Christmas Bird Counts? The key is to be ignorant in very particular ways at the moment of truth. What does a Common Greenshank sound like? Can a juvenile Greater Yellowlegs have pale green legs? When it mattered I didn't know. What distinguishes a female Black-Headed Grosbeak from an immature male Rose-Breasted Grosbeak? What does a Sedge Wren sound like? I could go on, but why bother? It's essential not to know these things.

Clearly, lack of retention plays a part. I'm like a law student who crams in enough to pass the bar exam but would inflict untold damage on trusting clients if allowed to represent them in court. When I study Kenn Kaufman's *Advanced Birding* or Pete Dunne's *Essential Field Guide Companion*, I highlight, take notes. Knowledge is there. Then it's gone, like a fleeing bird. The reason may be my age or the advanced age at which I took up birding. The root cause may be some random twist in my DNA. These aren't things I can take credit for.

Ignorance is necessary but not sufficient. As Oscar Wilde observed in *The Importance of Being Earnest*, ignorance is like "a delicate exotic fruit; touch it and the bloom is gone." Ignorance will wither and die without laziness to nurture it. And it's not enough to embrace laziness now and then, to be fickle and erratic as its caretaker. You must cultivate your laziness into a mindset, a habitual disposition to make thoughtless assumptions and ignore possibilities. Oh, there's a field full of Canada Geese. Oh, why sort through all those Herring Gulls? Thus have I passed over a rare Cackling Goose and a rare California Gull. It helps if the laziness is physical as well as mental. Why didn't I have my scope and Sibley when I needed to identify a greenshank? Both are too damn heavy, that's why.

In truth, it's hard to distinguish between laziness and lousy memory. In my profession, the study of literature, I retain all sorts of obscure allusions and nuances. But when I come upon certain articles in birding magazines—on raptor molts or conundrums in storm-petrel identification—I know that if I try to read them, my attention will flag, thought will wander like a vagrant, and so I don't bother, though I look at the pictures and captions. It's hard to separate cause from effect. Do I lose interest because I know I won't retain, or do I fail to retain because I'm unmotivated? I don't know, and I guess I don't care. I feel the same way if I try to immerse myself in mushroom varieties or strange attractors in chaos theory. I bird because it gives me pleasure, and there's little pleasure in homework that's likely to prove both boring and futile. I'm not a forager staking my life on the ability to distinguish edible from toxic fungi.

My crowning moment of laziness came one summer's day when I was blissfully bicycle-birding on the roads of Martha's Vineyard. Across a field at Katama Farm I saw a smallish raptor hovering in the distance. "Kestrel," I said to myself as I pedaled on with my binoculars stowed in my backpack. "Same kestrel," I said as I passed the bird again, a little closer this time, an hour later. "Looks a little hefty. Must be good hunting here." I take almost equal pride in the moment I scoped a certain plover on Plum Island—first of the year, I thought with pleasure—an hour before the Prodigy correctly identified it.

A retroactive caveat. At the risk of sullying my reputation as an honest reporter, I confess that the incidents in the previous paragraph did not in fact take place. I did ride across Martha's Vineyard and see a falcon hovering in a field, but that was weeks after Vern Laux identified the bird as a Red-Footed Falcon, unprecedented in North America. And I didn't scope a plover just before Rick Heil identified it as a Pacific Golden Plover. But if I had, I guarantee you I would've ticked it off as an American Golden Plover, and I swear on a stack of multicultural religious texts that I would have thought "kestrel" and merrily continued on past Katama Farm.

Some might argue that my appeal for recognition as a rarity-misser is simply an apology for mediocrity. After all, anyone can succeed at not finding birds. You don't even have to be a birder. But I'm something more or less than mediocre. I might be ignorant, lazy, and optically challenged, but I'm no slacker. I don't sit beside a computer screen waiting for people to report rare birds so I can leap from my chair to chase them. I go out in the field and look for hard-to-get birds, yet I aspire not to find and identify them. That's not mediocrity. It's zen.

Others might protest that my approach to the issue of reputation is too narrow. One can also gain respect by devoting oneself to the welfare of birds, striving to protect their habitats, and trying to prevent more oil spills. Yes, one can, but that sounds a lot like work. It also seems like unnecessary work, since most people who are that committed to birds have already solidified their reputations by finding various rare species.

Finally, some might raise a philosophical objection. If I failed to see or identify a rare bird, how do I know it was there? The answer is simple: I'm in contact with a spirit. Some call her Avis or Brid or Phoenix. To me she's simply the Goddess. She doesn't predestine bird sightings, doesn't reward diligence or punish laziness, though She does like to ask, "What have *you* done for birds lately?" Omniscient, the Goddess is expert at keeping lists, all sorts of lists, among them what I call my "potential life list." It includes every wild bird in whose presence I've been, every bird I've heard or seen or could've seen if I were paying better attention, whether I identified the bird or not. She's got a list for you too. Someday the Goddess will reveal my whole list. When She does, each glorious bird will appear before my eyes in a rapture of field marks, and I'll know what it is. But first I have to die.

Chapter 11

SYMPATHY

Birds in Nineteenth-Century Massachusetts Literature

As a teacher I knew about birds as literary symbols but knew almost nothing of actual birds. I'd taught Keats's "Ode to a Nightingale" and Shelley's "To a Skylark" with only a vague idea of what these birds look or sound like and no great desire to see or hear them. Then, a few years before I retired, I began birding. I've heard nightingales sing with "full-throated ease" along a shadowy Turkish stream. By a Mongolian lake a Eurasian Skylark rose higher and higher above me, almost vanishing, skylarking in courtship display as it poured forth "a flood of rapture so divine." Shelley's euphoric poem goes over the top—a lot of spiritual weight loaded on a little bird—but I understand now why these birds spurred the imaginations of poets.

After I retired I looked to combine my newfound love of birds with my long-standing love of literature. I hatched a plan to write a grand book tracing the history of American literature from a birder's perspective. After several editors persuaded me I'd never find a publisher, I kept reading anyway, partly as research for essays but mostly out of curiosity. In my pre-birder state, what had I missed in reading American literature? How well did writers know birds? How did they use birds in their stories and poems? Who was as oblivious to birds as I had been?

Massachusetts writers predominated in the American literary scene in the first century after the Revolution. Nathaniel Hawthorne, from Salem, lived for three years with his bride

Sophia in the Old Manse, a house Emerson owned in Concord, and here he took pleasure in the "winged people" all around him. In *Mosses from an Old Manse* (1846) he delights in the hummingbirds in the garden—"a joy to me, those little spiritual visitants, for deigning to sip airy food out of my nectar cups"—and breeding birds that "claim human friendship by building their nests under the sheltering eaves or among the orchard trees." Through walks with Thoreau, Hawthorne became more attuned to nature. On the Concord River he encountered a "shy kingfisher" that "flew from the withered branch close at hand to another in the distance, uttering a shrill cry of anger or alarm." His essay "Buds and Bird Voices" embraces the carefree spring days of birdsong: "The old paradisiacal economy of life is again in force; we live, not to think or to labor, but for the simple end of being happy."

Without a trace of the gloom of *The Scarlet Letter*, Hawthorne is as playful as Mark Twain when he imagines blackbirds in tumultuous political debates or catalogues the vices of crows: "A crow, however, has no real pretensions to religion, in spite of his gravity of mien and black attire; he is certainly a thief, and probably an infidel. The gulls are far more respectable, in a moral point of view." The birds around him discuss "the economy of life and love and the site and architecture of their summer residences." When they sing "like a brook let loose from wintry chains," he hears "a hymn of praise to the Creator" and wonders if birds might "partake of human nature, and possess the germ, if not the development, of immortal souls." Reviewing Hawthorne's book, Herman Melville wrote: "His wild, witch voice rings through me; or, in softer cadences, I seem to hear it in the songs of the hill-side birds, that sing in the larch trees at my window."

Hawthorne's interest in birds was intermittent. There's no hooting owl to enhance the dread in "Young Goodman Brown," no melodious songbirds to heighten the spring revelry in "The Maypole of Merry Mount." But in *The House of the Seven Gables* (1851) he uses birds to evoke characters and to illustrate a spiritually nurturing "sympathy" between people and nature. The heroine, Phoebe Pyncheon, a benevolent country girl named for a bird (also Hawthorne's pet name for his wife), moves about the house as gracefully as a bird and sympathizes with the "twittering gayety of the robins in the pear-tree." She sings like a bird "in whose small strain of music we recognize the voice of the Creator." In the end Phoebe helps two old "owls," her cousins Hepzibah and Clifford, to escape the plagued house and make a fresh start in the country. "We have flown far enough for once," Clifford says. "Let us alight, as the birds do, and perch ourselves on the nearest twig, and consult whither we shall fly next."

Kin to Phoebe in bird sympathy is Hilda, a "fair, pure creature" in *The Marble Faun* (1860) who is called "the Dove" and lives amid pigeons in a "virgin's shrine," the Dove-cote, an apartment high above Rome's "evil scents" and "moral dust and mud." These white birds associate Hilda with the dove's purity in Christian symbolism. Woman and pigeons live in a separate "moral atmosphere" where God keeps them safe. After Hilda witnesses a murder and feels tainted by her friends' sins, she's soothed by doves flying in through her windows like "winged messengers, bringing her what sympathy they could, and uttering soft, tender, and complaining sounds, deep in their bosoms." Synchronizing her moans with their coos, Hilda feels that her "incommunicable sorrow" has been "told to these innocent friends, and understood, and pitied." Hawthorne seems to present Hilda as a paragon of virtue, but many readers have found her self-centered, cold hearted, insufferably priggish, and even repulsive in her ignorant purity. Critic Emily Schiller asks, "If we hate Hilda so much, why do we assume that Hawthorne likes her?" It's a good question I can't confidently answer.

Whether Hilda is admirably pure or simply too damn pure for anyone's earthly good, Donatello in *The Marble Faun* is a good bird gone bad. He's identified with the title sculpture, "neither man nor animal, and yet no monster, but a being in whom both races meet, on friendly ground!" Birds recognize him as kin they need not fear. He feels sympathy with the trees. He calls to the "woodland inhabitants, the furry people and the feathered people, in a language that they seemed to understand." Like the faun, Donatello is a throwback to our species' innocent, premoral childhood, before we lost our natural spontaneity. When he declares his love for Hilda's friend Miriam, he shows "as little restraint as a bird pipes its notes, to a similar purpose," and one cheerfully singing bird flutters up as if to congratulate an old friend. Yet Hawthorne suggests that, like other "natural" men, Donatello is deficient in "the development of the higher portion of man's nature." When he kills a malefactor who has menaced Miriam with the "bony talons" of a predatory bird, the murder cuts Donatello off from both human and animal companions. While Hilda retreats to her dove tower, he flees to a dark owl tower, living with the tower's two dismally croaking owl proprietors. "They do not desert me, like my other feathered acquaintances," he proclaims. "This is my own abode, my own owl's nest!" Maybe owls are less morally discriminating than other birds. In a postscript Hawthorne emphasizes that his story is not a realistic novel but a romance. Its romantic owls and doves are not bound by the known behavior of actual owls and doves.

In contrast to the more citified Hawthorne, Herman Melville worked on whalers and on merchant ships in the South Pacific before he settled in Boston and eventually on a Pittsfield farm, and he took his readers to places that even modern birders call the last frontier—the vast oceans and remote oceanic islands of pelagic birds. In "Rock Rodondo" from *The Encantadas* (1854), we're at the end of the world, in another realm from garden hummingbirds and urban doves. Here, in the Galapagos, on a "Rock of vile Reproach, a dangerous and dreadful place," no humans nor songbirds live, only "innumerable sea-fowl" that gather on cliffs from leagues around to cry out in a "demonic din." In this "aviary of the Ocean," Melville marvels at how strange these birds are, how utterly removed from human life: "Birds light here which never touched mast or tree; hermit-birds, which ever fly alone, cloud-birds, familiar with unpierced zones of air." Pity the poor warbler that might land on Rodondo, for it would soon be overwhelmed by "locust-flights of strong bandit birds, with long bills cruel as daggers."

Melville finds beauty and awe in the Galapagos, but he's struck most by the predations of seabirds and what he considers their inexplicable grotesqueness. In the opening quotation from Spenser's *The Faerie Queen*, ravenous seafowl are a "nation of unfortunate and fatal birds." Species by species, Melville describes their ugliness. The pelicans, with "heavy leathern pouches" and "dull, ashy plumage," look "lugubrious" and "penitential." The penguins, hardly cute Disney characters, are "grotesquely misshapen," so unlovely and clumsy that "as if ashamed of her failure, Nature keeps this ungainly child hidden away at the ends of the earth." Only the lively, ubiquitous storm-petrel, known as Mother Carey's chicken, the "mysterious humming-bird of ocean," might be called charming if it had a little color. Melville doesn't speculate about why such weird birds exist, but his descriptions echo the theme of predation—and its cousin, "vulturism"—that emerges in his grand *Moby-Dick*, published in 1851.

Melville dedicated *Moby-Dick* to Hawthorne and, like Hawthorne, labeled it a romance. *Moby-Dick* is a metaphysically challenging book. Its bird symbolism, part of a larger scheme of animal and color symbolism, is complex, even contradictory. Certain passages suggest sympathy between birds and people, like the Nantucketer who "lives on the sea, as prairie cocks in the prairie," and is rocked to sleep on the waves along with "the landless gull." Ishmael, the narrator, says that some human souls contain the spirit of a Catskill eagle that "can dive down into the blackest gorges, and soar out of them again and become invisible in the sunny spaces." In the chapter "The Symphony," a flock of small birds frolic like "the gentle thoughts of the feminine air," in contrast to the murderous leviathans and sharks of the "masculine sea." But the "inscrutable sea-ravens" in "The Spirit-Spout" seem indifferent to human life as they sit each morning on the *Pequod* "as though they deemed our ship some drifting, uninhabited craft; a thing appointed to desolation, and therefore fit roosting-place for their homeless selves."

Melville's wondrously white albatross is a different bird altogether. Like sea-ravens, it lives in "exiled waters," but it dwells on a higher plane than either ravens or humans. In a long footnote to "The Whiteness of the Whale," Melville describes his first sighting of an albatross, a "regal" and "mystic" bird with "vast archangel wings, as if to embrace some holy ark" and inexpressible eyes that hold God's secrets. Transfixed, he loses "the miserable warping memories of traditions and towns," for the albatross lives amid "clouds of spiritual wonderment and pale dread." When the crew captured the albatross and then released it with a message tied around its neck, Melville envisioned the bird flying to heaven to "join the wing-folding, the invoking, and adoring cherubim."

The "horrible vulturism of earth" in *Moby-Dick* is embodied by scavenging "air-sharks" or "sea-vultures," black or speckled birds described with bitter irony as they pounce "most piously" on a whale's carcass, the "banquet" at the whale's "funeral." Melville also makes us feel the "unspeakably pitiable" suffering of a helpless animal when he compares a wounded, mute whale to "a bird with clipped wing, making affrighted broken circles in the air, vainly striving to escape the piratical hawks." Birds here are both victims and thieving scavengers. Ahab, his protagonist, struggling to comprehend Nature's mysterious workings and his own perverse soul, compares himself to both a predatory "victorious" fowl and a vulture that feeds on its own heart. "We are all killers on land and sea," Melville proclaims, and we humans are vultures too, feeding on dead flesh, but why has God fashioned a Nature where predation and vulturism are universal and survival requires pitiable suffering? How does the need to kill for sustenance turn into a perversion of human nature?

Melville wrote at a time when it was commonplace to vilify carrion-feeding birds, like vultures and ravens, often associated with Satan, and to condemn "vicious" birds of prey, like goshawks, that kill smaller birds. People now are more apt to view scavenging as just another way for birds to make a living, and to realize that charming songbirds are themselves predators. Just ask the caterpillars they eat. But neither we nor the songbirds can answer Melville's questions. Why have we been made this way? A decade later, in *The Origin of Species*, Charles Darwin provided part of an answer—the how, if not the why, of humans evolving from predatory ancestors—but it's an answer that's hard to square with the idea of a sympathetic God.

Some critics have complained that the Romantic birds in *Moby-Dick* are either unidentifiable or implausible in their habitats, like the black, red-billed "savage sea-hawk" with the hooked beak that steals Ahab's hat or the "sky-hawk" that goes down with the ship at the end. I'm inclined to cut Melville some slack, if only because he so powerfully captures the wild energy, independence, and frenzied flocking of hungry seabirds. He was honest enough to face the dark side of our kinship with birds. While Hawthorne found comfort in sympathetic bird neighbors—sweet singers, loyal mates, caring parents—Melville asked disturbing questions. How can we feel kinship with strange, predatory creatures that, for eons, lived and killed and died without any connection to humans? At story's end the sky-hawk leaves "its natural home among the stars" to follow the *Pequod*, becomes entangled in Ahab's flag, and drowns when the ship goes under, as if the ship, "like Satan, would not sink to hell till she had dragged a living part of heaven along with her, and helmeted herself with it." The sky-hawk's death isn't simply one bird's back luck, but the scene resists easy allegorical interpretation. Does it mean that, through our hubris or obliviousness, we will drag creation down with us? That remains an open question, for humans and birds alike.

If Melville was captivated by wild seabirds, then Henry James, raised partly in Boston, reminds us that some major American writers have had scant interest in birds anywhere or in nature generally. In *Nature's Nation* (1967) Perry Miller says that James "completely put aside the whole cult of Nature as a quaint 'moral passion.'" Birds were useful to him only to symbolize human qualities. In what sounds like a birdy book, *The Wings of the Dove* (1902), James's heroine, Milly Theale, isn't dove-like because she acts like a Turtle Dove but because a loving Christian God has given her metaphorical wings to escape "the fowler's snare" (Psalm 91) and "flee away and be at rest" (Psalm 55). Angelic, rich Milly spreads her wings to protect her friends both financially and spiritually. When she dies she spreads them wider to fly to "some happiness greater."

In his 1884 article "The Art of Fiction," James advised writers to be "people on whom nothing is lost"—excellent advice that he applied scrupulously to observations of persons but almost never to birds. His travelogue *The American Scene* (1905) describes natural landscapes from Concord, a "charming woody, watery place," to a "jungle" on the fringe of a Florida hotel, but birds are remarkably absent.

James's indifference to birds may annoy, but it's silly to judge writers by their knowledge or use of birds, since, especially in fiction, birds have limited potential as literary characters. Novelists have written birdwatching stories, but it's a rare writer, like William Wharton in *Birdy*, who's daring enough to tell a story about a deep connection between human and bird or, for that matter, between bird and bird. People may feel something like intimacy with birds, especially pets, but if birds have inner lives, they remain inaccessible to us. Birds can vocalize emotions and act them out through displays, but they can't articulate them in human terms.

Lyric poetry offers more fertile ground for writing about birds, since it depends less on characterization and social relationships, and it's more suited to expressing the feelings of evanescent encounters with birds. In the nineteenth century, as painters tried to capture the beauty of Massachusetts marshes and forests, poets here wrote about our region's birds. Among the first was William Cullen Bryant, a descendant of *Mayflower* immigrants, born in 1794 in a log cabin in Cummington, a frontier outpost in the Berkshires. As a child Bryant became a "delighted observer of external nature." During a long period as a New York City editor, he returned in summers to seek renewal in the Berkshire woods, where his poems are often set, just as Wordsworth, a major influence, found inspiration in the Lake Country. Biographer Gilbert Muller says that Bryant developed a poetic style "designed to capture the discrete particulars of Nature," though he was less interested in birds than the particulars of plants. Parke Godwin, his son-in-law, called him a "passionate botanist" who "knew the name of every tree, flower, and spire of grass."

The dominant themes in Bryant's poems are the healing qualities of nature, where a "sick heart" can escape suffering, and its revelation of a benevolent divinity. He depicts diverse American landscapes: a "wild wood" where birds "sing and sport in wantonness of spirit" in the canopy, an "unshorn" field where a "prairie-hawk" poses on high, and rocky isles where petrels skim the sea and screaming seafowl pile their eggs. In birds he finds "illuminations of moral truths," but they're just one element among many in harmonious scenes with squirrels, insects, laughing rivulets, contented trees, and tranquil rocks. His poems mention about thirty identifiable birds, like the Ruffed Grouse in "The Old Man's Counsel" that "wears a sable ruff around his mottled neck" and drums "a sound like distant thunder," but many of his birds are unspecific. "To a Waterfowl," his most famous bird poem, was occasioned when, on the seven-mile walk from his law office to Cummington, Bryant saw a single bird flying high in a red sky at dusk in December. Curious about where the bird is going, his narrator identifies with its solitude and toil on its life passage, but the emphasis is less on the unnamed bird than the invisible "power" that will guide both waterfowl and man to a "welcome land."

A departure from such reflective poems is Bryant's playfully anthropomorphic "Robert of Lincoln," about sexually dimorphic Bobolinks. The poem describes a vain, "gayly dressed" young husband who spends his days merrily singing, admiring his fine plumage, and boasting of his fearlessness. But when his Quaker wife, "pretty and quiet, with plain brown wings," hatches six young birds, Robert must forego "fun and frolic" and become "sober with work, and silent with care" as he gathers seeds for his hungry brood. "This new life," Robert thinks, "is likely to be hard for a gay young fellow like me," but the poem ends with the hope that when Bobolinks return the next spring, Robert will again "pipe that merry old strain."

Another lighthearted poem is "The Old-World Sparrow," in which Bryant parallels human immigrants to America to the House Sparrow, a "stranger bird" and "winged settler" that has been brought from Europe to a more welcoming New World. In the Old World the sparrow was trapped or poisoned for eating grain, but it will prosper in America as "the bane" of "insect legions" that strip fruiting trees. Given the sparrow's subsequent history, Bryant's optimism now seems misplaced, since House Sparrows were soon condemned as grain pests in North America and often exterminated, with some states putting bounties on their heads. Even today, many birders disdain House Sparrows as aggressive, non-native birds that outcompete native swallows and bluebirds, while in the land of President Donald Trump, some descendants of immigrants to our country have come to fear and disparage more recent immigrants as if they were invasive House Sparrows.

Bryant became known as one of the Fireside Poets, a group of friends (middle names mandatory) that included John Greenleaf Whittier, James Russell Lowell, Oliver Wendell Holmes, and Henry Wadsworth Longfellow—the first American poets to become internationally popular, read aloud by the fireside. Whittier, born in 1807 to a Quaker family on a Haverhill farm, called himself a "ruralist" and aspired to be an American Robert Burns. Like Bryant, he sensed the "sacramental mystery of the woods," but he distrusted the use of the natural world for spiritual symbolism and struggled to hear God's voice in nature. "Snow-Bound," his most famous poem, captures the rural isolation that many readers knew only too well, while using bird stories to locate his characters within nature and create a feeling of family warmth and continuity. A mother tells her children about the birds of her youth: hawks playing at twilight, loons laughing, and "wild-geese calling loud beneath the gray November cloud." The poem also reminds us that, to many Americans then, wild birds were sources of food as well as pleasure. The children's uncle, who knows all "the woodcraft mysteries" and comprehends the stories of sparrows, reminisces about shooting loons and teal and stealing eagle eggs.

Whittier, a man of duty, was a fervent antislavery activist during his career as a journalist, and many of his poems are polemical pieces written with no expectation that they would hold lasting interest. "What the Birds Said" is superficially a poem about spring migration, with birds flying north against an April wind, but these birds are singing about the horrors of the Civil War—towns on fire, children dying, the dead unburied. They also sing of the longing for freedom—"the freedman's song, the crash of Slavery's broken locks"—that makes the war necessary. A companion piece is Bryant's 1864 "Return of the Birds," another prowar nature poem. Bryant's birds have migrated too early, before winter has ended, for in "haste and fear" they fled battlefields further south, the towns burning, the dust of marching armies, and once bird-friendly fields torn up to bury the dead. Like Whittier, Bryant longs for a time when men will stop fighting and birds will again "warble, unafraid," but only after the conquering Union troops have "brought Glory to the brave, Peace to the torn and bleeding land, and freedom to the slave!" In the next century Roger Tory Peterson and Ludlow Griscom, the foremost American birders of their time, would offer a different slant when they described the remarkable adaptability of birds in wartime. Griscom was dumbfounded during World War I by a Eurasian Robin that sang from the remaining shrubbery moments after the Germans had shelled his company and destroyed a nearby church. During World War II Peterson was amazed by some Black Redstarts nesting in bombed chimneys amid the rubble in a blitzed part of London.

Thomas Wentworth Higginson, Cambridge born and raised, is now remembered mainly as Emily Dickinson's mentor, but during his lifetime he was known for his 1869 *Army Life in a Black Regiment*, based on his experience as colonel of the nation's first all-black regiment on the Georgia Sea Islands during the Civil War. Higginson had long been a militant abolitionist. He was indicted for riot, though never prosecuted, after a deputy marshal was killed when the Boston-based Vigilance Committee tried to free a jailed ex-slave in defiance of the Fugitive Slave Law. After his abolitionist friend John Brown was captured at Harpers Ferry, Higginson plotted an armed rescue, though Brown stopped the scheme. Both before and after the war, Higginson fought for a wide range of reforms including women's suffrage, desegregation, child labor laws, improved prison conditions, workman's compensation, restraint of monopolies, and anti-imperialism.

Such a résumé hardly fits the usual stereotype of a nature writer, yet in 1862, just before he left home to train former slaves to kill in battle, Higginson published "The Life of Birds," an essay so bright spirited, so removed from politics, that we feel as if we're back with Hawthorne in his garden paradise. Higginson imagines birds as exiles from another world: "So remote from ours their mode of existence, they seem accidental exiles from an unknown globe, banished where none can understand their language; and men only stare at their darting, inexplicable ways, as at the gyrations of the circus." He extols favorites like the Eastern Kingbird, with its "democratic habit of resistance to tyranny;" the Ruby-Throated Hummingbird, "like some exiled pygmy prince;" and the endlessly curious Chewink or Ground Robin (Eastern Towhee). He's amazed by birds' capabilities: their precise site fidelity, well-wrought nests, perfect eggs, and songs that are "the highest form of animal language." Writing three years after *The Origin of Species*, Higginson quotes Pythagoras—"the soul of our grandam might haply inhabit a fowl"—as he ponders the mystery of bird cognition. As mates and parents, he observes, "birds come nearest to man in their domesticity," yet the center of bird consciousness is "really farther from mine than the remotest planetary orbit." Quoting Darwin, he says that birds remind us "how profoundly ignorant we are of the condition of existence of every animal." I wonder which birds he saw, and what feelings they stirred, as he went off to war.

Like his fellow poets Lowell and Holmes, Henry Wadsworth Longfellow, also from Cambridge, has fallen out of fashion, but he was easily the most popular American poet of his time. Scholar, translator, and Harvard professor, Longfellow published a volume of antislavery poems, but unlike Whittier and Higginson, he rarely engaged in political activism. He was focused on creating national poetic sagas worthy of the grandeur of American mountains and rivers and the dynamism of American people. Poems like "The Sermon of St. Francis" and "The Herons of Elmwood," from *Birds of Passage*, emphasize our spiritual kinship with birds and their ability to transport us into the "joy of freedom" and "rapture of flight."

Birds both naturalistic and mythical figure prominently in *The Song of Hiawatha*, an epic poem set on the shores of Lake Superior and derived, with poetic license, from Finnish and Native American folklore. The ancient kinship between birds and people is dramatized through metamorphoses whereby humans, whether as punishment or through acts of mercy, become caged jays or great war eagles. Beautiful women are transfigured into birds and back into human form. Human characters are transformed into better-looking or tinier characters, while a Brant turns into a bigger, more imposing Brant. Migrating geese and herons "speak almost as a man speaks." Bluebirds and whip-poor-wills learn their "wild and wayward" songs from a human musician.

Hiawatha, an Ojibwe warrior, learns the language of birds—and how they build their nests and where they hide in winter—from his grandmother, Nokomis, who calls him "my little owlet." His story, the "song of Hiawatha," comes to us from Nawadaha, a musician who learned the ancient tribal legends from the songs of plovers, loons, and grouse. For Hiawatha, birds are sometimes enemies—like the mocking, scheming ravens and blackbirds that he ambushes, kills, and hangs on poles as a warning to other "black marauders"—but more often they're comrades. Gulls rescue him when he's trapped in the carcass of a giant sturgeon. Bluebirds and robins become his friends after they beg him not to shoot them. They sing in mourning when his dear friend dies and congratulate him when he returns home to marry his lover, Minnehaha. Hiawatha may now strike us a cliché—an Americanized Noble Savage, attuned to the wisdom of birds and woods, uncorrupted by Western civilization—but the poem reflects a widely felt longing, shared by writers like Cooper and Thoreau, for a life in harmony with nature in a land now crisscrossed by roads and railroads, with forests vanishing. *The Song of Hiawatha* was enormously popular, though it has been parodied almost since its publication, while folklorists like Stith Thompson have challenged its authenticity, and other readers object to Hiawatha's contrived conversion to Christianity at the end.

Longfellow died in 1882, before any organized bird conservation movement, but his fable "The Birds of Killingworth," from *Tales of a Wayside Inn*, anticipates later campaigns when conservationists tried to convince the public that birds were not pests but rather useful enemies of pests. The Killingworth farmers, supported by the Parson and Squire, denounce crows and other birds as crop pillagers. Charging birds great and small with "all the crimes beneath the sun," they doom all birds to destruction. The birds' defender, from the "hill of Science," is the Preceptor, who itemizes the sweet singers—thrush, oriole—that make birds "the Troubadours, the street-musicians of the heavenly city." He argues that a few handfuls of wheat or some cherries aren't worth the loss of such jubilant singers. Getting nowhere with his birdsong-versus-crops cost-benefit analysis, the Preceptor shifts to a warning: birds are "the wingéd wardens of your farms," and if they're slaughtered, their songs will be replaced by the "incessant whir" of marauding locusts and grasshoppers. But the farmers laugh at him, set a bounty on crows, and massacre all the birds in town. When summer comes, the warning comes true. Killington is overrun by insects, the land turned into a desert. It's the lesson of stories from *The Rime of the Ancient Mariner* to *To Kill a Mockingbird*: kill the birds, or at least the wrong birds, and there will be consequences. But Longfellow won't leave his readers with the threat of doom or a guilt trip. His farmers aren't exactly repentant, but the next summer the town imports a multitude of birds to bring a "new heaven" of joyous song to Killingworth and presumably eat more bugs.

Emily Dickinson saw many of the birds seen by her fellow poets, heard the same songs, and felt the same sympathy. But her bird poems stand out for their daring word choice and syntax, the unexpected turns of thought, and her skill at expressing the closeness she felt with the birds on her family's farm in Amherst. Dickinson once wrote to Higginson: "It is delicate that each Mind is itself, like a distinct Bird." The more we read her bird poems, the more we see her mind's distinctiveness, but the harder it is to encapsulate what birds meant to her.

Dickinson wrote before bird identification guides were widely available, but she knew the "spicing of Birds" in her patch and kept track of their comings and goings during the days and seasons. In a eulogy her sister-in-law, Susan, wrote: "So intimate and passionate was her love of Nature, she seemed herself a part of the high March sky, the summer day and bird-call." Dickinson gave crumbs to birds near her family's house and barn and filled a little tub with nectar for hummingbirds. She worried about backyard birds on days of extreme heat or frigid cold. In *A Summer of Hummingbirds* (2008), Christopher Benfey shows that fascination with birds was part of the bond Dickinson shared with a circle of family members and artistic friends like Martin Heade, who painted hummingbirds in Brazil, and Harriet Beecher Stowe, famous for *Uncle Tom's Cabin* but also the author of a children's story, "Hum, the Son of Buz," about a wounded hummingbird Stowe had rescued in New Hampshire.

Birds lightened Dickinson's heart. Through her poems we feel her joy both in birdsong and in her own playful inventiveness with language. Phoebes bring spring, the "time to strike my Tent-and open House—again." When her heart is heavy, a bird wends past her window and whistles an "Anodyne so sweet" to her "irritated Ear." Dickinson can hear the divinity in an oriole's song because the tune is also within her, but when a passing bird offers "specimens of Song" as if for her to choose, she's pleased to realize that the bird is shouting "for joy to Nobody but his seraphic self." She's uplifted by birds that sing "for nothing scrutable but intimate Delight" or give "Delight without a Cause" or "squander" song to stop the universe in its tracks. The world, she feels, is bountiful. Rather than go to church, she can keep the Sabbath at home, where she can "wear my Wings" while "going, all along" to heaven as God preaches in her orchard and a Bobolink serves as chorister. She feels affection even for less seraphic birds like the wary, velvet-headed little predator that came down her walkway, "bit an Angleworm in halves, and ate the fellow, raw."

Dickinson rarely left Amherst, and she loved the birds of her patch, like the robin, "my Criterion for Tune," because they shared her all-season "New Englandy" home. The robin too is a homebody that can "submit that Home—and Certainty and Sanctity, are best." She whimsically imagines one robin as a working-class "Gabriel in humble circumstances" with the punctuality and "oblique integrity" of a New England farmer maintaining "a small but sturdy Residence, a self-denying Household." In one early poem she cheerfully asks that someone feed the robins "if I shouldn't be alive."

Dickinson admires other bird neighbors for their brazenness or sheer energy. The Ruby-Throated Hummingbird never stops but partakes of nectar "without alighting and praises as he goes," while its spinning-wheel wing whir creates "dizzy Music" in her garden. The bird is a "little Tippler," an "Inebriate of Air," a "Debauchee of Dew." One hummingbird metaphorically sips Dickinson herself. The Bobolink she calls the "Bird of Birds"—brave, impudent, seditious, "attired to defy"—but what distinguishes it is joy. One swaggering Bobolink interrupts the "portentous" supplications of some dour Presbyterian birds to shout out "let us pray!" Equally resilient is the Blue Jay: neighbor, warrior, Brother of the Universe, braving New England winds to play in snow "when Heaven looked upon us all with such severity."

But the joy birds bring can be fleeting. Their dawn chorus, an "independent Ecstasy of Deity and Men," is a miracle, but it's gone by noon. The gayety of one navigating bird dazzles and then dissolves. In an early poem she overcomes "each little doubt and fear" to find faith that the robin, "which for myself doth sing," will return to sing for her again. But later she fears that robins might not return after their "last Experiment" at her home, and if they do come back, she might not be there to hear them. In poem 1463 (in the numbering sequence used by editor Thomas Johnson) a hummingbird flies a "Route of Evanescence with a revolving Wheel." This glimpse of beauty, says Benfey, became her "signature poem." She sometimes used the poem as her calling card, signed "Humming-bird," "as though she herself were its evanescent subject." In 1850 Dickinson wrote: "All we secure of Beauty is its Evanescences."

In other moments her pleasure in birds is bittersweet, part of a struggle between hope—"the thing with feathers that perches in the soul"—and despair. In poem 1655 a passing bird leaves her feeling insignificant: "My practice how absurd, superfluous my whole career, beside this travelling Bird." In poem 1046 she's stirred by "Instincts for Dance" and an "Aptitude for Bird" as she strains for breath, but her soul has turned numb, her brain has "dropped," and her nerve lies in marble. She also grapples with emotional paralysis in poem 768 as she remembers a day when hope kept her warm and then a day of despair when "Nature froze—icicles upon my soul." She remained immobilized while "birds went praising everywhere." Nature may be the "Gentlest Mother," but in poem 743 she has become deaf to birds and can dwell with Mother Nature only as a fellow mourner who shares a "wiser sympathy" based on knowledge of death. In poem 1764 the sweet, sad, mad songs of birds in spring make her think only of lost loved ones. She almost wishes "those siren throats would go and sing no more." When her father died, the birds in her yard and nature itself seemed alien. "The birds that father rescued are trifling in his trees," she wrote in a letter. "How flippant are they saved! They were even frolicking at his grave. . . . Nature must be too young to feel, or many years too old." But when her mother died, shortly before her own death, Dickinson found solace in the thought that her mother had "soared from us unexpectedly as a summoned Bird."

Sometimes bittersweet birdsong makes her "Heart put up its Fun and turn Philosopher." When birds "declaim their Tunes" for "utter Jubilee" as if to mock her grief on a "Morning after Woe," does it mean that nature doesn't care? Why must birds on a summer morning "stab my ravished spirit with Dirks of Melody"? She believes she'll find an answer only in death, when "Flesh and Spirit sunder," just as death alone holds the secret of why "Christ robs the Nest" and "smuggles" baby robins to eternal rest. In poem 690 Dickinson questions a God that provides cherries to robins, provides eagles with robins to strangle, and provides humans with sustenance only when it's too late to taste the sweetness. "Was God so economical?" In poem 376, when God ignores both her prayers and a bird's hunger, she feels that a more charitable Creator would have left her unborn, "in the Atom's Tomb," rather than give her "this smart Misery" of life and reason. In one early, lighthearted poem, she fancies she could bribe a passing bird to tell her the secret of the Skies and the Father, but she decides it's "finer" not to know. After her father's death, she can manage only stoicism. Living, she thinks, hurts worse than dying, but rather than fly to heaven as some birds migrate before winter to "a better Latitude," she'll remain with the birds in her yard, shivering for crumbs. "We—are the Birds—that stay."

Dickinson also identified with birds in her own striving to become fulfilled as a poet. "The world is sleeping in ignorance and error," she wrote in a letter around 1850, "and we must be crowing cocks, and singing larks, and a rising sun to awake her." Like a wren that "goes seeking around," she might be on a "timid" quest, but "her pride aspires." While God has given others a full loaf, she has just a crumb and a "Sparrow's chance," but she feels rich nonetheless in her "poignant luxury." As shy as a phoebe, she can still make "a little print upon the Floors of Fame." In one letter she describes bluebirds agitated and tired as they work "exactly like me," but later she's heartened by the "conscientious Voice" of a bluebird that "will soar unmoved above ostensible Vicissitude." In poem 250 she acknowledges her own obscurity as a poet, while other birds pass by her "on their way to Yellower Climes." Yet she's determined to "bring a fuller tune," however late: "I shall keep singing!"

Though obscure until well after her death, Dickinson did bring a fuller tune and is now the most loved and most influential of American poets. And her love of birds anticipated generations of women who would compose bird poems, write bird books, organize the country's first conservation movement, and join with men nationwide to form birding clubs. That's a story for another chapter.

Chapter 12

FOR BIRDS AND PEOPLE

The Brookline Bird Club

In June 1913 thirty bird-lovers gathered at the Brookline Public Library to found the Brookline Bird Club in order to "study, observe, and protect native song birds and to encourage their propagation." A front-page *Brookline Chronicle* story reported that the club was formed "to study the 'little brothers of the air,' arouse a sentiment for their preservation, arrange free lectures for the people, and plan other ways of education in bird life." The BBC wrote a constitution and set annual dues at fifty cents, twenty-five cents for "juniors"—boys and girls under fourteen but "old enough to go alone on street cars." A highlight of club field trips that fall was a Hooded Warbler in breeding plumage at the Boston Public Garden. A 1913 *Boston Globe* photo showed a BBC group at Chestnut Hill: men in suits and ties, women in plume-less hats and bulky ankle-length dresses, and one junior birder with a tam o' shanter in the front row.

Its tradition of nature study made Massachusetts fertile habitat for one of the country's first bird clubs. In 1818 the state had passed the nation's first law protecting some songbirds ("non-game" birds) from shooting. Roger Tory Peterson considered Massachusetts the cradle of American ornithology, for in 1873 the Nuttall Ornithological Club had been founded in Cambridge, and from Nuttall emerged the American Ornithologists' Union. The Massachusetts Audubon Society was established in 1896 to fight against the plume trade. The *Brookline Chronicle*, with a little hometown bias, boasted in 1916 that Brookline was "probably the center of bird interest in the United States." The town had its own bird warden, outlawed the use of firearms or traps to kill or catch birds, and by 1915 it was supporting 150 bird-feeding stations. After winter storms American Crows would trail the grain-distributing sleigh from stop to stop.

One might envision the club's progenitors as whiskered good old Yankee boys, but in fact the Founding Fathers were mostly Founding Mothers. The prime mover was a woman, Mary Moore Kaan, as was the first trip leader, Edith Andrews, and eight of the first eleven directors. Recreational birding opens a window into a period when American women, at least those with leisure time, were determined to get out into the world and become more active physically as well as intellectually and politically. They rode bicycles, went camping, danced more freely, and began to wear less restrictive clothing. Better, more affordable "opera glasses" brought more women into birding. Florence Merriam Bailey joined other Smith College girls on "bird rambles" and went on to write *A-Birding on a Bronco* and *Birds through an Opera Glass.* Field guide author Frank Chapman felt "astonishment, joy, and chagrin" when his bride Fannie mastered the art of bird-skinning on their Florida honeymoon. In 1902 teacher Nell Harrison wrote indignantly about women's exclusion from scientific egg collecting: "Men can go freely into the fields and follow the birds everywhere, while fashion and conventionality debar women from the same privilege." Professional ornithology remained a predominantly male domain, and some ornithological clubs barred women into the 1970s, but in 1901 Bailey, Mabel Osgood Wright, and Olive Thorne Miller became the first women elected to the American Ornithologists' Union, and two decades later Grace Snow became the BBC's ornithologist.

Women were already a force in bird conservation. Two Boston women, Harriet Hemenway and Minna Hall, had led the Audubon campaign against the plume trade—what Chris Leahy calls "the first successful wildlife protection movement." At tea parties they'd shame their high-society friends for gratifying their vanity at the expense of beautiful birds. Hall wrote a letter scolding First Lady Helen Herron Taft for wearing a plumed hat at the 1909 presidential inauguration. Poet Celia Thaxter chastised any woman who'd wear "a charnel house of beaks and claws and bones upon her fatuous head."

With the women came the children. Members of modern birding clubs often bemoan the lack of young birders in our midst, but by 1920 juniors represented almost 30 percent of club membership. BBC founders, the *Brookline Chronicle* reported in 1926, believed they had a "sacred obligation" to cultivate young birders. Members were urged to bring juniors on field trips, and women were especially intent on converting children into birders, for they felt that even boys who shot or stoned birds "could be made over into conservationists." Many women had joined men to set up Junior Audubon clubs, and birding books by women were often aimed at children, whose creativity and self-reliance could be nurtured through engagement with nature. This focus on children reflected the turn-of-the-century "back to nature" movement, spurred by a widespread concern that city children, and urban residents generally, had become estranged from outdoor life. Many children had never spent a night outside a city and couldn't identify even the most common birds or trees. Harvard president Charles Eliot wrote in 1914 that without the consolation of natural scenery, "the evils which attend the growth of modern cities and the factory system are too great for the human body to endure." Projects like Fresh Air Charity were established to help children whose parents couldn't afford to leave the city on vacations or send children to summer camps. Eliot told a Girls' Camp Association that the "organized summer camp" was "the most important step in education that America has given the world."

The BBC Junior Department, with its own bulletin, was led by Horace Taylor. The *Chronicle* noted in 1926 that Taylor took "especial charge of these young people, leading them on instructive bird walks and continually counseling them in the best methods of bird study and bird protection." He offered bike-birding trips in Cambridge and Boston, lessons in drawing birds and conducting censuses, field contests in bird identification, and visits to the Harvard Museum of Comparative Zoology and the new aviary at the Franklin Park Zoo. The BBC nurtured many eventual leaders of American ornithology and conservation. Maurice Broun, the first warden at Hawk Mountain Sanctuary in Pennsylvania, began birding at age thirteen in the Boston Public Garden when he came across a friendly BBC group who showed him a Magnolia Warbler. Richard Pough, a founder of the Nature Conservancy, led BBC trips as a biology student at MIT. Roger Tory Peterson joined the club in the early 1930s when he taught science at the Rivers Country Day School in Brookline, shortly before he published his first field guide. Chandler Robbins, who joined at age twelve and remained a member until his death eighty-seven years later in 2017, went on to organize the North American Breeding Bird Survey and pioneer the study of how forest fragmentation displaces birds.

The BBC welcomed all comers on field trips to "know birds and enjoy them," but BBC leaders considered bird conservation the club's ultimate purpose. What state ornithologist Edward Howe Forbush called the Epoch of Popular Bird-Study went hand in hand with a gospel of bird protection. Edward Baker, the first president, spelled out the club's goals as stimulation of interest in bird life but also protection of local wild birds and the establishment of a bird sanctuary. In 1913 the

Christian Science Monitor reported that the BBC followed "all legislation that would affect the welfare and culture of birds." Its lobbying to stop the importation of feathers pitted "friends of birds" against the French Syndicate of Feather Workers.

Birds were threatened from all sides. Hundreds of thousands were killed for their feathers, used in plumed hats that were still being worn by would-be-fashionable women from art patron Isabella Stewart Gardner to factory workers like the Lowell girls. Market-hunting was at its peak. Boston's Locke-Ober restaurant served Upland Sandpipers and now extinct Eskimo Curlews, while one Boston Harbor restaurateur boasted he could instantly produce any edible North American bird. Brochures from "naturalists' supply" stores listed the going prices for eggs stolen from nests. At one BBC meeting, attended by two hundred people, Forbush made a case for preserving birds that eat harmful insects, though some members resented the need to prove birds' cost-effectiveness. Winston Packard and Ernest Baynes were quoted in the *Chronicle*: "All but particularly thoughtless or particularly stupid people must be interested in birds entirely apart from their economic value, and to many they are the source of the greatest joy."

BBC bulletins reported the club's conservation activities. The club lobbied successfully for a law to stop the shooting of Bobolinks, worked to protect coastal tern colonies, and, as members of the Federation of New England Bird Clubs, allied with Mass Audubon and the Essex County Ornithological Club to stop development on Plum Island and procure land on the island for a wildlife sanctuary. The BBC, one bulletin reported, had joined the campaign to "stop the iniquitous practice of abandoning housecats, THE GREATEST ENEMY OF BIRDS," while members became combatants in the Great Sparrow War, in which defenders and attackers of House Sparrows vilified one another—and even the sparrows themselves—as liars, traitors, and murderers. At a 1913 meeting, the *Chronicle* reported, Taylor insisted on the "imperative need of getting rid of the dirty, noisy English Sparrows." The stunned reporter noted that the sparrows "had not a friend in the company to stand up for them."

BBC membership rose quickly—to 558 by 1928—and soon spread far beyond Brookline. In December 1913 the club offered its first trip to Lynn and Nahant Beaches, traveling by boat from Rowe's Wharf in Boston and then by narrow gauge railroad. The first Cape Ann trip, via a Boston-Gloucester freight boat, was in early 1916. The volunteer trip leaders weren't experts, but in a period of intense controversy over the reliability of sight records (as opposed to specimens collected), they were encouraged to be careful in bird identification and maintain exact counts of species seen, even House Sparrows. Some "walks" were long, demanding hikes, like the round-trip trek, sometimes on snowshoes, from the Ipswich railroad station along the Crane dunes to Essex Bay. A March 1916 trip report illustrated the hardiness or madness of birders: "We tramped through the fields of snow, over the hills and around the swamps, with the wind blowing the snow in our faces. . . . Most enjoyable." Club members went out again the next day and were delighted to find a Northern Shrike nabbing and eating a House Sparrow.

Fellow humans also presented challenges. A 1916 group at Jamaica Pond had to contend with children frolicking in the parkway along with "barking dogs, nursegirls pushing squeaky baby carriages, equestrians, motorists, ball-players, picnickers, and what-not." In 1919 a BBC member named Nuthatch wrote a fanciful trip report about a group of hunters, the Jungle Klub, riding borrowed circus pachyderms to the Lynn marshes to shoot Jungle Kreatures, only to be frightened off by weird, opera-glass-wearing bipeds who muttered incomprehensible things like "whatawonderfuljunco."

Long before birdsong apps and fancy slide slow presentations, early club lectures included bird mimicry by noted "whistlers" Arthur Wilson and Charles Gorst, who produced "operatic airs with Victrola accompaniment." Club director and "dramatic soprano" Edith Torrey sang Shakespeare's "Hark! Hark! the Lark." Lecture topics ranged from the focused "Hunting without a Gun" to the less focused "Random Observations on Birds." Bird conservation and field identification were regular lecture topics. In 1914 Forbush used a "stereopticon" for illustration (it malfunctioned); in 1918, "lantern slides." By the late 1930s "Kodachrome pictures" provided the graphics.

A 1925 bulletin proclaimed that the club was flourishing, with large attendance on field trips. That year the BBC offered three-day excursions to Cape Ann and to New Salem in central Massachusetts, where a group found nesting Olive-Sided Flycatchers. The first all-automobile trip, to Artichoke Reservoir in West Newbury, didn't occur until 1930, but as early as 1918 some members had driven to Ipswich for the dunes walk. Members also went birding internationally. In the 1920s BBC president Raymond Talbot led nature tours to Europe, a mix of birding, hiking, and sightseeing. The seventy-day 1926 tour steamed out of Montreal on the Cunard line's S.S. *Ascania* and crisscrossed northern Europe by rail and motorcar at a cost of $980 per person.

Closer to home, 1926 bird highlights included scarce Red-Headed Woodpeckers nesting near the Brookline library, a rare Arctic Three-Toed Woodpecker in Wellesley, nine Snowy Owls in three locations on one November day, and a Northern Goshawk biting off a rooster's head in a Wellesley barnyard. A 1928 *Christian Leader* article, "An All-Day Trip in Agawam," gives us a feel for a typical BBC outing of the period, to Ipswich (once named Agawam) in May. To join the group the author, one Johannes from Brookline, must overcome "trip resistance"—the "natural human dislike of spending a few hours on company tension with strangers." Tension is eased by the friendly leader, an unnamed Waltham librarian who "put himself out" to help beginners see birds. Johannes divides participants into birding types: the convivial, talky ones; the skeptics, needing rigorous proof for each identification; the "go-alongs" who take the leader's word for any identification; and the diehards rushing headlong into bramble thickets. He notes that the group's "traditional New England reserve" is instantly dropped when they come upon a Yellow-Breasted Chat. Some participants stop to play with children or dogs. Others, presumably not the diehards, stray off in search of ice cream. At day's end, while waiting for a boat on Plum Island, they get a close look at a Piping Plover. Johannes closes with the hope that sportsmen and naturalists will join hands to save this struggling species.

In a fiftieth anniversary address in 1963, Larry Jodrey conjured up visions of BBC trips long before his own days as a birder. Members would travel by train from Brookline to far-flung locations like Newburyport. After long days in the field, they'd eat clam chowder and warm themselves around fireplaces in boarding houses. Birding was challenging, with cruder optics and few reference books. Casual clothing was hard to come by, much less modern designed-for-birders outfits with big pockets and detachable leggings. Members wore old business clothes, the women "crowned by hats not always currently in style" but without earrings, ornaments considered in poor taste on birding walks. "Jewelry and finery," Jodrey said, "were reserved for the indoor meetings to which members customarily wore their dressiest outfits, rendering themselves sometimes unrecognizable to friends who were accustomed to seeing each other in birding garb."

BBC members also came to know the bittersweetness Jodrey expressed, "a touch of sadness in recalling pleasant trips to many once delightful places which are now, on account of their development as residential and commercial areas, no longer birding territory." In 1928 the *Brookline Chronicle* reported, "The march of civilization has ruined many of the locations which were once favorite haunts of the birds." Puttenham Meadows, a sanctuary in Brookline established in 1926, became a "huge disappointment" and was converted to a municipal golf course. Club trips to the Belmont Hills stopped in 1934. In 1930 members were among the last people to see the sole remaining Heath Hen on Martha's Vineyard, the "last specimen of its kind," one participant reminisced, and a bird seen with "great satisfaction." The BBC was also losing its founders. When she died in 1931, Mary Moore Kaan was eulogized in a bulletin as a pioneer who'd "instigated" the club "for the sake of the birds themselves" and "for the sake of the people."

From its beginnings the club reflected our country's political and social history. Soon after the United States entered World War I, the BBC called for a boycott of "war wings," feathers sold to women by the Naval Reserve in the name of national service. Congress finally passed the groundbreaking Migratory Bird Treaty Act in 1918 not for simple bird conservation but partly to protect crops and ensure food to sustain the war effort. For many members the impact of war was personal. In 1918 the *Chronicle* published a letter from army private E. Saxe, who thanked the BBC for trip reports in the newspaper and asked for identification help with a "warbler-type" gray and white bird singing at dawn just after his company in France had been gassed in trenches by the Germans. The bird had dipped and risen while "singing wildly" a series of rich notes "from bass to high C." Saxe's comrades were amazed that the warbler seemed so "unconcerned about its surroundings and unknowing of any strife." After the war some veterans returned home to go birding with a vengeance. Eventual BBC president Leslie Little "looked up the club almost the moment he got out of the army." Other young birders had been sacrificed to war. Barron Brainerd, a club director and birding prodigy, did not die in combat, but his 1919 obituary hints at a hard struggle and decline precipitated by his service in the war. It took months before his father, John, the BBC president, could bring himself to lead another bird walk.

The 1930s, the years of the Great Depression, stand out as a difficult yet dynamic decade in BBC history. Some members were forced to drop out. Others requested more "ten-cent" trips to local spots that required no more than ten cents in carfare. BBC leaders had to point out that many once "fine birdy" local places had been ruined by development. Though there was less money for bird protection, the bulletins expanded beyond lists of trips and meetings to cover conservation issues in more depth. Bulletins also featured instructions on how to prepare "Christmas pudding" for chickadees, Grace Haskell Story's "Italian sonnet" about birding the Ipswich dunes, and quotations from naturalists like Thoreau: "I would rather never taste chicken meat nor hen's eggs than never to see a hawk sailing through the upper air again."

The Depression was a period of widespread political anger and activism, when many Americans felt that their government, or capitalism itself, had failed to protect people from economic catastrophe or to safeguard the nation's wetlands and other natural resources. Wardens were still confiscating dead birds whose feathers were intended for the plume trade. The end of the Heath Hen, once abundant in Massachusetts, aroused fears that other species, like the Ivory-Billed Woodpecker, would soon become extinct. Dust storms and drought in the West not only displaced people but decimated populations of waterfowl and songbirds. There was truth behind the Texas joke: "It's so dry that the birds are using barbed wire to build nests."

During the 1930s the BBC fought conservation battles on many fronts. It opposed the practice of baiting ducks to shoot them, proposed a tax on bird-killing housecats, and resisted a proposed highway that would have connected Ipswich to Plum Island and fragmented prime bird habitat. It expressed outrage over damage done to shorebirds and seabirds by waste pumped overboard from oil-burning vessels. A 1930 bulletin listed by species the many oil-soaked birds found dead at Chatham Beach and Monomoy Island. The BBC also joined state and national campaigns to stop the "wanton killing" of raptors and criticized the spreading of "prejudice and false propaganda" about hawks and owls. In 1930 it supported a federal Bald Eagle protection bill and, the *Chronicle* reported, resolved that "the names of all hawks and owls should be omitted from the list of birds not protected by law." In 1934, while celebrating the foundation of Hawk Mountain Sanctuary, Raymond Talbot defended the "much maligned" American Crow and pointed out that many "innocent" birds were victimized by crow shoots that even now are still held across our country. Many club members were hunters, but they insisted that any hunter should be able to "prove that you know the birds when you see them." Some bulletin appeals went beyond birds altogether, such as an attack on dog racing.

The BBC also renewed efforts to nurture young birders. Guiding the way was Talbot, BBC president for sixteen years and one of its most committed leaders. Talbot had started birding at age eight during a long convalescence from appendicitis and soon became known for his toughness in the field. A Boston University professor of Romance languages, he traveled the world, sending home letters about birds in Saharan sandstorms and Wallcreepers climbing cliffs in the Pyrenees. At his 1958 memorial service he was described as "outspoken in support of his moral convictions" and sensitive to "the beauty of color and sound, of landscapes and living things."

In 1928, as a Mass Audubon field agent, Talbot began writing *Bird News for the Schools*, distributed free by the BBC to every high school and junior high in the state, with sponsored prizes for student articles on bird study and protection. "It's always fair weather when bird-lovers get together," Talbot rhapsodized, even when the "mean, disagreeable" New England wind penetrates the marrow. He fielded questions from his young readers: Do birds like to live in bird houses? Do they talk among themselves? How many birds does the average cat kill each year? Why do you like hawks so much? One student asked: "Is it possible to see an Ipswich Sparrow?" Talbot answered: "Possible, though not easy." Another asked why a "stray Arkansas Kingbird" (Western Kingbird) was still hanging around Cambridge in December. Talbot responded: some bird questions can't be definitively answered. Talbot reached out to young birders with unflagging energy. For years the BBC conducted bird walks for school, church, and scout groups, and in 1940 alone Talbot gave thirty-two bird lectures at twenty-one summer camps.

In a 1934 *Bird News* piece on Martha's Vineyard—a spot "almost sacred for bird-lovers"—Talbot wrote, in bold type: "America must learn, before it is too late, the lesson of the Heath Hen and of those other birds which Americans have destroyed. We must protect and save the birds we have left." He criticized the press for glorifying an estate guardian who'd killed a Snowy Owl. In one of his last pieces, about a birder indifferent to conservation, he concluded: "I have failed utterly if any large proportion of my readers really are convinced that conservation is of no concern to a bird club."

As our nation entered World War II, the BBC reached the end of an era. The bulletin, which became the "blue book" in 1941, was reduced, listing trips and statistical reports but without the poetry and conservation appeals. Talbot stepped down as president, and *Bird News* was discontinued in 1943. The bird highlight of 1943 was a rare Arctic visitor, a Gyrfalcon, in Newburyport; in 1944, also in Newburyport, an extremely rare White-Tailed Sea-Eagle, a record now questioned for insufficient documentation. That year, in 142 trips, the BBC found a record-high 236 species. Yet the war's last few years had brought security regulations, gas rationing, and restrictions on "pleasure driving." In 1944 field glasses were forbidden on the traditional boat trip to Provincetown, and all boat trips were eventually suspended, as were coastline walks. Birders wandering about with binoculars were sometimes suspected of being spies assisting German submarines. The club struggled to find trip leaders. But some members who served in the armed forces managed to get themselves stationed in bird-rich tropical areas. "Birds were the breath of life in their nostrils," wrote Roger Tory Peterson, "while some of their fellow soldiers, lacking this consuming interest, almost went mad." Servicemen overseas were not supposed to reveal exactly where they were stationed, but some birding soldiers revealed their locations by writing home to tell knowledgeable friends which species they'd found. Meanwhile, the use of diagnostic marks for birds in Peterson's field guide had become a model for plane-spotting aircraft identification.

In 1945 Douglas Sands, "just out of the Army," entertained BBC members with a slide show on the "Fauna and Flora of the Galapagos Islands." The Provincetown boat trip, with binoculars allowed, resumed in 1946. Wartime was over.

The years since World War II have brought great changes to the BBC. For a while the club stagnated. Membership dropped to a low of 325 in 1947. The 1960 statistical report notes, without explanation, that the club had undergone a "year of turmoil," and one bulletin that year listed several trips with "leader to be chosen from among those present." But there was a steady surge in membership throughout the 1960s and 1970s, peaking at over 1,600 in 1977. By its fiftieth anniversary the BBC had sponsored 5,243 trips and seen all 282 species on the Mass Audubon state checklist, as well as 57 write-ins. By 1972 the BBC could call itself "America's Most Active Bird Club." It offered what the *Boston Globe* called "a feverish field trip schedule," sponsoring 219 trips that year with 301 species seen. In 1967 *Time* ran a feature article on birding, generously estimating that over eleven million Americans were now birdwatchers. Birding had seemingly become fashionable, though birders, especially teenagers, were still mocked as nerdy or effeminate, and, as Jodrey noted, witty civilians would still roll down car windows to holler "tweet, tweet, quack, quack" at roadside birders with binoculars.

The club expanded its range to include regular trips to Boston Harbor islands and Nantucket, camping on Cape Cod and in the Berkshires, and out-of-state trips to the Isle of Shoals and the Maryland shores. A 1970 group studied specimens at the Harvard Museum of Comparative Zoology and wryly added some extinct species to the BBC life list. Walks at Mount Auburn Cemetery became a popular tradition. *Boston Globe* articles called the cemetery "one of the most persistently birded areas in the country" and described "bird chasers and meadow haunters" at Mount Auburn, some with "Caution: Birdwatchers" bumper stickers and one with a PETREL license plate. BBC walks sometimes drew an "unwieldy 100 or more" participants.

One recruiting agent for the club was the "find of the century," a Ross's Gull discovered at Newburyport Harbor in 1975. A first record for the Lower Forty-Eight, this rare pinkish Arctic gull made the front page of the *New York Times* and inspired John Updike to write a *New Yorker* article about his failed attempt to find it. The gull was seen by thousands of birders and curiosity-seekers from across the country. The next few years brought a spectacular string of rarities: a Black-Browed Albatross that swooped close to a fishing boat out of Rockport, an Ivory Gull in Salisbury watched by thousands of birders in one weekend (it "was fed bologna sandwiches but did not beg"), and a White-Tailed Tropicbird found barely alive on a Byfield playing field after Hurricane Gloria in 1985. Some years were busts, like 1978, with extremes of cold and heat, drought, and dismal migrations, but in "mind-boggling" 1979 the club's annual summary cited an "inexhaustible flow of rare discoveries." With birding you take your chances.

The statistical reports in club bulletins also demonstrate how quickly bird distributions can shift. The 1945 report highlights included Common Eider, Harlequin Duck, Purple Sandpiper, and Northern Mockingbird—all species now common in our state. Shifts in distribution were also reflected in the reports of the Essex County Ornithological Club's annual May canoe trip on the Ipswich River, often joined by BBC members and, dating from 1907, among our country's longest running bird censuses. To modern Massachusetts birders, the canoe trip reports from the 1930s are striking for both the absence of now common species—Blue-Gray Gnatcatcher, Carolina Wren—and species once routine but now rare in Essex County and even in the whole state. Golden-Winged Warblers and nesting Vesper Sparrows were seen every year, Sedge Wrens most years. The canoe trip reports illustrate both the declines of wetlands and grasslands birds and the expansion of ranges by new arrivals. Eastern Meadowlarks were last found in 1986, American Bitterns in 1987. Firsts included Snowy Egret in 1968, Northern Cardinal in 1969, and Turkey Vulture in 1979.

For decades BBC outings were recorded in vivid detail by statistician Mary Lou Barnett, citing field card comments that were often "witty, poetic, and occasionally philosophical," though she had to admonish some trip leaders—like one who'd reported 125 rare Loggerhead Shrikes—to proofread their cards. Her reports often describe "indefatigable" and "doughty" birders up against the elements: gale-blown on Crane Beach, frostbitten at Mount Auburn, in "snow up to the knee" on Plum Island, and, in Marblehead, finding fog, heavy surf, and surfers—but no birds. In 1966 an eager "sheriff's posse" braved ice, soaking mist, and blinding sheet, "beat the bushes and crawled in the snow," to find "sweet Victory"—a rare Rock Wren in Rockport. One frigid morning Larry Jodrey expressed a feeling known to all Cape Ann winter trip leaders—the hope that no one will show up. His friend Jerry Soucy—bulletin editor, field trip coordinator, mentor, philosopher—swore off boat trips: "I have spent too many tortuous hours on rocking boats and so I depend on coastal storms to bring pelagics to me."

Other challenges came from gas shortages, Plum Island hunters, civilians, and fellow birders, like the guy who tested a leader's aural skills by joining a Plum Island auto caravan on his Harley, and the notorious Mrs. Nudge-In, who squeezed right behind the leader's car on any caravan she joined. In Boxford a farmer sent his daughter out with a broom to scare off a rare Western Meadowlark luring birders to the edge of his land. A surly Nantucket man came out with a gun in one hand, a glass of whiskey in the other, as birders studied a Jackdaw, a rare vagrant from Europe, that wasn't even on his property. Some members were unfazed by any obstacle. In 1969, when below-zero weather scared off everyone else from the New Year's Day walk at Crane Beach, the leader headed out anyway and found eighteen species on his six-mile trudge. "Mr. Jameson," reported Barnett, "said he enjoyed his walk." In 1978 Herman Weissberg found a scarce Acadian Flycatcher singing in West Newbury the day before he went into a hospital for open-heart surgery.

Beasts, birders, and civilians all conspired to add comedy to Barnett's reports. At Mount Auburn, when the leader called out a Worm-Eating Warbler, a novice birder famously asked, "*What* is that worm eating?" One overexcited leader, trying to help his comrades see a rare Cattle Egret in Rowley, set up the group's only scope in a manure pile. In Sherborn club president Eliot Taylor whistled at dusk for a whip-poor-will. A donkey responded. At Mount Greylock a club member was asked to move his car so some people could jump off the mountain. The member obliged, and six hang gliders appeared and jumped. The last glider flailed into some bushes but took flight with the assistance of birders, who carried on to find the Mourning Warbler they were after.

The last few decades have been marked by changes in communication and technology that help BBC members and other birders to find birds, identify them accurately, record findings, and share sightings. A big step in the late 1960s was the Voice of Audubon—for years the voice of Ruth Emery, also a BBC leader, known for being helpful and gracious to all callers, even the woman who swore she'd just seen an extinct Passenger Pigeon. In 1973 BBC leaders helped to found the journal *Bird Observer*, still New England's most comprehensive source of field data. A Bird Alert Hot Line was set up to get word of rarities out quickly. Another innovation, the club's CB radio patrol, was illustrated by a radio message in the 1985 statistical report: "Come in, Barn Owl. We're at the salt pans. The Tundra Swan has just landed." In 1996 Barbara Volkle, later a club president, organized MassBird, a popular LISTSERV for sharing sightings across the state and into neighboring states. Trip leaders now send trip lists to eBird, a joint project by the Cornell Lab of Ornithology and National Audubon that compiles sightings nationwide and serves as a vast resource of bird-finding information.

BBC leaders, through periodic self-examination, have found that the club remains sound. We offer, as one director put it, the "pleasures of group birding, the opening of doors on the world of nature with no strings attached." Newcomers feel "not intimidated but welcomed." Trip leaders, all volunteers, are friendly and knowledgeable. Current president Neil Hayward, like his predecessor, Dave Williams, continues a long line of dedicated, foresightful presidents. Members talk about the fun they've had on club trips and the opportunities to find new birds, birding locations, and birding companions. Jodrey liked to reminisce about old-time trip leaders like Clara de Windt, known for her "bright scarlet snow-bunny suit" (her "winter plumage"). She "would have made a figure descending the grand staircase of the Metropolitan Opera," but most important, she exemplified the "you show me your birds, I'll show you mine" spirit of club birding. Past president Steve Grinley recalls the camaraderie of Mount Greylock campouts, when groups would gather around fires to cook dinner, share wine, and relive the excitement of finding Bicknell's Thrushes still nesting on the summit near Bascom Lodge. Some longtime members worry that, while the Internet has made it easier to find information and chase rare birds, birders might lose the spirit of sharing that has marked the BBC. Yet they're grateful that the club has elevated their lives and introduced the delights of birding to thousands of others.

In 2013 the BBC celebrated its one-hundredth anniversary as one of the country's oldest, largest, and most active bird clubs, still leading annual trips close to the record high of 290 in 2000. To commemorate our founders, fellow director Diana Fruguglietti and I led a walk that retraced the steps of the very first trip—around Fresh Pond, then called "the

Cambridge marshes." The club retains "Brookline" for name recognition, but we long ago expanded far beyond Brookline to offer diverse excursions throughout eastern Massachusetts, across the state, and north into New Hampshire and Maine, trips for beginners and limited-mobility birders, conservation-oriented searches to document species on the state endangered list, and impromptu chases of rarities like a Northern Lapwing in Bridgewater in 2012 and a Fieldfare in Carlisle in 2013. In the past decade, largely through the work of the unsinkable Ida Giriunas, another past president, the BBC has achieved a national reputation for leading birding boat trips to and beyond Stellwagen Bank in search of shearwaters, petrels, jaegers, and any rare seabird.

But we face challenges, especially the dwindled role of young birders in the club. In 1966 Barnett praised the "tenacity and bravado of our more youthful leaders." At a seventy-fifth anniversary gala, Larry Jodrey recalled when Dick Veit, Chris Leahy, Peter Alden, and Simon Perkins—all prominent leaders in conservation and international bird touring—were young club members, "looking quite innocent in those days, full of wonderment." Yet by the 1970s adolescents had become scarce in bird clubs. But there have been encouraging developments, like the recent spread of young birders' clubs and the Cornell Lab's Young Birders' Network. The BBC now offers annual scholarships for young birders to attend National Audubon's Hog Island camp in Maine, and we donate money to support bird study in schools. Some members, like Jim Berry, make it a point to recruit and mentor the birders, ornithologists, and conservationists of the future. Still, it will take sustained commitment and our founders' sense of mission to keep bringing new generations into the birding fold.

The BBC, like the birding community generally, also remains overwhelmingly white. We welcome everyone and offer regular trips to urban parks and nature centers, yet, like environmental groups across the country, we've struggled to appeal to an ethnically diverse population. Beyond personal preferences, there are cultural and historical reasons why few black Americans have become birders: a severance from nature after the great migrations from the rural South to cramped northern cities, a lack of exposure to birding mentors, a reluctance to venture down trails or once segregated beaches that might be unwelcoming or unsafe. The Fledgling Birders Institute now sponsors an annual Focus on Diversity workshop to "promote effective outreach to more diverse audiences with birding opportunities, outdoor recreation, and conservation messages." It's a matter of inclusion and reciprocity. Birding has brought us pleasure, and we want to share that pleasure widely, as others shared their expertise and enthusiasm when we were novices. We also need a broader base to support bird conservation—people who want to protect birds because they've learned to care about them.

Conservation remains an ongoing concern. Over the years the BBC has tried to realize its founders' ambition to focus on bird protection. In the 1940s, with Mass Audubon and other bird clubs, it helped establish the Parker River National Wildlife Refuge to provide feeding, resting, and nesting habitat for migratory birds. In 1962, when Rachel Carson published *Silent Spring*, the BBC joined the campaign against indiscriminate use of pesticides. In recent decades we've donated funds to protect Least Terns and Purple Martins, contributed to land trusts and initiatives to preserve habitat at shorelines targeted for dredging, and supported programs like the Birders' Exchange and research at Manomet Bird Observatory. We've also provided leaders and participants for annual Christmas Bird Counts, the nation's first Breeding Bird Atlas—sponsored by Mass Audubon—and the more recent atlas, and more localized breeding bird censuses.

Some threats to birds have moved the BBC to action, but in other periods the club has languished. For over fifty years each bulletin announced that the BBC was "open to all who are interested in birds and their protection," but in 1965 the phrase "birds and their protection" was changed to "birds and nature." In 1968 the club formed a conservation committee (now the Conservation and Education Committee), led by Joe Kennelly. He urged members to lobby for a state endangered species bill and against rescindment of the Wetlands Protection Act. The disastrous *Argo Merchant* oil tanker spill in 1977 prompted an internal debate over political activism. A group spearheaded by Soheil Zendeh and Craig Jackson wanted to circulate a petition to the secretary of the interior to "stop the leasing of offshore tracts for drilling of oil in the North Atlantic-Georges Banks area." But others argued that the BBC should stick to birding and not align with any political causes. Club directors permitted the petition to be circulated at the annual meeting, but they resolved that, out of fear of entanglement in seemingly endless controversies, "we should not get involved with politics."

Bird conservationists no longer have to wage attacks on the plume trade or pervasive market-hunting, at least not within this country, but there's no shortage of threats to birds. Nationwide, groups like the American Bird Conservancy work to oppose legislation or deregulation that would jeopardize birds and their habitats. In 2016, as chair of the BBC Conservation and Education Committee, and with support from state ornithologist Drew Vitz, I organized the Association of Massachusetts Bird Clubs, an alliance of around twenty clubs from the Berkshires to the South Shore. Birders, like any community, need organizations to bring people together and reach out to new people. We also hope to unite on behalf of bird conservation through citizen science projects and advocacy. If birders won't organize to protect birds, who will?

In 1975 Helen Kaan donated five hundred dollars in honor of her mother, founder Mary Moore Kaan, to help keep BBC dues affordable. It was "wonderful," she wrote in a letter, "that the club has kept its original character and purpose through all these changing years." The BBC had fulfilled her mother's hopes. At the seventy-fifth anniversary, Larry Jodrey reminded club members of their debt to their forebears and their obligation to carry on traditions of conservation and encouragement of youth. "Generations go swiftly. Others will take our place. We only share our heritage; we share the earth, for a brief bit." His wisdom still holds.

Chapter 13

MR. FORBUSH AND MR. WHITE

For a bird-fancier from the Bay State, I was slow in getting to Edward Howe Forbush. I was put off by the monumental weight of his three-volume *Birds of Massachusetts and Other New England States*, published between 1925 and 1929, the first comprehensive study of our region's birds. Fourteen hundred pages—that's a lot of damn bird-lore to lift. I also assumed that his work would now be dated, supplanted by recent scientific discoveries and current knowledge of bird distributions. But in 2012, when I agreed to write a hundredth-anniversary history of the Brookline Bird Club, I knew I could put him off no longer. The preeminent New England ornithologist of the early twentieth century, Forbush had spoken at the club's first annual meeting, and he'd led the now-defunct Federation of the Bird Clubs of New England, which got the Massachusetts legislature to fund publication of his work. In my research his name kept popping up.

As I curled my way through the first volume, I was more than pleasantly surprised. Here was a great nest of curiosities. Northern Fulmars, cliff-dwellers and carrion-feeders that tend to stay far offshore, were once widely hunted for their oil, used for lighting and medicinal purposes. Common Ravens were merely "accidental visitors" a century ago but had once been permanent residents in our state. Common Loons and Trumpeter Swans had once nested on many ponds and lakes in Massachusetts. Rather than rendering his information obsolete, the datedness of Forbush's work added a new dimension to my understanding of the birds I saw or didn't see in our state each year. Killdeer, now common breeders here, had been "practically extirpated" as New England nesting birds. Dickcissels had almost disappeared from Massachusetts coasts for reasons "that must be left to conjecture." Avian life is dynamic. Terms like "common" and "rare" are relative and transitory, contingent on birds' adaptability and on changes wrought by humans that have stressed this adaptability to the limit. To protect the birds we have now, we need to know where these birds have been, geographically and historically.

I skimmed the sections where Forbush tries to prove that birds we love for their beauty or songs are also good because they eat bad bugs—the subject of his earlier *Useful Birds and Their Protection* (1908). I recalled a wry comment in Thoreau's journals: "It is as if the question were whether some celebrated singer of the human race—some Jenny Lind or another—did more harm or good, should be destroyed, or not, and therefore a committee should be appointed, not to listen to her singing at all, but to examine the contents of her stomach and see if she devoured anything which was injurious to the farmers and gardeners, or which they cannot spare." But I understood the fixation on economics. Forbush was writing at a time, not fully past, when legislation to protect birds depended on proof that birds would eat pests, spare crops, and save Americans money.

The facts in Forbush's work will remain useful as long as New Englanders care about birds, but what really got me was the man's style: effusive, at times overreaching, but rising into lyricism as he describes birds in their habitats: the American Bittern, "a hermit, dwelling in swamp and fen," that "excites suspicion and superstition" (described by Thoreau, Forbush says, as "the genius of the bog"); the Cooper's Hawk, a "forest rover" that is "cradled in the windswept woods, and fledged amid the creaking and groaning of great trees"; and Snow Buntings, intrepid Arctic breeders that signal seasonal change in New England when they "ride down on wintry winds and whirl about the fields amid the driving snow." Forbush wonderfully captures the Winter Wren, *Troglodytes troglodytes*, a Greek name for a caveman who creeps into holes: "This little Brownie of the forest creeps like a woods mouse under the roots of trees standing on banks overhanging the water, in and out of brush heaps and wood piles along river bottoms and on the banks of woodland brooks, cautious and furtive—an absurd little creature, its stub tail turned up over its back at the least provocation, until it seems as if the bird would tumble forward, pushed over by the efforts of its own tail, or overbalanced by the bobbing of its head." People just don't write this way about birds anymore. Must science and poetry never mingle? Can't we gush over what we love?

I soon discovered I wasn't the first writer to like the Forbush style. One fervent admirer was E. B. White. Three decades after his death, White is still known for his children's books, like *Stuart Little* and *The Trumpet of the Swan*, and his classic work on language usage, *The Elements of Style*, coauthored with William Strunk. A longtime *New Yorker* contributor, he's still considered a master prose stylist. And when White struggled with his own work, he turned to Forbush. "When I am out of joint," he writes in "Mr. Forbush's Friends," from a February 1966 *The New Yorker*, "from bad weather or a poor run of thoughts, I like to sit and think about Edward Howe Forbush." For more than twenty years, White went back to Forbush time and again for "refreshment and instruction."

White sometimes wrote about birds, as in his comic poem on song identification, "A Listener's Guide to the Birds," but he wasn't really a birder. "Although not a student of birds," he says, "I am thrown with them a good bit. It is much the same sort of experience as being thrown with people in the subway. I gaze at a female, and am filled with curiosity and a wish to know more than I do about her nesting site, breeding habits, measurements, voice, and range." To satisfy his lecherous curiosity, White laments, he has "nothing to help me but my imagination," but if a bird intrigues him, he can turn to Forbush "for help in comprehending what I have been looking at." He's fascinated by the peculiar questions Forbush raises. Is the occasional haplessness of Cedar Waxwings caused by gluttony or intoxication from fermented fruit? White is less interested in the sections on economic status, where we see "Mr. Forbush the partisan wrestling with Mr. Forbush the scientist." Yet he praises Forbush's determination to defend even unpopular species like crows and jays, birds with police records: "He was the champion of birds as well as their interpreter. In his role as defense attorney for the birds, Mr. Forbush is not merely spirited, he is wonderfully resourceful."

What White especially relishes in Forbush are the "Haunts and Habits" sections, when Forbush cuts loose, "dropping his tight scientific detachment and indulging himself as stylist, enthusiast, and footloose reporter." White quotes a passage on Holboell's (now Red-Necked) Grebe, a species that John Smith probably saw and the first entry in the three volumes: "A bright clear day in January, a gentle breeze, a river mouth where the rippling flood flows into a sparkling sea, a lazy swell washing gently on the bar where a herd of mottled seals is basking in the sun, Old-squaws and Golden-eyes in small parties—such a scene at Ipswich is a fit setting for the great Grebe that winters on our coasts." The Forbush style, White concedes, may become self-indulgent, "a rich prose occasionally touched with purple," yet he's won over by its vividness and enthusiasm for birds. If the prose is "occasionally overblown," White says, "this results from a genuine ecstasy in the man, rather than from lack of discipline. Reading the essays, one shares his ecstasy."

White is also charmed by the bird reports from "Mr. Forbush's large company of informers, or tipsters: people who at one time or another wrote him or phoned him to tell of an encounter with a bird—a strange doing, an odd fact, a bizarre occurrence." Some of these reports came from "professional bird people" and nature writers, like Olive Thorne Miller, but most were passed on to Forbush by "hundreds of amateurs and strangers, who by reporting some oddity of bird behavior or recording an unlikely arrival have achieved immortality; their names are embedded in the text of *Birds of Massachusetts* as firmly as a bottle cap in a city pavement, and they are for the ages." These tipsters, "bright of eye, quick to take pen in hand," are the "friends" in the title of White's essay, and he devotes a good half of the essay to condensed versions of their bird tales, like these:

> Reverend J. H. Linsley. Opened the stomach of a gannet, found bird. Opened stomach of *that* bird, found another bird. Bird within bird within bird.
>
> Mr. Stanley C. Jewett. Asserts that wounded red-breasted merganser at Netarts Bay, Oregon, dived to submerged root in three feet of water, and died while clinging there. Apparent suicide. May 1915.
>
> Mr. J. A. Munro, of Okanagan Landing, British Columbia. Watched male bufflehead, far gone in passion, dive under another male, toss him into air. Sexual jealousy.
>
> Mr. George W. Morse, of Tulsa, Oklahoma. Saw great blue heron strike at small fish between own legs, tripping self up. Heron was carried downstream in capsized position with legs in air. It held on to the fish.
>
> Mr. W. L. Bishop. Found ruffed grouse submerged in brook, except for head, to escape goshawk.
>
> Mr. T. Gilbert Pearson. Lady of his acquaintance, while sitting alone in her room, was startled when beef bone

fell out into hearth. Went outside, discovered turkey buzzard peering down chimney. Carelessness on part of bird.

Mr. M. Semper, of Mapes P.O., British Columbia. Was at neighbor's house sharpening a mower sickle, saw golden eagle seize neighbor's little girl, Ellen Gibbs, by arm. Mr. Semper kicked eagle with no effect. Girl's mother appeared, decapitated eagle with good effect.

Dr. H. F. Perkins. Found yellow warbler's nest six stories high with a cowbird's egg on every floor. The warblers, each time they discovered a stranger's egg in the nest, built on top of it, thus burying the egg.

Mrs. George H. McGregor, of Fall River. While sitting on front porch one evening, heard catbird sound "Taps." Believes bird picked it up from hearing it played at burial services in nearby cemetery.

Miss Elizabeth Dickens. While on Block Island saw brown creeper climbing cow's tail.

Mrs. Olive Thorne Miller. Reported case of female tufted titmouse stealing hair from gentleman in Ohio for use in nest building. Bird lit on gentleman's head, seized a beakful, braced itself, jerked lock out, flew away, came back for more. Gentleman a bird lover, consented to give hair again.

White doesn't question the reliability of the informants' reports or comment on the risks of drawing lessons about bird behavior from anecdotal evidence, but, taken as a whole, the accounts illustrate how, long before eBird, birders belonged to a loose community of information-sharing enthusiasts, contributing bits of observation to our understanding of birds. Grouped together by White, with abrupt shifts from gannet stomach contents to a suicidal merganser, the reports also oddly resemble certain modernist literary inventions in which themes emerge, with a cumulative emotional impact, from an assembly of small, seemingly unconnected stories. This is the format of Félix Fénéon's *Novels in Three Lines*, a collection of three-line news items that were published anonymously in the French newspaper *Le Matin* in 1906. Fénéon's tiny, true tales are self-contained, the characters in them unrelated, but, collected, his "novels" elaborate motifs of violence, political conflict, infidelity, and madness:

> A criminal virago, Mlle Tulle, was sentenced by the Rouen court to 10 years' hard labor, while her lover got five.
>
> Because of his poster opposing the strikebreakers, the students of Brest Lycee hissed their teacher, M Litalien, an aide to the mayor.
>
> Nurse Elise Bachmann, whose day off was yesterday, put on a public display of insanity.
>
> A complaint was sworn by the Persian physician Djai Khan against a compatriot who had stolen from him a tiara.
>
> A certain madwoman arrested downtown falsely claimed to be Elise Bachmann. The latter is perfectly sane.
>
> Reverend Andrieux, of Roannes, near Aurillac, whom a pitiless husband perforated Wednesday with two rifle shots, died last night.
>
> Women suckling their infants argued the workers' cause to the director of the streetcar lines in Toulon. He was unmoved.
>
> Scheid, of Dunkirk, fired three times at his wife. Since he missed every shot, he decided to aim at his mother-in-law, and connected.
>
> Mme Vivant, of Argenteuil, failed to reckon with the ardor of Maheu, the laundry's owner. He fished the desperate laundress from the Seine.

> Sand and only that was the content of two suspect packages that yesterday morning alarmed Saint-Germain-en-Laye.

It would be both fanciful and anthropomorphic to make a cross-species comparison: passion-mad Buffleheads versus vengeful human cuckolds. Unlike Fénéon's miniatures, the reports collected by Forbush were composed by many individual informants, without design, political motive, or thought about what these anecdotes might signify if considered collectively. And they often depict bird behavior that is peaceful and benign. Yet in the examples that White extracts from Forbush, the repeated instances of predation, risk, and rivalry exemplify both the intensity of birds' lives and our own fascination with mayhem and weirdness, whether human or avian.

One day in early April, after a fierce New England winter, I left my house with a mission: to find a Wilson's Snipe. In truth I was searching for a new season, since snipe, like Eastern Phoebes and Red-Winged Blackbirds, are among the first reliable signs that spring will actually return. At a favorite snipe spot, the Common Pasture in Newbury, an always soggy meadow, I found another snipe-seeker, a familiar face with a name I couldn't recall, common in the birding world. He introduced himself, Tom, and reminded me that he'd joined several of my BBC walks. We'd seen each other's posts on MassBird. We're the descendants of Forbush's friends, but instead of sending our bird stories to Forbush, we share reports on a birding LISTSERV.

Tom and I scoped the area, finding and admiring a Blue-Winged Teal, uncommon in our region, a handsome male in breeding plumage with a diagnostic white crescent moon on his face. We turned our attention to snipe. They're pudgy, long-beaked shorebirds, like pot-bellied Pinocchios, but cryptic and hard to detect, patterned with the colors of a wet spring field. Eventually I spotted one, subtly jerking as it probed for bugs behind two Kildeer a hundred yards out. I gave directions, and my comrade saw the bird too. I thought of White, who'd found "pure pleasure" in Forbush's description of a snipe: "When the spring rains and mounting sun begin to tint the meadow grass, when the alewives run up the streams, when the blackbirds and the spring frogs sing their full chorus, then the Snipe arrives at night on the south wind." For White, Forbush was a man for all seasons, a man who "carries his readers into seasons yet to come."

My friend and I scanned the rest of the meadow. Where there had been only grass, water, and camouflage, we were now finding birds. "One snipe," I said. "Seven snipe. A field full of snipe. And a Pectoral Sandpiper."

"Yes." Tom grinned. "Yes, it must be spring."

Chapter 14

THE GREAT MARSH

Shorebird Swarms and Swallow Waves

Mary and I looked out past a tidal channel to soothing salt marsh. I heard songs I couldn't identify. We chatted with another couple, new BBC members who wondered what to expect on a Plum Island field trip. We didn't know. We were novices too.

We stopped talking when our commander, Bill Drummond, turned off his walkie-talkie and called our troop to attention. A rare bird, a Loggerhead Shrike, had just been seen at a nearby marsh called Plumbush. Instead of heading into the refuge, we'd form a caravan and drive back out, closing ranks in case of civilian cars on the road. Several vehicles would have CB radios, set to the birders' channel, in case the shrike was found in transit. If we spotted it, we should flash our headlights. If we saw it once we were all on foot again, use hand signals—two arms straight up for a definite shrike, one arm for an iffier bird. Don't shout, don't make needless noise, don't flail about. Spooking the bird would constitute insubordination.

"Loggerhead?" Mary asked in our car.

"Beats me. Paul Bunyanish?"

She flipped through our old Peterson guide. "It's like a mockingbird with a mask. It looks just like this other type of shrike."

"Well, I'm not flashing my lights. Not unless it lands on our hood with a sign: 'I am a Loggerhead Shrike.'"

At Plumbush, along the Plum Island Turnpike, we eased out of our cars and fanned out for a search. Minutes later we quick-footed back toward Bill's upraised arms. Mary and I looked where others were looking. "Get on this bird," Bill commanded, "if it's the last thing you ever do." We finally spotted it, alone on a wire, bold like a mockingbird with a hard black mask right through its eye and a nasty hook at the end of its beak. The shrike dropped into marsh grass and returned, empty-beaked, to its wire.

"Butcher bird," said a guy beside Mary.

"What?"

"The shrike. It kills other birds, then it impales them." He grinned, as if cuing Mary to show some feminine revulsion. Mary didn't blink. Two other guys high-fived. Mary and I eyed each other. This wasn't exactly the NBA, but we liked to see people having fun. It was a cool bird.

The Loggerhead Shrike, which our group saw in May 1998, is the only bird I remember distinctly from my first official bird outing in the Great Marsh. The species hasn't been seen since in Essex County, and it wasn't until years later, in Texas, that I watched a shrike pounce on a Bushtit, carry its prey to a barbed wire fence, and impale it, not for sadism or storage but to keep its meal fixed to one spot. The morning's other birds have blurred together with warblers and waders from other outings, often guided by Bill Drummond. Former BBC president, leader of countless trips, Bill is loved for his generous mentoring and teased about his military regimen on field trips. "Get on this bird if it's the last thing you ever do," is his famous command, used to keep his troops intense, whether they're birders on the edge of an Ecuadorian cliff, as we later were, or students in his math class looking for an oriole he's just spotted outside the window. To live, Bill needs birds.

The Great Marsh, the largest continuous salt marsh system in our state, extends from southern New Hampshire to Gloucester, where it's part of my patch. It comprises more than twenty thousand acres: marshlands sheltered behind barrier beaches, estuaries, islands, Plum Island Sound and Essex Bay, and tidal rivers winding inland. The Agawams, led by their sagamore, Masconomet, once held all the territory along the coast from the Merrimack River south into Cape Ann and west to modern-day North Andover and Middleton. After diseases had decimated the native population, farmers and fishermen from Europe colonized the area. Salt marsh hay was used for roofing, bedding, and livestock feed. The marsh remains vital for commercially harvested fish and shellfish. Most plants are obligate species that can live nowhere but salt marsh. There are obligate marsh birds too—the Willet, the Saltmarsh Sparrow. Well over three hundred bird species have been found in the Great Marsh: residents, breeders, and migrants along the Atlantic Flyway. The Parker River National Wildlife Refuge is probably the best-known birding destination in Massachusetts. The birds, the white-tailed deer feeding warily at fields' edges, the red foxes, the fossorial Eastern spadefoot toads, and migrating monarch butterflies—each animal here has its own span, its own dictates, but they're moving through one story in a sea-land.

Since I settled in Gloucester in 1972, I've told people I'll never leave the ocean, but I also mean I can't imagine leaving salt marsh. In *Life and Death of the Salt Marsh* (1969), John and Mildred Teal write that the marsh "reaches as far inland as the tides can creep and as far into the sea as marsh plants can find a roothold and live in saline waters." It's this reaching and creeping I love, life grasping for rootholds, the endless rise and fall of water, the marsh inching inland and receding, the boundaries ever shifting, plants ever colonizing, like eelgrass, capable of complete submersion, animals finding homes, a world in flux. On a gray mudflat under solemn clouds, the sun comes out and transmutes a mud puddle into a reflective pool of sky, shining cloud, and a Great Blue Heron lifting off. Mary's by my side, light passing through her hair. Feeling swoops into space inside me. Around us ocean flows into bay, estuary into river, marsh into solid land. Each day is as changeable as the seasons, each season distinct, the sumac reds and matted grass chartreuses in autumn as beautiful as our maple forests. I take Mary's hand.

Plum Island is a long barrier beach between the ocean and Plum Island Sound and the Plum Island River. In 1942 the U.S. Fish and Wildlife Service established a refuge on the island, and for birders "Plum Island" has become synonymous with the refuge. The dunes are stabilized by beach grass, beach pea, and beach heather: visitors must stay on boardwalks to protect the fragile cover. During nesting season most of the beach is off-limits to protect Piping Plovers. Behind the dunes, swaying cordgrass and sedges, laced with tidal creeks, stretch toward the mainland. Stands of pine and Eastern red cedars grip the sand and rise above marsh flatness. In the underbrush are thickets of beach plum, for which the island is named, a favorite food of the Agawams. In the 1950s the Fish and Wildlife Service built dikes to create the North and South Pools to provide nesting areas for freshwater marsh birds and feeding grounds for migrating shorebirds and waterfowl. Refuge staff now engage in on ongoing battle with invasive plants like phragmites and purple loosestrife, which have taken over much of the marsh and dry out the habitat, making it unlivable for native plants like common cattails.

Birds frequent the island in all seasons, and birders go from station to station, habitat to habitat, looking for the specialties at each station and following up reports from other birders. At parking lot 1, where our first BBC trip started, communal Purple Martins, sturdy and glossy dark, fly in and out of white gourds. They're early spring migrants from the Neotropics.

Guardians of their community, like my friend Sue McGrath, have affixed fake martins to the gourds to welcome them and scare off House Sparrows. During spring and fall migrations, hawk-watchers stand by the gourds and scan for raptors like American Kestrels and Sharp-Shinned Hawks. Across the road, by a boat ramp, I listen in spring for grunts or clicking castanets at the edge of marsh across the narrow Plum Island River—sounds of the leggy, long-billed, cryptic Clapper Rail, a salt marsh specialist I first saw here but haven't seen anywhere in Massachusetts for years.

The flat road passes salt pans and curves through woodlands. On one bike ride, as I passed gatherings of egrets white as a Pentecostal congregation, I braked for a rare White-Faced Ibis in the salt pans. The bird seemed curiously unwary, spaced out. Without binoculars I could make out the thin white facial border that distinguishes it from a Glossy Ibis. The next day I watched a Facebook video of the bird. There was the ibis, bobbing in a pool to the sounds of wind and the chatter of ornithology students, when the soundtrack erupted with screams. "Oh my God!" "What the—." "Noooooooo." A Peregrine Falcon (later determined to be one-eyed) swooped into view, landed on the ibis, thrashed it around in the water, calmly sat on its victim to drown it, and tore into the flesh on its neck. "This is so messed up," cried one student. "I can't bear to watch." "I can't look away," said their teacher. Laughter, groans.

In May flocks of wandering warblers can show up anywhere in roadside thickets on the refuge. Birders string out along the road, tracking warblers by sight and song—a sharp-looking Magnolia Warbler with a black mask over its yellow throat and black racing stripes on its flanks, a Prairie Warbler moving among shrubs with its buzzy ascending-the-scale song. In mating dress the warblers are a gallery of fine facial designs, bright throats and epaulets, vivid yellows or oranges playing off blue or black. While our fellow mammals *eek* and *aarf* and *oomph*, these animals sing. They're sensitive to too-close proximity but not shy about self-advertisement. One May morning, when a big orthopedic boot grounded me from the BBC bike ride, I drove slowly down the refuge road, stopping for birdsong, and then clomped my way as daintily as possible to the ends of the boardwalks at Hellcat Swamp. Northern Waterthrushes were singing everywhere, some hidden, some almost underboot, some squabbling over territory. Careful not to double-count, I tallied forty-five on the refuge, a new record for the species in one day in Essex County.

Each warbler has its own voiceprint, simple, quizzical, or nimble. In recent years scientists have refined the study of spectrograms, graphic representations of animal sound frequencies. Spectrograms, says birdsong expert Nathan Pieplow, "encode a bird's intentions; they draw its inner state. Each species has its own symbols for aggression, alarm, sexual ardor, and the hunger of begging nestlings." For Pieplow spectrograms have the beauty of calligraphy. Since he realizes his hearing will grow less acute with time, it gratifies him to know he'll still be able to watch the birds' signatures scroll past on a screen, "the elegant autographs of meadowlarks, the graffiti tags of grackles."

Late May brings the look-alike, sound-different *Empidonax* ("master of the gnats") flycatchers: Least, Willow, Alder, Yellow-Bellied. On one ride I heard fifteen emphatically sneezy Willows—*RITZbew!*—between the entrance and Hellcat parking lot, where the paved road ends. Even on quiet days the Hellcat boardwalks are never completely dead. If you can't find a catbird or towhee here in May, the world is about to end. On one of my first BBC trips, our leader thought he saw an Olive-Sided Flycatcher, a species that neither I nor the other participants, two elderly women, had ever seen. To verify, we needed to see the bird's diagnostic vest or hear its song, often represented phonetically, and rather arbitrarily, as *quick, three beers*. The bird didn't show itself. Exasperated, our leader stopped coaxing it and commanded it to sing. "Come on, fella, let's hear the fucking *quick, three beers*." The women and I looked at one another: this was a different way to call in a bird. Silence in return—no fucking *quick, three beers* for us.

The Marsh Loop boardwalk at Hellcat twists through the freshwater North Pool, where water is shallow enough to support dense, rooted plant cover but deep enough to inhibit growth of woody plants. Red-Winged Blackbirds cry out from the reeds. Marsh Wren acrobats, splayed on reeds in iron crosses, sing continuously, sometimes matching the riffs of competing neighbors, as stride piano players will "cut" one another to demonstrate superior technique. Least Bitterns, small, ochraceous, clinging to dense reeds in shadows, seem so at home in a New England marsh that it's hard to believe some winter in the Andes. Their genus name *Ixobrychus*, "reed roarer," is derived from a folk belief that, to make their low cooing calls, bitterns blow into hollow reeds. The American Bittern, larger, stretched skyward, still and patient as a penitent, relies on posture and camouflage to go unseen. Even when standing more or less in the open at the edge of reeds, it seems extraordinarily confident that no one will notice it. If a predator gets too close, the bittern will crouch, ruffle its feathers, spread its wings, and wield its long bill as a weapon. Its belching "song" has engendered a host of nicknames—thunder-pumper, bog-bumper, stake-driver, dunk-a-doo. The song inspired Theodore Dreiser, no one's idea of a nature writer, to invent the spooky "wier-wier" bird that torments the protagonist at Big Bittern Lake in *An American Tragedy*.

Some years I can't find any bitterns at Plum Island. Freshwater marshes are disappearing from our state—drained, filled, developed—and many obligate freshwater breeders, like bitterns, are on our state endangered list. But in spring 2004, when refuge staff kept the level of water high within the dikes, the North Pool became, for a season, a marshland of old. Least Bitterns, probably two pairs, were confirmed as nesting. Adult Soras and Blue-Winged Teal were seen with downy young and juveniles—the first evidence in years of either species breeding on the refuge. A female "mystery rail," impossible to identify definitively as either Clapper or King, finally revealed her identity when she engaged in courtship play and copulated with a larger male King Rail. Freshwater species like American Bitterns, Common Gallinules, and Pied-Billed Grebes were found as well, without evidence of breeding. This season of discoveries was documented in *Bird Observer* (October 2004) by Tom Wetmore, who maintains a website of Plum Island sightings. A big, white-bearded, gregarious guy, Wetmore epitomizes the camaraderie of refuge birding. It's a rare day on the island when I don't run into him, and he's always got birds to share. For years I've reminded him that I'm the senior John Nelson, but he met the other first, so I remain John Nelson 2.

Whether friends or strangers, birders on the refuge often share reports—a rare Gray-Cheeked Thrush just ahead, a Hooded Warbler seen at dawn—or they shake their heads over the absence of "good" birds to report. Judging any report requires a quick, sharp evaluation of the reporter. Is this person truly bird-wise? Did this person actually see the bird? Does the person know that other thrushes are often misidentified as Gray-Cheeked? A reporter's degree of confidence is not a dependable gauge. One day I drove to a patch called the Old Pines to see if the Ospreys had returned to their platform nest. In the parking lot I was accosted by a giddy couple who'd just found two Bald Eagles on the nest. I walked to where I could see the nest and raised my binoculars. "Ospreys," I told the couple. "Wonderful birds. They breed here every year."

No, they insisted, Bald Eagles. I opened my Sibley guide and pointed out differences between Ospreys and Bald Eagles. No, Bald Eagles. I set up my scope, at 32× magnification, and let the couple view the birds at their leisure. Bald Eagles. Identification errors are commonplace in birding, from inexperience, inattention, or wishful thinking, but here was such intransigence, such denial of disconfirming evidence, that "error" hardly seemed the word. Eyesight should learn from reason, Johannes Kepler proclaimed. Sometimes the eyes refuse the lesson.

In late summer the Bill Forward Pool, separated by a dike from the North Pool, becomes a hot spot for migrating shorebirds, called "wind birds" by Peter Matthiessen because winds carry them across the world. I've seen Spotted Sandpipers bob their butts from my patch in Gloucester to the banks of the Rio Negro in Brazil, and I've watched Curlew Sandpipers, in every plumage variation, from Mongolia to Ghana to Plum Island. Like many birders, I've known frustration in identifying shorebirds, especially the small "peeps," but I try to embrace the challenge—the study of size, shape, bill length and straightness, nuances of browns and grays, streaks or lack thereof, preferred depth of water, and rhythm of feeding technique, like the sewing-machine style of dowitchers. I try to watch with an artist's eyes. David Sibley learned the fine distinctions among shorebird shapes and postures by painting the birds. Sophie Webb, a field guide illustrator, says that when she draws a bird, she can grasp "how a bird moves, its habits and structure, in an almost internal way."

Beyond identification dilemmas, it's fun to watch shorebirds use their bodies to communicate attitude. They fluff up like kittens on guard, cock their heads as they jostle, and threaten through posture. If a Peregrine Falcon flies overhead or for no evident reason, a ripple of panic or "dread" might course through a flock, turning a scattering of birds into a tight, twisting swarm. In *The Wind Birds* (1973) Matthiessen describes how shorebirds "whirl off in small groups, by species rather than individuals, according to a wariness which seems to increase with the species' size. . . . They close again, for the wind birds are formation flyers; whirling down across the water gleams and shining mud, they twist and flare in a semaphore flight which turns the flock from light to dark to light again." Poet Amy Clampitt marvels at the "calculus," the "tuning," the "unparsed telemetry within the retina" that enables shorebirds to whirl in these tight flocks. Swarm scientists, who range from robot programmers to cancer researchers, have studied shorebirds to figure out the neural mechanisms that trigger a multitude of discrete entities to form an instantaneous, coordinated collective.

In November I'll come to the refuge hoping to find a vagrant flycatcher in the dunes or a rare Western Grebe at sea, but birds of prey are the main draw in late fall and winter. Northern Harriers, with a distinctive (but not unique) white rump, glide and wobble low over the grasses, then pounce. They're alert for stirrings that, even if I could fly, I'm sure I wouldn't see. The gray males, smaller than the brown and orange females, are called Gray Ghosts. Rough-Legged Hawks, tundra breeders that come in light and dark morphs, helicopter and hover above Cross Farm Hill. A Peregrine might launch into a flock of Eurasian Starlings as they swarm across the sky. Civilians might fear for the starlings, but birders here will root for the Peregrine. Starlings are disliked by many North American birders as an introduced species that outcompetes native birds and, in lockstep hordes, can dominate a marsh or meadow through sheer numbers.

There's something about raptors, a mix of self-reliance, flight power, and searching intensity, that makes us stand back in awe, yet beckons us to enter their inscapes. In *H Is for Hawk*

(2014), Helen MacDonald describes her identification with Mabel, a Northern Goshawk she adopted: "I look. There it is. I feel it. The insistent pull to the heart that the hawk brings, that very old longing of mine to possess the hawk's eye. To live the safe and solitary life; to look down on the world from a height and keep it there. To be the watcher; invulnerable, detached, complete." But becoming the watcher unsettles her own sense of identity. "Hunting with the hawk took me to the very edge of being a human. Then it took me past that place to somewhere I wasn't human at all. . . . Every time the hawk caught an animal, it pulled me back from being an animal into being a human again." As MacDonald watches Mabel clutch a prostrate rabbit, she reaches the limit to her identification with any bird: "Now I see that I am more of a rabbit than a hawk. Living with a hawk is like worshipping an iceberg, or an expanse of sliprock chilled by a January wind. . . . I love Mabel, but what passes between us is not human."

And there are owls on the island, like the crepuscular Short-Eared and diurnal Snowy. The nomadic Short-Eared Owls, round headed, flat faced, fly like buoyant barrels. Snowy Owls, white or sooty-white, are the Moby Dicks of owls, big and stout, though lighter than they look when fluffed out in the cold. Long sighted, with big, heavy eyes, they depend on touch when hunting prey hidden under vegetation or snow. One fine day, at dusk, I saw the two together, a Snowy rising from dunes behind me, crossing the marsh with slow, stiff strokes, a Short-Eared barreling just under it toward Cross Farm Hill. I looked around, wanting to share these owls, but no one else was in sight. The Snowy landed on an Osprey platform. The Short-Eared disappeared over the hill.

Mary has her own owl story. She rarely goes birding on her own except by chance, but one winter day, when I was laid up after a surgery, she itched to see a Snowy Owl, so she took my scope and drove to Plum Island. Her first hour was frustration—is that an owl or another owl-shaped icy lump?—but then she hooked up with two other birders, who soon showed her a Snowy swiveling its neck out in the marsh. One birder slapped the back of his buddy, a well-traveled South African who'd now seen every owl in North America except a red-morph Eastern Screech-Owl.

"I can show you one," Mary said. "If the sun's out, he's there every day. Guaranteed. He pokes his little head out and basks."

"Where?" asked the South African.

"Not too far. I can take you there."

The buddy pulled her aside. "You can't guarantee an owl."

"But if the sun's out," Mary protested.

"You can't guarantee an owl."

She led the other birders' car out of the refuge and toward a side street in Essex. She was having doubts. What if clouds came? What if the owl were sleeping in? Should she speed up and ditch these guys? But when they got to the hole, the sun was out, the owl was there, and the two birders were high-fiving. I've heard the story a hundred times, but I love the end, when Mary smiles and frames her face with cupped hands, like a screech-owl snug in its hole, heavy-lidded from the warmth of our sun.

Many rarities, like the Loggerhead Shrike, have been found on the refuge, and birders are quick to spread the news by word of mouth, cell phone, and eBird. Bird Watcher's Supply and Gift in Newburyport, owned by Steve Grinley—a longtime BBC trip leader and generous supporter of the birding community—has long served as command central for rarity reports. Sometimes, when I stand on the dike by the Bill Forward Pool, specters of rare birds will wing by me: my first Fork-Tailed Flycatcher, a South American visitor looking like an Eastern Kingbird elongated in Wonderland; a striding, elegant

Tricolored Heron fanning its wings to shade its view; American Avocets with baby blue legs and thin, upcurved bills, like specialized dental picks; and a lost one-eyed White Pelican that stayed a whole summer, alone, dwarfing the herons that fed alongside it. One morning, near Mass Audubon's bird-banding station, I joined forty roadside birders vying for angles to see a vagrant southerner, the notoriously hard-to-see Swainson's Warbler. On a scale from "killer look" to "better view desired," my glimpse was just satisfactory, but many never saw it at all. My first Harris's Sparrow, in contrast, was an exhibitionist. When it hopped through the legs of one observer, it was instantly named the Bill Buckner Bird—a joke any Red Sox fan should get.

In 2013 I was among many birders who saw a Common Ringed Plover and a Red-Necked Stint at Sandy Point State Reservation, on the southern end of the island, past the refuge border. Both species are extremely rare Eurasian vagrants. Both were discovered, about five weeks apart, by Suzanne Sullivan. How had she picked these birds out from the hundreds of lookalike peeps and Semipalmated Plovers wandering the mudflats? One day I met Suzanne, a lively, friendly woman, and asked her. Her answer, modestly delivered, was unsurprising: knowledge of field marks, awareness of possibilities, attention to detail, patience—more patience than I've got. I felt as I had when I'd talked to a birder who'd picked out an Anhinga within a long string of migrating cormorants. Birding humbles. There are reasons why birders like me don't find the rarities.

From Sandy Point you can look south to Crane Beach Reservation, between the mouths of the Ipswich and Essex Rivers. The beach fronts the ocean along the Castle Neck peninsula, a barrier between the Atlantic and Castle Neck River, tidal salt marsh, and small islands. Hog Island and the Crane Wildlife Refuge estuary can be reached only by boat. In 1910 Richard

Crane Jr., the son of an industrialist who'd made his fortune through indoor plumbing, bought eight hundred acres on the Castle Hill drumlin and later acquired the land that forms the three-thousand-acre Crane Estate. He built a huge Stuart mansion—the Great House—atop the hill with a view up the coastline from the Grand Allee, a long lawn, bordered by spruce and a statue gallery, that rolls from the mansion to the sea. Castle Hill, Crane Beach, and the refuge were eventually donated to the Trustees of Reservations, which manages the beach and marsh to preserve wildlife.

Crane Beach, three miles of sand backed by dunes and woodland, is one of our state's glories. Robert Frost strolled the beach on winter visits. Ipswich resident John Updike wrote his poem "Seagulls" about a gull flock here which "came in such a rush, and seemed so precious and perishable," that he jumped up and scratched the poem's first lines on a piece of charred wood from a campfire. The beach was part of the Ipswich patch of Dr. Charles Townsend, a founder of the Essex County Ornithological Club in 1916 and author of the 1905 *The Birds of Essex County*, among the first comprehensive studies of birds within a single county anywhere. An intrepid all-around naturalist, Townsend hiked and camped in the dunes, canoed through the marshes, and swam in the ocean in all seasons. His descriptions of bird behavior, always observed with thoughtful attention to detail, have been modeled by Jim Berry, former president of the ECOC and Townsend's heir in his exhaustive study of the county's birds.

Each June Jim and I lead a trip at Crane Beach, cosponsored by the BBC and ECOC. Actually, Jim leads the trip; I tag along as his quippy sidekick with a scope. It's an easygoing outing, a few hours until sunset, and it draws a mix of serious birders, beginners, and beach-lovers who'll watch birds now and then. We look for three targets, all breeding birds. The sand-colored

Piping Plovers can remain invisible until we get close and they skitter off. With binoculars we'll search a roped-off area higher up the beach for nests inside wire enclosures built to protect the chicks from foxes, skunks, and people. Least Terns, our second target, circle us, screech, scold us, buzz us, ignore us, and fly back to screech some more. Counting them all is a challenge. Further down we scan for fresh holes in the dunes and, we hope, our third target, Bank Swallows, maybe carrying food to nestlings as they did when Mary found some at Wingaersheek.

Each Crane outing brings some new adventure. One evening we raced back to our cars when lighting bolted over Plum Island and black storm clouds came at us hard from up the coast. The next year, as we lingered for a last look at the becalmed sweep of coastline under a setting sun, Miles Brengle and Nathan Dubrow, Jim's avid, ever-alert young proteges, spotted some uncommon Caspian Terns and Lesser Black-Backed Gull lounging on the beach. Some years back, my friends Jennifer and Mark Joseph brought along their five-year-old daughter, Brenna. Her eyes grew big when we hoisted her up to the scope to see a four-legged Piping Plover—a parent huddled over a new offspring. That year we ended the evening with a stroll along the Grand Allee. Mark still remembers a sun-bathed Indigo Bunting singing at last light from a spruce above a Roman statue.

Some years we return to our cars on paths through the heather woodland, a good place to compare the performances of two local mimics, the thrasher and mockingbird. How songbirds evolved to mimic other birds remains one of ornithology's great mysteries. Mimics are samplers, not copycats; they string together songs and other sounds in mixes particular to their species and themselves. They may even pass along old snatches of songs from birds now gone from an area. Brown Thrashers sing more individual motifs than any other species yet studied.

Northern Mockingbirds seem like self-amusers; they'll dance in the air or mock for themselves if there's nothing else to do. Thomas Jefferson called his pet mockingbird "a superior being in the form of the bird." Are mockingbirds trying to improve the songs they hear? It would be interesting to study their spectrograms and compare their motifs to the originals, like Carolina Wren songs, for variations in pace and inflection. Last year, as a finale, a small group of Common Nighthawks—the "bull-bats" less common here now than in Eliot's time—wheeled and buzzed above us at dusk. Their genus name *Chordeiles* means "a dance with music in the evening." I'm still waiting to hear a mockingbird mimic a nighthawk.

West of Plum Island is Newburyport Harbor, an estuary fringed by marsh at the mouth of the Merrimack River. In late summer at low tide, thousands of shorebirds might spread out over the vast tidal flats, spaced according to foraging preferences. A patient scan might pick out an uncommon Hudsonian Godwit or Ruff. In late fall the harbor is taken over by gulls and waterfowl. One day, while scoping a crowd of American Black Ducks at Joppa Flats, I glimpsed the powder blue head and orange shield of a drake King Eider, usually a duck of open ocean. Not trusting my eyes, I spent fifteen minutes relocating the bird and then rushed into Mass Audubon's Education Center. A small gang of visitors and staff members, all hot for a King Eider, followed me back.

Another day I found a Black-Headed Gull amid a group of similar Bonaparte's Gulls at harbor's edge. After I posted a report, a friend sent me a private message asking how I knew that my gull was in fact a Black-Headed. Doubting a fellow birder's report can be tricky, ego-threatening business, but he explained that he'd twice seen other birders misidentify a Bonaparte's as a Black-Headed in exactly this spot. He was satisfied when I itemized my bird's field marks. The next spring, also in a private message, I questioned a novice's sighting of two Seaside Sparrows at Brace Cove at Gloucester. I didn't tell him he was wrong. Instead I pointed out, diplomatically I thought, that Seaside Sparrows are salt marsh obligates and that, the previous day at Brace Cove, I'd seen two Savannah Sparrows, also with yellow above the eye. I was trying to be helpful, not pedantic, but the man never posted another sighting.

Across the Merrimack from Plum Island, and reaching the New Hampshire border, is Salisbury Beach State Reservation, where a creek winds through marsh just inland from a long stretch of beach. Beachgoing campers keep birders away in summer, but we come each winter to look for "winter finches" like White-Winged and Red Crossbills. The crossbills are stocky, parrot-like seedeaters named for oddly crossed bills adapted for extraction of conifer seeds. They're sociable nomads that wander the northlands in search of cone crops. Some years they're here in numbers; other years they're absent. The reservation also draws wintering birds of prey. A Short-Eared Owl and Northern Harrier, carrying on an age-old rivalry, might swoop and lunge at each other in a dogfight. This is *my* marsh; these are *my* prey. No, it's *my* marsh.

In spring and summer I bike through the Great Marsh listening for the bacon-sizzling hisses of Saltmarsh Sparrows and checking bridges over the Parker River for nesting Cliff Swallows. Wilson's Phalaropes, at their easternmost breeding outpost, sometimes feed in a Rowley marsh, recognizable by their jerky, dizzy spinning and the ripples around them. Along with a few other families, like jacanas, the three phalarope species are polyandrous. The female mates, lays eggs, and leaves the male to find a new mate. The male does all the incubating and feeding. "The fair sex conducts the courtship," wrote nineteenth-century ornithologist Elliott Coues, "and several of them may be seen in spring pursuing a modest male, who undertakes the role of St. Anthony without success, and when captured, submits with what grace he may to incubating such eggs as his flourishing partner assures him are his own." A female might badger and thump a male until he consents to sex or risks drowning. Some early ornithologists mistook female phalaropes for males because, well, they didn't act female. The confusion is understandable, since female phalaropes are atypically larger, more colorful, and more pugnacious than males, though they give themselves away by laying eggs. Franz de Waal observed a similar reaction in male primatologists who, confronted by mutually masturbating male bonobos, insisted on labeling the behavior "sham" or "pseudo" sex to distinguish it from "real" heterosexual sex. I've yet to meet the woman who doesn't feel a sisterhood with the table-turning, tit-for-tat phalarope females.

One day, as I rode past the sunlit haystacks and rosy clouds of a Newbury marsh—a scene painted by Martin Heade in the nineteenth century—I drifted into fantasy. The scattered songs I heard, with aircraft hum as a backdrop, swelled into a great chorus. The flight calls of migrating shorebirds filled the skies. Before killing shorebirds became illegal, the birds here were decimated by market hunters. Matthiessen describes "fire-lighting," in which men in punts found shorebirds resting at night, blinded them with bright beams, and then came ashore to wring their necks. In daytime, the swarming of shorebirds enabled hunters to kill many birds with a few shots into a flock. Chris Leahy describes the abundance that we've lost: "The sky-darkening legions of plovers and godwits and whimbrels and dowitchers that once connected Arctic nesting grounds with winter quarters in the southern temperate zone have never been resurrected."

Last September, after a knee replacement, I returned to Plum Island to try some biking again. It was the season for one of the great bird spectacles, the migration of Tree Swallows over coastal dunes, in the many thousands, on their way to southern wintering grounds. The swallows will take breaks, lining up on telephone wires, but as I biked they were all on the move, in swarms, riding currents above, behind, and alongside me. Up ahead, the swallow wave was so dense that some photographers had stopped their cars to take pictures. I rode into the heart of the wave, exhilarated, as if the swallows might lift me off and carry me with them, south over the Great Marsh toward the Caribbean. In the spring they'd bring me back.

Chapter 15

SAUNTERING THROUGH A GRAVEYARD GARDEN

She was orphaned at age six in North Carolina. At eleven she was bequeathed to a five-year-old white girl. James Norcom, her owner's father and father of eleven slaves, pursued and pressured her as soon as she reached puberty. Beauty, she wrote, curses a slave girl, without protection from harassment or rape: "Slavery is terrible for men, but it is far more terrible for women." Norcom forbade her to marry the freedman she loved and threatened to kill her and any man she tried to marry. Desperate for a guardian, she became the lover of a young white lawyer, Samuel Treadwell, who fathered her son and daughter. In a scheme to free her children, she pretended to escape and then hid in her grandmother's attic for seven years, contortioned in a nine-by-seven crawl space, three feet high at the highest point, with a trap door but no windows. Her presence in the garret was a secret kept even from her children. She could hear them playing outside but couldn't see them. She used a gimlet to drill peep holes in the walls. She watched her son get bitten by a dog. Treadwell eventually bought her children, as she'd hoped, but he never freed them.

I stood in the Clethra Path at Mount Auburn Cemetery, beside the grave of Harriet Jacobs, author of *Incidents in the Life of a Slave Girl* (1861), a book I'd taught in an American literature course. "Patient in tribulation," reads her headstone, "fervent in spirit serving the Lord." Above me, an Indigo Bunting sang two-note phrases. Jacobs must have heard birds from her garret, maybe Indigo Buntings, but she doesn't mention them. The songs of free birds may have tormented her. Eventually she escaped north, rescued her children, and worked in Boston as a nursemaid for Nathaniel and Mary Willis, who purchased and freed her. Jacobs met Frederick Douglass and women writers active in the abolitionist and suffrage movements, and she helped former slaves and orphaned children who'd found their way to Boston. To write *Incidents* she had to overcome the shame she'd felt as a white man's mistress. She appealed to the sympathies of white women in the North. In 1870 she opened a boarding house in Cambridge and befriended Mary Walker, another escaped slave who'd long been separated from her children. At Walker's gravesite here, a stone dove arches its neck and stretches its wings from atop a marble obelisk.

I strolled down Sycamore Avenue to the statue of a tall woman with hanging braids and intricately carved wings, a trumpet in one hand, the other raised toward heaven. Sculpted by Martin Milmore to honor his daughter Maria Coppenhagen, the winged woman is one of many angels here: soul-carrying angels, sword-wielding angels, child angels, angels guarding, praying, and pointing. A Great Crested Flycatcher *wheep*ed from near the memorial to Mary Baker Eddy, founder of Christian Science. Strange ringtones at odd hours led to a legend that Eddy had been buried with a telephone, but in fact, when her tomb was being constructed, a phone was installed for security guards protecting her casket from vandalism until it could be moved to the finished gravesite.

Mount Auburn Cemetery, in Watertown and Cambridge, is famous for the people buried here, its monuments, trees, and birds. Orioles and tanagers feed on blossoming fruit trees in an urban oasis of landscaped hills, pine stands, and redwood dells. Blue Jays stand guard on statues of flying cherubs. Chimney Swifts twitter over mausoleums with Corinthian columns. Our country's first landscaped garden cemetery, Mount Auburn was inspired by Père Lachaise in Paris and called "Sweet Auburn" from Oliver Goldsmith's poem "The Deserted Village." It was among the first graveyards to be known not as a "burying ground" but a "cemetery" or "sleeping place," where the dead could find peace and the living awaken to divinity within the cheering light of Nature. Reporting on the opening service at Consecration Dell in 1831, the *Boston Courier* noted the "music of the thousand voices which joined in the hymn, as it swelled in chastened melody from the bottom of the glen, and, like the spirit of devotion, found an echo in every heart, and pervaded the whole scene." British observer Harriet Martineau wrote: "A visitor from a strange planet, ignorant of mortality, would take this place to be the sanctum of creation. Every step teems with the promise of life. . . . Humanity seems to be waiting, with acclamations ready on its lips, for the new birth."

Mount Auburn embodied a new way of looking at death in a young, optimistic country. "The terror of death had given way to romance," says historian Louis Masur. "Surrounded by the peaceful solitude of nature, the city of the dead became a city of eternal life." Martineau viewed the cemetery as a rebuke of dour New Englanders "whose fathers seemed to think that they lived only in order to die." Puritan headstones had accosted visitors: "Stop here my friends and cast an eye / as you now, so once was I / as I am now, so must you be / prepare for death and follow me." Doug Chickering, a birding friend with relatives buried here, describes old "slate headstones with the grinning images of skeletons and crude angels that bear testimony to a much harsher, frightening view of death among the stern and hardy Puritans. One didn't contemplate paradise but instead feared hell." Mount Auburn, by contrast, offered a chance to contemplate "paradise," from the Persian for "magnificent garden."

People came here for meditative walks and social mixing in a garden open to all races, classes, faiths, and circumstances. Mount Auburn became the third most popular American tourist attraction after Niagara Falls and Mount Vernon and a model for the Emerald Necklace in Boston and Central Park in New York. And as a vast garden where, Martineau wrote, "every bird to which the climate is congenial builds its nest," it attracted birders. In 1832 Thomas Nuttall brought John James Audubon here to show him his first Olive-Sided Flycatcher. The cemetery staff now consider birds the primary tourist attraction, and the Friends of Mount Auburn welcome birders.

Leaving Jacobs's gravesite, I heard a squeaking Black-and-White Warbler and the high, thin, fading *see see* of a Blackpoll Warbler, a ventriloquist who invariably spins me in circles trying to locate him. Blackpolls are long distance champions, migrating from Brazil to as far north as Alaska. Black-and-Whites are shorter distance, more leisurely travelers. Both warblers would soon head north, for it was late May, near the end of spring migration.

I wasn't exactly birding that day, more like sauntering, a term from Thoreau's "Walking." Mount Auburn, with its winding paths and curiosities in any direction, was designed to saunter, to lose yourself in attentive roving while knowing that, with Harvard Square a few miles away, you won't get lost. Thoreau walked here as a Harvard student: "I love to wander and muse over them in their graves. Here are no lying or vain epitaphs. There is room enough here. The Loosestrife shall bloom and the Huckleberry bird sing over your bones." A few years earlier, before it was a cemetery, Emerson described students in the "wild lands" of Mount Auburn "so happy they do not know what to do." One day he heard a Black-Capped Chickadee and "then a far-off tree full of clamorous birds, I know not what, but might hear them half a mile." He lay down in a sunny hollow, opened his eyes, and "let what would pass through them into my soul." A year after the death of his young first wife, Ellen, he went to the cemetery to have her coffin reopened so he could gaze upon her.

I don't know if Hawthorne ever came here, but his story "A New Adam and Eve" (1843) depicts a carefree Adam and Eve strolling through an Auburn-like garden: "With light hearts—for earth and sky now gladden each other with beauty—they tread along the winding paths, among marble pillars, mimic temples, urns, obelisks, and sarcophagi." Emily Dickinson visited when she was sixteen. "It seems," she wrote, "as if Nature had formed the spot with a distinct idea in view of its being a resting place for her children, where wearied and disappointed they might stretch themselves beneath the spreading cypress and close their eyes 'calmly as to a night's repose or flowers at set of sun.'"

Near Bigelow Chapel I heard an emphatic *chip*, then a jumble of song, and tracked down a necklaced Canada Warbler in the shaded understory. I'd seen this warbler two weeks earlier in Windsor, Ontario, where my brother had Ralph lived and died, as I cut across a field while out walking and composing his eulogy. We'd seen the warbler together at Point Pelee, a birding hotspot near Windsor he'd known I would like.

I stopped at the Sphinx, Milmore's massive statue of a resolute woman with a lion's body, its tail curled on muscular haunches, and an eagle's head atop a layered Egyptian headdress. "American Union preserved," reads the inscription, "American slavery destroyed, by the uprising of a great people, by the blood of fallen heroes." Peaceful it may be, but Mount Auburn is filled with monuments to the spirit of righteous militancy, soldiers for God and freedom, clear-eyed warriors with terrible swift swords. Julia Ward Howe is buried here, identified on her headstone as a daughter and wife but remembered for "The Battle Hymn of the Republic," written in 1861 and using the music from "John Brown's Body." "Let the Hero, born of woman, crush the serpent with his heel," the hymn urges; "let us die to make men free." One who died in the Civil War was Robert Gould Shaw, the white commander of the all-black Fifty-Fourth Massachusetts Regiment, the subject of the film *Glory*: In May 1863 a huge crowd lined Beacon Street in Boston to watch the soldiers march in blue past the State House. Shaw was killed in action eight weeks later, his body never found. Around a bend from the Sphinx, a bronze tablet commemorates him. One day, in late autumn, I'd come here after a report of a rare Ash-Throated Flycatcher, in the same genus as the Great Crested. I found the bird perched on the black wrought iron fence that encloses Shaw's cenotaph.

Finding gravesites with recognizable names is a Mount Auburn tradition. Past Shaw's cenotaph, the simple headstone for Dorothea Dix contains only her name. Superintendent of Union army nurses during war, Dix went on to crusade for humane care of the mentally ill. "I come as the advocate of the helpless, forgotten, insane," she wrote, "in cages, closets, cellars, stalls, pens!" On the Pyrola Path, I stopped at the Margaret Fuller memorial. A protégé of Emerson, Fuller edited the literary journal *The Dial*, but she wearied of the Transcendental Club in Concord—"this playground of boys" she called it—and wrote a groundbreaking feminist tract, *Women in the Nineteenth Century*. "We would have every path laid open to Woman as freely as Man." Fuller and her husband drowned in a shipwreck, their bodies never found. Their two-year-old son Nino, also drowned, was buried under a white marble cenotaph with Fuller's face in bas-relief profile.

Jacobs, Howe, Dix, and Fuller are all listed among the "noted persons" in Mount Auburn's brochure. In their midst are gravestones for now-forgotten women who died young in childbirth or are noted merely as "Sarah, his wife" or named without dates of birth and death. One headstone says simply: "She Tried." The cemetery's first president, Joseph Story, believed that monuments to the dead should help us know "our own destiny and duty." I find it hard to visit these sites without succumbing to self-appraisal. Have I tried? Have I been a crusader in the great struggles of our time? Not often enough. Headstones summon us to remember the dead and carry on for the sake of the living or those not yet born, but we don't know who will remember us or why.

In *Birds and Birding at Mount Auburn Cemetery* (2004), Chris Leahy calls the cemetery a "hallowed shrine of American ornithology." Buried here is William Brewster: first curator of birds at Harvard, a founder of the Nuttall Club, first president of Mass Audubon, and president for forty years of the American Ornithologists' Union. He also chaired the AOU Committee on the Protection of North American Birds, which, Leahy says, "marked the formal entry of professional ornithologists into the field of conservation." Like many birders of his time, Brewster started by shooting birds for sport and skins and by collecting nests and eggs. Whether by foot, carriage, or canoe, he learned to watch birds with great concentration. In *A World of Watchers* (1986), Joseph Kastner describes the remarkable "avian empathy" that allowed Brewster to get close to birds: "At a vireo's nest, where a female is sitting on four eggs, he strokes the bird's back without arousing a protest." Brewster also felt empathy for fellow birders. When Nuttall members became too frail or sick to go birding, he often took care of them in his Cambridge house. His grave is marked by a rough stone with one smooth face for an inscription from the Song of Solomon: "For lo, the Winter is passed, the rain is over and gone, and the time of the singing of birds is come."

Not far away, on Palm Avenue, Ludlow Griscom is buried. Griscom, more than anyone else, trained modern birders, through example and cross-examination, to become scrupulous observers. Roger Tory Peterson considered him the court of last resort in all matters of field identification. In his 1955 *The Birds of Massachusetts*—coauthored with Dorothy Snyder and dedicated to Griscom's wife, Edith, a "patient and long-suffering ornithological widow"—he would label as "unacceptable" any "sight record of a species difficult to identify, regardless of date, place, or previous records, by an observer or observers of unknown competence or known incompetence." Griscom wouldn't tolerate sloppy sight records, and some birders feared his notorious "retort discourteous." His simple stone, with his last name only and no dates, is hidden in shade under a false cypress, a welcoming place for birds seeking cover.

As I stood by Griscom's grave, a Red-Tailed Hawk screamed overheard. In *The Lively Place* Stephen Kendrick says: "To be reading a worn epitaph and look up and see a red-tailed hawk surveying his territory from a funereal urn is to really know Mt. Auburn." My hawk was soaring, not perched, and Griscom has no epitaph, but close enough. Paul Roberts, a past BBC president and dean of Massachusetts hawk-watchers, notes in an essay on Mount Auburn raptors that Red-Tails began moving east in Massachusetts only near the end of the twentieth century and didn't nest in the cemetery until into the twenty-first century. The first breeding pair were named Hamlet and Ophelia.

Sauntering isn't Griscom-style birding, but weeks earlier, at the peak of spring migration, I'd come to Mount Auburn for a more typical outing, a BBC trip led by Linda Ferraresso, another former club president. The cemetery, a stopover on the Atlantic Flyway, has been designated an Important Bird Area, among the best places in our state to find migrating songbirds, and Mount Auburn trips are a long-standing club tradition. Former president Bob Stymeist, the mayor of Mount

Auburn, has led BBC trips here for more than five decades, in some years almost daily in spring, and he's seen more than two hundred species in the cemetery, close to the total number ever recorded here.

By six about forty birders, as sociable as waxwings, had gathered by the Egyptian Gateway at the main entrance. Club walks here start early; by noon, only the permanent residents may still be active and singing. I checked the chalk board inside an alcove for the previous day's bird reports. Nothing that exciting, but with fog the night before and a wind shift to the southwest, today's weather offered a fair chance for a migrant fallout. Linda, in a cluster of chatting birders, caught my eye and waved. The cemetery's website asks birders to "gather in only small, quiet groups, not large loud crowds," but that's a hard rule to follow on a sunny May morning when Linda is leading a trip. An excellent field observer, she's a woman with energy, focus, and high social intelligence. If Linda can't engage you, make you feel welcome, and elicit a few clues about what makes you tick, then you can't be engaged. I smiled at her and waved at other familiar faces. Certain birders I know only from Mount Auburn walks. They're always here. They may live inside the cemetery.

Linda gathered the group for the customary introductions. It was good to attach names to some recognizable faces, but there were too many names to remember. A woman passed around baggies with home-baked treats. "Birds await us," Linda announced as she led our parade along the usual route past Story Chapel and up Indian Ridge, an esker left behind by a stalled ice floe, now a paved path bordered by maples, black oaks, and flowering dogwood. We found our first scattering of migrants—Northern Parula, Red-Eyed Vireo, Yellow-Rumped Warblers—by tracking songs to singers. It can take years of listening to all the song elements—timbre, pitch, melodic line and pattern, timing—until the bird music is sorted into mental spectrograms, the identifiable songs of species. In *Mr. Palomar* Italo Calvino's protagonist listens to blackbirds and wonders: "And what if it is in the pause and not the whistle that the meaning of the message is contained?" Some songs still stump me. I heard a Magnolia Warbler or a Chestnut-Sided and finally found both high in an oak. The quality of movement can offer clues to identification. Vireos seem as methodical as shoppers with lists; warblers flash and perform arabesques. In his essay on warblers in the cemetery, Wayne Petersen explains how different species minimize squabbling through variety in foraging. They're not all going after the same bugs in the same way in the same spots. The ubiquitous, ever-on-the-move Yellow-Rumped Warblers, or "butterbutts," both delight and distract. My stepson Chris once sent me a photo of a warbler at his suet feeder in Florida. "Is this," he asked, "a yellow-dumped warbler?" Yes, a Yellow-Dumped indeed.

Linda, attuned to the shyest, least self-assured members of our group, helped them locate and identify birds darting around in treetops, and she complimented them on their sightings. As a leader you want everyone to see every bird well. Some more experienced birders, quicker to find birds, eased down the path to see what else was around. I pointed out a Wood Thrush, bold spotted, upright as a robin, by the plot where Longfellow is buried with two wives and four children. His first wife, Mary, died in childbirth; his second wife, Fanny, died in a fire. After he'd bought the plot, Longfellow watched workers excavate his grave: "I looked quietly down into it without one feeling of dread. It is a beautiful spot."

At Halcyon Lake a Black-Crowned Night-Heron, a species from an ancient bestiary, was hunched and poised over a reflection of itself in the shadows beneath overhanging willows. A butt-bobbing Spotted Sandpiper teetered across mud near the Eddy Memorial. Baltimore Orioles, black with orange fire, whistled in the canopy. Stunning birds—it's hard to turn away from them, however common. Linda called out an Orchard Oriole, smaller and nimbler than a Baltimore, warbler-like, a gothic chestnut and black. Its species name *spurius* is Latin for the son of an unknown father; an old common name was the Bastard Baltimore. One highlight of the atlas was finding a pair of Orchard Orioles at a nest in Whipple Woods, one of the secret places in my patch.

At Auburn Lake an Eastern Phoebe hawked insects from a horse chestnut by the bridge. Tree Swallows, sipping on the wing, skimmed the water. Birds were everywhere, a feeding frenzy in surround sound. Linda noted songs, called out names of warblers, and tracked their movements: Black-Throated Green at three o'clock, Black-Throated Blue below it, a Nashville up high, a Common Yellowthroat low in a shrub, a Yellow by the water—all variations on the theme of New World warbler evolution. A black-capped Wilson's Warbler acrobatically caught an insect. A Northern Waterthrush tail-wagged at pond's edge. A Blackpoll spun me around. A Rose-Breasted Grosbeak, with its red badge of courage, landed in a bald cypress. The young woman beside me was laughing, dazed by the riot of birds. "Oh, look," she said, touching the arm of the guy next to her. "What a beauty." A redstart fluttered across a limb right over our heads. The guy shook her off. "I need a Bay-Breasted," he told her. She turned to me as if to ask: why does somebody go birdwatching if he doesn't like to watch birds? "Don't mind him," I said. "Redstarts are great." We watched the redstart naked-eye. Seen without binoculars, it became an animal moving through its realm, not a display of field marks.

Our group was almost relieved when the wave finally passed. We moved on feeling post-orgasmic, reliving this or that sighting, happily complaining about the occupational hazard of warbler's neck. Mourning Doves scratched around beneath the bird feeders near Brewster's gravesite. Bands of birders wandered the walkways, headed up slopes, stopped to look up and point, as if there were nothing more natural than to stroll through a cemetery with binoculars. In May only the most furtive bird could avoid being seen here by some birder. A few people casually tagged along with us. We were halted by a three-part song, rapid-fire, enunciated, climaxing in staccato—a Tennessee Warbler in a treetop. Uncommon here, the Tennessee seems a drab thing, gray and dull olive, vireo-like, but as bird-banders know, if you get close enough, any bird becomes a wonder of weaving and subtle shading.

We headed up Harvard Hill, donated to Harvard College in 1833 and still reserved for Harvard people, though space is tight and entrance requirements tough if you want to join the Harvard Club of the Dead. Behind me, a couple joked about a snobby Harvard alum on MassBird who was seeking other Harvard types to go birding with. I laughed along: a Harvard degree isn't a birding credential. There had once been seven hills here, "abrupt heights and deep hollows," Brewster wrote, "covered by heavy and perhaps primeval forests," but the other six were leveled, and the forests are now thoroughly managed. The cemetery contains nearly seven hundred species and varieties of trees, and arborists and horticulturalists carefully structure the plant community to support birds and other wildlife. In May azaleas bloom in white, pinks, and reds. Lilacs and viburnums are in flower. Mount Auburn's website lists plants blooming by location and month.

Another warbler flurry met us up the slope. A Scarlet Tanager, saturated in sunlight, rasped from a treetop. I'd once found a scarce Summer Tanager in exactly this tree, and I searched now with a birder's irrational hope that, since the tanager had once liked this spot, it would return at just the moment I was looking for it. We crossed over to the Dell, a steep, shaded hillside leading down to a vernal pool, where endangered spotted salamanders breed each spring. A Hermit Thrush and Ovenbird sang from somewhere near the murky water. We joined some people watching a resident Great Horned Owl. We waited a while for it to do something exciting—hoot, preen, cough up a pellet—but the owl slept on.

We climbed the steps to the base of the imposing Washington Tower, built of granite in the 1850s at the summit of Mount Auburn. Beyond, a city panorama spread out: the columns of Harvard Stadium in the foreground, the Hancock and Prudential towers above the horizon, and far off, glinting in sunlight, the golden dome of the State House. A few of us took a break to sit on a bench and absorb the view. "The older you get," said a woman beside me, "the more your eyes want to see the world." She was tall and bony-slim with silver hair and penetrating eyes. "My friend likes to say, 'God always answers our prayers. Sometimes the answer is no.'" She laughed, and I laughed with her. The Scarlet Tanager was now at eye level. It was joined by a Blackburnian Warbler, its fiery orange concentrated in its throat. "Simply lovely," the woman said.

Near Margaret Fuller's cenotaph we stopped for more warblers, still beautiful the second or seventh time around. At the edge of Willow Pond, a Green Heron, already stretched, grew ever more elongated. We could feel its anticipation. A female Baltimore Oriole collected fibers to weave a nest hanging above the water. We'd lost cohesion, people drifting off to look at birds, flowers, monuments, but we coalesced when Linda called out a Cape May Warbler: streaked below, face rouged brown, our rarest warbler of the morning. "I guess that will have to do it," she said after everyone had seen the Cape May. It was almost nine. "Some of us have jobs." Others groaned about having to work too. We thanked Linda—great morning, great birds, eighteen warbler species—and said our goodbyes. The tall woman shook my hand. "It was nice to share a moment with you."

Someone had heard a report of a Mourning Warbler back near the Dell, and a few of us tried in vain to find it. Eventually we separated, and I sauntered back toward the entrance. I was hoping to hear a cuckoo. I passed one of the many dog statues in the cemetery. One year I'd seen a young man enrapt as he stroked the stone fur ruff of a Newfoundland sculpted centuries ago. It must have been 2004, the year the Red Sox finally won the World Series: the cemetery was festooned with Sox paraphernalia to share the celebration with loved ones who'd waited long in vain. That day I'd chatted with an old security guard who itemized some of the things his crew had found on the grounds: Sox jerseys, panties, medical waste, a trash bag filled with four calves' heads.

Down another path, people were circled around a gravesite. A pale, auburn-haired girl in a long black dress bent down to drop a dark red rose on the casket. The lacquered wood gleamed in morning light. Death draws people into a circle. Then the circle breaks up, and people are left to grapple with their loneliness or regret or rage. I've heard stories of clueless birders intruding on grief, raising binoculars to watch some bird perched above mourners around an open grave, but I've never witnessed it.

At Bigelow Chapel I picked out the bride in a long, flowing gown, lacy and scalloped, amid a wedding party gathered beneath the gothic spires. A Yellow-Billed Cuckoo sang above them. It might seem strange to marry in a cemetery, but what better place to commit yourselves "'till death do us part" than a garden of birds and monuments to the generations? Mary and I were married in my sister Joan's backyard. People laughed and danced, children played, birds sang. It was a joyous day. I can't describe how beautiful Mary looked. In my dreams we become birds, usually cranes or storks, flying over green pastures to the end of all land.

Two years after my brother and Joan died, in a time of one death after another, I published an essay, "Parting Words," about eulogy-writing. At the end I joked that if I predeceased Mary, I'd made her promise to tell the gathering what every dead male intellectual would like to believe: that his spouse loved him more for his body than his brain. Whether she holds to her promise, I'll never know. Last year, when Mary was very sick, she tried to get me to face the reality that one day she'd be gone. I heard her. All I could summon was dread. I'll grieve when I have to. She's doing better now. This morning we watched a pair of Red-Tailed Hawks fly over our house.

Chapter 16

DEATH AND THE ROSE-BREASTED GROSBEAK

I wrote my essay on eulogies after a ten-month span when my only brother and three remaining sisters all died. Within a few years before that, I'd lost close friends, two nephews, and a stepson. Time was rushing ahead. Who's next? Some deaths were more or less expected. Since I'm the youngest by far of seven children, it's not surprising I would outlive my siblings. My oldest sisters, Rosie and Carlotta, were both in their upper eighties when they died. The sudden death of my stepson Tommy, at age thirty-three, was a blow. Mary and I were still reeling. For the living, no two deaths are alike. Each is interlaced with a weave of sweet and painful memories, dreams realized or not, twisting patterns of love, lost promise, strands of guilt, empty days, sorrowful yearnings, circling thoughts, and hopes that we can somehow commune with those who are gone.

I also birded a lot that year—for the atlas, at Mount Auburn, and traveling around and out of the country in pursuit of new birds. When Mary and I reached Tennessee to find my sister Joan much sicker than we'd known—she died weeks later—I was still abuzz over a bird from a pelagic trip out of North Carolina, Swinhoe's Storm-Petrel, the first North American record. When Rosie died I was in full bird-search mode in the Philippines. When Ralph died, I scrambled to catch a flight to Windsor, attended wakes and a funeral, delivered a eulogy, went to an Irish pub with his son, caught a flight home at dawn, and spent the day finding birds for our Bird-a-thon team. I was glad to have something to do with myself.

I usually didn't think about death while I was birding. Near home, on foot or bicycle, I moved through a familiar scape of sight and sound, and potential sound, with near constant concentration. If I were someplace where I didn't know the songs—a tributary of the Amazon—I was still listening and at full visual attention for most of each day and into the nights. Edward O. Wilson in *Biophilia* (1984) calls it the "naturalist's trance." Gretel Ehrlich writes in *The Solace of Open Spaces* (1985), "Animals hold us to what is present." Iris Murdoch describes a day when she was feeling anxious and resentful until she became entranced by a hovering kestrel: "The brooding self with its hurt vanity has disappeared. There is nothing now but kestrel."

Birding blessedly distracts. Other pastimes, I guess, could serve the purpose, like the tennis games I used to play, or online poker, or Big Days at yard sales. But I never think of birding as a distraction. A distraction couldn't offer such moments of discovery—a Capuchinbird's shocking air raid siren song in a remote Brazilian forest or, at home, a baby hawk flapping and hopping with ungainly resolve and rising in first flight. That spring I spent hours in our yard watching birds' family lives. A pair of Pine Siskins, uncommon breeders in our county, bred in the woods beyond our pond: first the male and female daily at our thistle feeder, then the male in courtship antics—its call a joyriding *zhreee*—then the female carrying grass to build a nest, and, weeks later, the female stuffing food into a fledgling's gape. When a hailstorm hit, I fretted over birds still incubating, battered by hailstones as they sheltered their eggs.

Distractions don't always work. Sometimes grief overtook me, no matter what birds were around, whether siskins at home or a wondrous blue Celestial Monarch flitting through a canopy on Mindanao. I didn't break down sobbing. I was immobilized, disoriented, the last sibling standing, lost. Or I was possessed by a restlessness, uneasy, searching, for what I'm not sure. "No one ever told me," wrote C. S. Lewis after his wife died of cancer, "that grief felt so like fear."

Sometimes a bird set me off. My loved ones weren't birders, but certain birds, to this day, remind me of each of them. With my friend Steve, it's the Carolina Wren and Northern Mockingbird, for both sang the whole time—the mockingbird echoing the wren's *teakettle teakettle teakettle*—as we circled his gravestone on a frosty morning. With Joan—beautiful, spirited, elegant in hip waders, a woman who reached out to people—it's any kingfisher, for she could fish expertly whether on a rocking ocean or in a fly-casting stream. With Ralph it's the Canada Warbler. The words for his eulogy came easily. My brother, a political science professor, was a kind, smart, witty, and faithful man. In my book *Cultivating Judgment*, on how to teach critical thinking skills, I'd used him as a model to emulate.

Rosie is brought back by Dark-Eyed Juncos, birds I was surprised to see in July on out hike up Roan Mountain in Tennessee, months after they'd left our yard. I'd forgotten that juncos are altitudinal migrants. Rosie liked their energy, their blithe acceptance of cold and wind, the white flashing in their tails. For her eulogy I wrote a poem, "Woman of a Garden," comparing her tending of her garden to her loving cultivation of her eleven children. For years she'd helped to preserve birds as a volunteer at a nature center, and at the Field Museum of Natural History in Chicago she'd led groups of children and elders to see the bird specimens. Carlotta appears with a flock of terns that called out and streamed over as we strolled along a breakwater in Provincetown, before disease began to claim her. Which species I can't say, since I wasn't a birder then, but it doesn't matter. "My, aren't they grand," she said. Carlotta, a sensitive heart, a nurturing teacher, had a feeling for beauty in all its forms.

I like to think of my stepson Tommy as a closet or incipient birder. We never went birding together, but Mary trained him to look out for Red-Tails, and he'd indulge me with a smile and show of interest when I went on about birds. He loved creatures generally and had adopted an ailing macaw from the animal shelter where he worked. One day he called me. He sounded excited. He'd been out in the woods and had seen some really cool birds. What were they? He described field marks. His attention to detail amazed me. I can't remember all the species now, but one was unmistakably a Rose-Breasted Grosbeak. We made plans to go birding together the next morning. When I got off the phone I proudly told Mary, "I've turned Tommy into a birder." She nodded, then burst out laughing. What? "He didn't see a grosbeak," she said. He hadn't been in the woods at all. With some coaching from her he'd been putting me on. I was touched nonetheless. He'd cared enough to play out his role expertly and string me along.

I didn't think of my loved ones every time I saw these birds. Joan liked goldfinches, just as she hated the turkeys invading her yard—almost fifty on one day—but with all the finches at our feeders and the female turkey that visited daily, pausing to defecate on the flat rocks around our pond, I'd have been grief-struck all day long if every goldfinch or turkey prompted thoughts of her. Rather, birds and my departed had taken up residence together in a dense, tangled, unconscious habitat of feeling and memory. Through birds the fullness of love, of grief, became fuller.

One morning before dawn I lay in bed, unable to get back to sleep. From the stillness outside came a song, slurred and wavering, a Veery, a thrush I'd never heard in our woods. I remembered Edna St. Vincent Millay's "This Is Mine, and I Can Hold It." A beautiful thrush song makes her feel like a vessel about to shatter, for all her senses "have broken their dikes and flooded into one, the sense of hearing."

The Veery stopped singing and then started up again. I thought of another man lying in darkness and listening to a thrush. I'd first taught Keats's "Ode to a Nightingale" decades earlier, long before I knew about birds or felt ringed by death. Keats wasn't a birder in the modern sense, skilled at identifying species, but he had that rare quality birders strive to achieve, the ability to stay attuned to the slightest movement, sound, or shift in light—the naturalist's trance. "Nothing seemed to escape him," wrote Joseph Severn, his friend and eventual nurse, "the song of a bird and the undernote of response from covert and hedge, the rustle of some animal, the changing of the green and brown lights and furtive shadows, the motions of the wind—just how it took certain tall flowers and plants—and the wayfaring of the clouds." Keats knew how it felt to be circled by death. His father died when he was eight; his mother, when he was fourteen. For months, as his brother Tom wasted away from tuberculosis, Keats stayed by his side, nursing him and becoming so distraught, so exhausted, he could barely write letters, much less the poems on which he'd focused all his ambition. "I have never known any unalloy'd Happiness for many days together," he wrote his betrothed, Fanny Brawne. "The death or sickness of someone has always spoilt my hours."

Tom died when Keats was twenty-three, not long before he wrote the "Ode to a Nightingale." In the poem Keats never mentions his brother by name, but the youth who "grows pale, and spectre-thin, and dies" is certainly Tom. The ode is set on a spring night. The poet's heart aches as he listens to a nightingale sing in an ecstasy. The song stirs intense yearning. He longs to escape with the bird and "leave the world unseen."

He wants to forget what the nightingale will never know—the "weariness, the fever, and the fret" of life, the palsy of the old, the sickness that steals the young. Knowing he can't forget, he imagines himself dying, that very moment, a painless death as "easeful" as the nightingale's song. He envies the bird's freedom, not from death, for the bird will die, but from awareness of death. But eventually the nightingale flies off. The music is "fled." The poet is left, as we all are, with his "sole self." The ode ends with a question: "Was it a vision, or a waking dream?" In a sense Keats has flown with the bird: he has transformed its song into a poem. In a world of death, two consolations, if that's the word, have come together, the evocative beauty of birdsong and the power of human language to express the feelings the song evokes. Yet his helplessness, and ours, to fend off death remains.

Keats seemed to know that his own time was brief. He composed this ode shortly before he contracted tuberculosis while on a walking tour in northern England. In early 1819 he wrote that he wanted to "moult" like a bird into a fresh body. By July he no longer "hoped for fresh feathers and wings: they are gone, and in their stead I hope to have a pair of patient sublunary legs." He was living what he called a "posthumous life" when the ode was published the next summer. He died the following February, before his twenty-sixth birthday. When doctors opened his body, the cells of his lungs were so destroyed they could not understand how he'd managed to stay alive the last few months.

The music of my Veery fled, or I fell back to sleep. When I got up, Turkey Vultures were riding thermals over our house. Each year they seemed to arrive earlier and stay longer. A few now winter here. In earlier ages their unseasonable appearance would have been an ill omen, a warning that death was close. In his poem "Under the Vulture-trees," David Bottoms tries to give vultures a more benign spin. Hundreds of vultures, perched by a river, become "transfiguring angels" with "surprisingly soft faces, like the faces of the very old who have grown to empathize with everything," and "with mercy enough to consume us all and give us wings."

If you've lost a son or brother, or fear that your own time is near, the mercy of carrion-feeders may not provide much comfort, but the need for relief can make us desperate. What do we do with our minds, Keats asks, when our hearts are plagued by sorrow? How can we fly when the "dull brain perplexes and retards"? How can we stop thinking about what we've lost and know we will lose? In her poems about birds and death, Mary Oliver asks the same questions. In "The Return" she asks: what can offer us "deliverance from Time"? What can we do with the knowledge that "death is so everywhere and so entire"? "*What good is hoping? . . . What good is trying? . . . What good is remembering?*" Answers to such questions are a lot to ask of a bird, whether thrush, vulture, or the herons and hummingbirds in Oliver's poems. It's not enough to be distracted or to yearn to fly and forget. We want to be transformed. We want birds to give us faith that we too shall rise. In "And the Thrush Said" a bird says to Keats: "O fret not after knowledge. I have none."

With thrush and vultures gone, I ate breakfast. At our window feeder a bird joined me, feeding nervously on sunflower seeds. I studied it: big pink bill, oversized head with bold stripes, buffy streaking on its breast. It was an immature Black-Headed Grosbeak, a species so rare in our state that once I got the word out, birders would be trooping to our yard to see it. Then I noticed the faint, splotchy red wash on its breast. The Latin name for the genus, *Pheucticus*, means "painted with cosmetics." It wasn't a rare bird after all, not a Black-Headed but a far more common Rose-Breasted Grosbeak, virtually identical as a juvenile except for that slightly blushing breast, which turns bloodred on an adult male. Still, I was pleased. I'd heard grosbeaks singing in the neighborhood and known a pair must be nesting nearby, but I'd never found the required proof—adults building a nest or feeding young—to confirm their breeding status for the atlas. Here was proof indeed.

For a while, in a trance, I watched the bird. It was a scruffy little thing, eyes darting, unsure of itself, probably just fledged. If it were human, it would have acne and a cracked adolescent voice. But in a few weeks it would gather itself and fly, alone, across plains and seas, to a land it had never seen, the Cayman Islands or the Chiriquí highlands of Panama. The next spring it might find its way back to my patch. I thought of Tommy, his sly smile when I let him know I was on to his joke. Yes, you had me fooled, boy. You didn't see a Rose-Breasted Grosbeak. You were just having some fun with your old man. How often I regretted the journeys he'd never take, the adventures he'd miss because his life ended too soon, too soon. How seldom I remembered the journeys he did take, to China to perform with his karate group, to Caribbean islands with the girls who could never resist him. He struggled so hard to believe in himself, find himself, lose himself—drugs, too many girls—but he knew joy, and in moments he was beautiful, stroking the sick macaw on his shoulder or, master of self-defense, poised on one leg with arms outstretched like a crane about to lift off. At Mount Auburn, by an Irish cross with a spread-winged bird of prey and a tree stump with climbing vegetation, all in stone, I'd shivered with a mother's anguish as I stood over a stone crib for a dead infant.

The grosbeak leaped to a perch near the feeder. I got up for a closer look. The bird detected movement but didn't take off. The moment felt intimate, light. I asked the bird no questions, expected no revelation. I didn't envy it, didn't ache for wings to fly south with it. Mortality rates are high for young birds, whatever the cause on the death certificate, hurricane, cat, juvenile pilot error. One day, maybe soon, this bird wouldn't make it. But until that time came, it would be a creature of vitality and beauty, ever striving. I remembered another Keats poem, "Ode on Melancholy." Grief can't be escaped. You can't silence "the wakeful anguish of the soul." No, you must yield, let it come, all of it, with eyes and heart open, and "glut thy sorrow." Wish for no grief, no fear, and you wish for no life at all. I didn't want to flee my dead. I wanted them with me—son, brother, sisters, friends—with birds singing. I glutted my sorrow.

The grosbeak flew off. I heard other birds nearby, a goldfinch, a Carolina Wren's bright *teakettle*, something stirring in a bush. Ridden by loss, Keats still listened for all the signs of life around him. I embraced the day, or tried to.

Chapter 17

CAPE COD

Following Footprints and Bird Tracks in Sand

One August morning sixteen of us waded with spotting scopes from the shore of Morris Island in Chatham to climb aboard a boat for a ride to the end of South Beach. Squeezed along fiberglass benches, we were a gaudy bunch, decked out in Hawaiian shirts and leis for the BBC's annual South Beach Safari. I sat beside Laura de la Flor and Mark Burns, our leaders and innovators of many club traditions: tropical New England safaris, the Plum Island bike ride, celebrations of equinoxes. Waiting for us might be a reported Wilson's Plover, Black Skimmers, some rarity incognito amid bird multitudes. Our long trek across shadeless sand and briny mud would be lightened by esprit de corps. But we were also saddened. Steve Leonard, a safari regular and good friend to many of us, had died two weeks earlier.

The boat left the island. Salt spray tickled our faces. A White-Winged Scoter scooted by. Harbor seals lazed on a sandbar. Land came closer on one side, receded on the other. Someone pointed out North Monomoy Island. Was that South Monomoy further out? I could never get my bearings here. The light, the tides, the constant shifts of perspective all fooled with my sense of distance and orientation. A good fisherman would know the landscape of the sea floor and the signifying shapes of water, birds could read colors and patterns beyond human perception, but I couldn't fathom which passageways led to ocean and which didn't. In a few years, through wind and tides, South Beach would become attached to South Monomoy, while a new breach would open up farther north. The simplest certainty—that's land, not water—seemed an illusion.

Glaciers and their retreat formed the landscapes and seascapes we now see on Cape Cod, Nantucket, and Martha's Vineyard. Advancing ice sheets dug, scraped, pushed, and dumped land and leveled ancient hills into coastal plains. Stellwagen Bank, now out to sea, may have once been connected to the lower cape. The lobate front of the last ice sheet scalloped bays and sounds. Irregular glacial advance and retreat shaped the rough triangles of Nantucket and Martha's Vineyard, the arc of the Elizabeth Islands, and the arm of the cape. Retreating ice left behind heaps of debris, or "till": gravel, sand, and erratics from as far north as Katahdin in Maine. Terminal moraines—elongated, rounded ridges of rock formed at the ice front, now the highest points of land—mark the cape and its shoals as the southern terminus of glacial movement.

In her history of Cape Cod, *The Narrow Land* (1934), Elizabeth Reynard tells a Wampanoag story of the cape's creation. Maushop, a young giant later called Moby Dick, couldn't sleep in the oppressive summer heat: "On such nights he made a bed of the lower Cape; of the cool lands that lie narrowly between ocean and bay. There his body twisted and turned, changing position, seeking repose, until he shifted the level sand into dunes and hollows." Moby Dick also became a name for the great ice sheet that shaped the land: "The vast Moby Dick of glaciers, pushing dark silt before it, ploughed homeward to the sea to die. With transparent lips it sucked the ocean, while its gaunt sides withered inward, leaving around them a narrow shroud rimmed by tallow-white beaches, plumed with blue fire of waves and flanged by the smoky sea."

As we crossed a channel, Laura floated a lei and asked for a moment of silence. We bowed our heads. Some people wept.

I remembered Steve grinning as he called out "Turdus migratorius!" to greet a passing American Robin and declaring to a group of baffled birders that a second rail skulking in reeds at Plum Island wasn't another Clapper but a scarcer King Rail. When we lifted our heads, Linda Ferraresso gazed heavenwards. "I can see Steve up there now, cornering Audubon. 'John James, can I talk to you a minute about the bill shape on your female Solitary Vireo?'" Steve was a Griscom-style stickler, not one to tolerate slipshod observations, whoever the offender. No doubt he rubbed some birders wrong, but his sarcasm went hand in hand with a passion for birding and a belief in upholding standards. He had a probing mind and good heart.

I think of Steve when I come to Cape Cod, for he taught me about the birds here, but I also remember the writers who explored this land before me. Thoreau was disoriented too. "To an inlander," he wrote in *Cape Cod* (1865), "the Cape landscape is a constant mirage." A flat stretch of sand seemed to slope upward toward the ocean. A close windmill or herd of cows seemed far off on the horizon. A family a-blueberrying amid dwarf bushes became a race of giants. He too was confounded by the inlets around Chatham, where the slightest channel was dignified by a name.

I'm not an inlander like Thoreau—or haven't been for half a century—but coming from what some people call the "other cape" (Cape Ann) I'm an outsider here, off my patch. Visiting this cape is like meeting a distant relative who's viscerally familiar but has some strange habits. Our Great Marsh has barrier beaches and channels, but on Cape Ann I've got granite underfoot. Here the bedrock is too deep to reassure. Storms wreak havoc on Cape Ann—toss riprap ashore to crush houses, float trucks into harbors, drown men at sea—but I don't worry that the barriers will relocate or that the cliff at Halibut Point will collapse into a rock pile. Here the borders between sea and sand never stop roaming. The rocks seem like vagrants waiting for an ice floe to carry them home. In the 1870s an eroding cliffside migrated toward the twin lighthouses of Chatham, over two hundred feet back from the beach, until one lighthouse fell over the edge. Maps of Chatham over the past century recall the earliest maps of New England, as if the mapmakers were trying to refine the sketches of their predecessors. Wait, this inlet should be over here; this is a shoal, not an island; that shoreline faces in a different direction. Beaches change shape like a man on a binge or a diet. Fossil pollen and spores found in greensand suggest that, through continental drift, the cape and islands were once much closer to the equator, subtropical in climate. On South Beach I can feel our continent still drifting.

On his three visits here, Thoreau felt that he'd put all of America in back of him. Behind the cape, he wrote, "the State stands on her guard, with her back to the Green Mountains, and her feet planted on the floor of the ocean, like an athlete protecting her Bay." Cape Cod was isolated. Fishermen were more likely to sail to China than go to Boston by land. Off-cape visitors were rare enough that Thoreau and his traveling companion, William Ellery Channing, were suspected by some locals of being bank robbers. It would be generations before Henry James, in *The Bostonians* (1886), could describe the cape as an escape for city people who "wanted to live idly, to unbend and lie in hammocks, and also to keep out of the crowd, the rush of the watering-place." When I'm drawn here I find Thoreau a congenial guide. Other writers, like John Hay and Mary Oliver, may describe the cape more knowingly, more lovingly, but Thoreau offers the fresh eyes of a fellow outsider. Recalling the great explorations of Alexander von Humboldt and Darwin, he came here to explore. Looking for birds, he found "crow-blackbirds" hopping about in dry fields, a Black-Throated Bunting (Dickcissel) in shrubbery, the eggs of Killdeer and Common Nighthawks, and an Upland Plover (Sandpiper) "whose quivering notes were ever and anon prolonged into a clear, somewhat plaintive, yet hawk-like scream, which sounded at a very indefinite distance."

Thoreau found wildness here he didn't expect: whales and human wreckage cast up ashore, seals he'd associated with "the Esquimaux and other outlandish people," and great gaps between offshore vessels "like the spaces between the stars" on an immense ocean as "wild and unfathomable," as humbling, as Mount Katahdin. "Creeping along the endless beach amid the sea-squawl and the foam," he wrote, "it occurs to me that we, too, are the product of sea-slime. It is a wild, rank place, and there is no flattery in it. . . . There is naked Nature—inhumanly sincere, wasting no thought on man, nibbling at the cliffy shore where gulls wheel amid the spray." In spirit I follow his wandering footprints along "footpaths through which the sand flows out and reveals the nakedness of the land."

I feel the lure of discovery whenever I cross the Sagamore Bridge over the Cape Cod Canal, a deep channel that was once an outlet of glacial Lake Cape Cod. In 1717, to keep wolves off the cape, the town of Sandwich proposed a border wall along the whole length of what is now the canal, but it abandoned the project for fear that a wall would keep wolves on the cape, not off it. Cape Cod marks the northern limit of the ranges of some bird species as well as many plants. On my first bird trips here, Steve, former BBC president Joe Paluzzi, and Susan Hedman showed me a Yellow-Breasted Chat and Northern Bobwhite, birds tough to find anywhere north. Steve liked finding birds for others and, better yet, teaching them how and where to find birds on their own. When he showed me my first Grasshopper Sparrow, a flat-headed, buffy-breasted little bird he'd scoped at Crane Wildlife Management Area in North Falmouth, Steve was laughing. He could see the sparrow open its mouth, but he could no longer pick up high notes like its thin insect trill. Steve learned all he could about birds and amplified his knowledge through careful field observation. God help anyone who called his birding a "hobby."

At Marconi Station in Wellfleet—part of the great marine scarp from Eastham to Truro—I learned to identify Vesper Sparrows by their flashing white outer tail feathers, their shuffling gait, and three-part whistle-warble. When we heard a bobwhite, its call unmistakable even to a novice, I pursued the sound through shrubs and stunted trees until I saw a neckless, tailless quail-thing running away from me. We found few birds on the White Cedar Swamp Trail, where the cedars are so closely spaced, the shade so dark, that few flowering plants grow, but I learned that this woodland was the most reliable place in the state to find a Chuck-will's-widow, the whip-poor-will's more southerly nightjar cousin. I returned alone one night and ran into a birding friend, Lenny Jackson. We should have been content to hear the bird's rhythmic, onomatopoeic song, but the sound sucked us deeper and deeper into a stumbling chase through dense thickets in darkness. The bird taunted us, now close, now further off, until we were utterly lost. We never did see it. It never stopped singing.

Some of my cape trips have been rarity chases: a Little Egret that missed the sign for Europe, a migrating Gray Kingbird that overshot Florida, a Bell's Vireo's that outwaited many other birders until only I was still there to see it. I swear that vireo winked at me. Any report of a rare bird poses a dilemma. Was it a fly-by or found in a place where it might stick around? Should I get there at dawn the next day or wait for confirmations and risk the chance that it's a two-day wonder? How long should I wait at a stake-out until I try other likely spots? Depending on success or failure, I've congratulated myself for brilliant strategies and upbraided myself for miscalculations.

Many rarities have been found on the islands, which means a pricey ferry ride and at least a whole-day commitment, so I've ruled the islands off-limits for chases. Mary doesn't believe me. I don't blame her: it depends, I guess, on how rare the bird is.

The fun of a chase includes fellow chasers, often friends from around the state that I see only when we're looking for rare birds. One day I came across Steve while we were searching for Cave Swallows on the cape. I gave up after a while and checked Marconi, where I found a rare Scissor-Tailed Flycatcher, reported a week earlier but not seen for days. When Steve arrived at Marconi I showed him the flycatcher—a juvenile with its tail still elongating—and then he drove back to share the news with the folks still hoping for swallows. Whenever rare birds were found, Steve would use every available means—phone, car, feet, Pony Express—to get the word out.

The oddest "chases" are backyard stakeouts, like the one for a vagrant Broad-Billed Hummingbird frequenting a feeder in November in South Yarmouth, as if the cape were next door to Nueva Laredo. A few of us, all strangers, were there one morning when the bird showed up. We danced about as if we'd all bet on the same longshot at the track. Sometimes word leaks out of a rarity hanging around someone's yard, but the homeowner doesn't want a horde of binocular-wearing outlanders traipsing through the neighborhood, so, to our chagrin, birders are disinvited. But the South Yarmouth folks, thrilled by rare-bird serendipity, welcomed all visitors, arranged a sem-circle of viewing chairs, and set up a heat-lamped feeder cover to keep the hummingbird cozy in their yard. One winter day another cape homeowner saw me shivering in her yard, like some lost, hopeful beggar, as I waited out a Western Tanager. She gestured me inside, gave me a cup of coffee and a blueberry muffin, and set me up in front of her picture window.

In February I sometimes come to the cape for the BBC duck prowl. Steve used to say, "Get your ducks in a row early"—that is, find the various duck species before migrant songbirds arrive. Falmouth, with its many ponds and a long coastline along Nantucket Sound, offers a nice variety of both freshwater and sea ducks. Our leader, Eddie Giles, club president during our one-hundredth anniversary, is a gregarious guy who likes to lead people on "prowls" for ducks, owls, or whatever. We crisscross roads reminiscent of Wampanoags and early English settlers—Sippewissett, Teaticket—as we prowl for ducks from Siders Pond in Falmouth to Mill Pond in Marston Mills. "You do what?" my prebirding self might wonder. "In winter?" But he was a callow young man. Among duck beauties the Northern Pintail is all elegance, streamlined, low-riding, with a long, pointy tail and white neck arcing gracefully into a narrowing white stripe. The Canvasbacks and Redheads are handsome cousins with a family resemblance, but distinctive in color and profile, the larger Canvasback with a ski-sloped face, chestnut head, and bright white "canvas" body. Both species are scarce in the East but still common breeders in Midwestern prairie potholes. With ducks, as with birds generally, rarity is relative. On the cape we'll search for a scarce Eurasian Wigeon keeping company with its common baldpate cousins, American Wigeons, but on a winter tour of Holland, my British companions kept sorting through the everyday Eurasians with the remote hope of finding a single American, designated a "rare straggler" in *Birds of Europe*.

In winter the cape is stark, raw, the summer people gone, tourists few, and many locals struggling to find work. Birdsong is scant, the plants dormant under frozen mud, the shorebirds long gone from the ponds, though a few Great Blue Herons are still here, chancing the elements while their fellows have migrated south. In "Herons in Winter in the Frozen Marsh" Mary Oliver describes two herons on the cape "mired in nature, and starving," hunkered as they stand to attention in "stubbled desolation" until the marsh softens. In *The Primal Place* (1983) cape resident Robert Finch describes the victims of a long freeze on the cape: "Grebes huddled in a single remaining patch of water less than four feet across. Their lives had been whittled down to this one small opening against the encroaching ice, an opening so small it was conceivable that only their collective body heat was keeping it open." Rump footed, the grebes struggle to take off from land or ice and may paint themselves into a corner by taking refuge in any open water. Finch also describes Canada Geese trapped by the freeze: "Migration was now their only chance, but most had become too weakened by hunger to attempt it. Their strategy of waiting it out was proving fatal."

In summer I come to the cape on safari, though the reshaping of South Beach has made access difficult and BBC groups might trek elsewhere around Chatham and beyond. We meet at the Monomoy National Wildlife Refuge headquarters, past a causeway through marsh, where in 2002 birders discovered Gerard Manley Hopkins's "windhover"—a rare Eurasian Kestrel. To civilians, our pack of birders might look like lost pleasure-seekers in search of a luau, but our safaris take us to great congregations of terns and shorebirds. The Red Knots—known for their huge gatherings during migrations to eat horseshoe crabs at Chesapeake Bay—like the mussel beds. Their temporary neighbors, the oystercatchers, don't exactly "catch" but rather probe, stab, and hammer. Piping Plovers and Least Terns feed along the wrack line, where knotted wrack—dead seaweed—accumulates at the highest tide line. We scan inlets for the scarce bigger shorebirds: graceful Hudsonian Godwits, their long bills probingly upturned;

Marbled Godwits, tawny and bulkier with straight lance-like bills; and on inland flats, Whimbrels with long, downcurved bills. We sort through scores of "peeps," Least and Semipalmated Sandpipers, looking for one that has the droopy bill and reddish scapular of a rare Western Sandpiper. The year Steve died, one sunbaked safari-goer staggered through a crowd of Semipalmated Plovers and asked them, "Why can't one of you be a Wilson's Plover?" The Laughing Gulls laughed at him. If a Laughing Gull's laugh sounds too hollow, not piercing enough, we'll check to see if it's a rare Franklin's Gull. We have found some rarities, like a Little Stint, a peep from Eurasia that had joined a shorebird flock along Morris Island. We've also come across birders, stifling their smugness, who've told us that, a mile back, we walked right by a rare Sandwich Tern.

From the beach, amid shells carried by both southern and northern currents, we scan the ocean for jaegers, the local pirates. The nimble Parasitic Jaegers chase terns to steal their fish. The bulkier Pomarine Jaegers, more easily outmaneuvered, will follow trawlers for discarded catch. Bullies the jaegers may be, but just as cowbirds are obligated to parasitize, so jaegers were born to rob lunches. From inland-facing shores, we sort through the hundreds of camped-out terns, trying to isolate those that aren't Common Terns. The Roseate Terns, with black bills and distinctive harsh cries, are only faintly rosy but paler and slighter than Commons. The scarce Black Terns merely hint at blackness when not in breeding plumage. A possible Arctic Tern might set off a prolonged debate about worn plumage, carpal bars, and the bird's leg length.

Watching terns, I think of John Hay watching terns. Born in Ipswich, Hay came to the cape in 1942 to study with writer Conrad Aiken, served in World War II, and spent the rest of his life in a home he built in Brewster, where he wrote about the "great house of nature." To Hay, terns were "a great tribe of searchers" adapted to all the elements of flight and shoreline, their movements rhythmic as the seasons, their feathers contoured for "the flow and stress of the atmosphere." The Arctic Tern, which "experienced more daylight than any creature on earth," is "a bird of light, engaged in an ancestral practice that challenged the planet." Roseate Terns knifing through the air evoke William Blake's "arrows of desire." Hay loved the names for terns: medricks, mackerel gulls, striking peters, paytricks. In *Spirit of Survival: A Natural and Personal History of Terns* (1974), he describes terns as an intricate, reciprocal, striving "society," the pairs bonding through complex ceremonial courtship, their offspring begging for food and then learning to fish as hungry impatience became concentrated into skill through trial and error.

As ancient travelers, Hay felt, terns "tie all skies together" and trigger what he calls the "psychic receiver in us, the biological inheritor" that's "ready for each scent, sound, and motion within the trees." Life on earth, he believed, is a "depth of alliances." Birds and people alike know "constant inner relocations." Tern behavior might seem stereotypical, but they're responsive, anticipatory spirits: "Their repeated rituals and migrations, their passionate, seasonal needs, are part of a world of search and discovery." To watch the terns, to share their world, is "to extend your weather, and your range." But Hay feared that people were losing their knowledge of wildlife and their place in nature. "Timberdoodles, shitepoles, ragged robins, skunk coots, wall-eyed herring and quawks are disappearing into books," he wrote. "We were turning into perpetual migrants with no recognizable place to go, continually exchanging houses and land, so that Cape Cod could be the same flat, insulated place we were trying to make of Arizona."

North of Chatham, Fort Hill in Eastham offers a glorious view of long barrier spits, an inlet into Nauset Harbor, and wide expanse of salt marsh. The coastal plain extends seaward and underwater to the continental shelf. The inlet has shifted over centuries. "What the Ocean takes from one part of the Cape it gives to another," wrote Thoreau. In the seventeenth century, he noted, Eastham voted that, to protect crops, "every unmarried man in the township shall kill six blackbirds, or three crows, while he remains eligible; as a penalty for not doing it, shall not be married until he obey this order." But the blackbirds continued to "molest the corn." Thoreau concluded that "either many men were not married, or many blackbirds were."

Nauset Harbor is where Champlain and his crew were astonished by Black Skimmers when he mapped this part of the cape in 1605. A boat trip, like those run regularly by Mass Audubon's Wellfleet Bay sanctuary, is still the best way to see the birds out in Nauset Marsh. On the grasslands of Fort Hill, Eastern Kingbirds, kestrels, and occasional bobwhites feed in fields of beach pea and Queen Anne's lace. The trail winding into the marsh below the hill might lead to a cryptic Virginia Rail, a scarce Nelson's Sparrow (a close relative of Saltmarsh Sparrow) in fall migration, or even a rare Yellow Rail. Black-Crowned Night-Herons bark like stray dogs as they glide by the marsh in the evening.

As the Chatham terns recall John Hay, so the Nauset dunes conjure his comrade in spirit, Henry Beston. In 1925 Beston, a Harvard graduate and an ambulance driver during World War I, bought land in Eastham and had a carpenter build him a small house on a sand mound thirty feet from the ocean, a place where he could be alone "beyond the violences of men" on a "last fragment of an ancient and vanished land." His record of his year there, *The Outermost House* (1928), is about solitude, but it's not a book that gazes inwards. All the drama and mystery are in the dunes, the waves, the great rivalry between ocean and beach, the hazardous migrations of shorebirds, and the struggles of men and birds alike to survive the fury of winter storms.

Beston calls himself a "scholar with a poetic joy in the visible world." He marvels at shorebird synchronicity and the enigma of bird tracks in sand, beginning nowhere, leaving a trace of alighting wing, then vanishing into "the trackless nowhere of sky." He learns that creation is dynamic, ongoing. After songbirds leave the cape in late summer, they're replaced by Arctic seabirds migrating thousands of miles "from the nest-strewn crevices and ledges of Atlantic rocks no man has ever named or scaled." Beston exclaims, "What a gesture of ancient faith and present courage such a flight is, what a defiance of circumstance and death—land wing and hostile sea, the fading land behind, the unknown and the distant articulate and imperious in the bright, aerial blood." Birds connect him to earth's rhythms and humble him: "In a world older and more complete than ours, they move finished and complete, gifted with extensions of the senses we have lost or never attained, living by voices we shall never hear. They are not brethren, they are not underlings, they are other nations."

Beston, like Hay, was appalled to come upon seabirds dead in the sand or doomed from oil spills. He brought one oil-soaked Dovekie home to save it, but it wouldn't eat. Birds, he believed, were highly adaptable, but there were dangers—oil slicks drifting into their sleep—no bird could guard against. Like Hay, Beston also feared that people were becoming alienated from nature, "piteously ignorant" of both the "great earthly realities" and their own natures. "The world to-day is sick to its thin blood for lack of elemental things," he wrote, "for fire before the hands, for water welling from the earth, for air, for the dear earth itself underfoot." Humans were losing their "animal faith."

Wellfleet Bay Wildlife Sanctuary, up the coast from Eastham, is part of a vast estuary with salt marsh, moors, pinewoods, and a beach along the bay. Bobwhites used to visit the feeders at the nature center, but they've been replaced by bands of Wild Turkeys feeding alongside the finches and sparrows. Twice I've come to the nature center for rarity stake-outs. The first day that I was able to drive after a hip dislocation was also the first day in many weeks that a rare Lazuli Bunting failed to show up at the feeders. I had better luck with a Hoary Redpoll, a little finch with a pushed-in face, stubby yellow bill, red cap (poll), and frosty (hoary) body. The Hoary is cousin to the darker, streakier Common Redpoll. Both are Arctic breeders that occasionally "irrupt" south in winter searching for food, though Hoary Redpolls rarely get as far south as our state.

The sandplain grasslands and coastal heathlands preserved at Wellfleet Bay are types of natural communities dwindling on Cape Cod. The trails here offer a spectrum of birds in their varied habitats: migrant warblers in woodlands, Eastern Bluebirds and Prairie Warblers breeding in fields, egrets and Glossy Ibises—and on one visit a few rare White Ibises—feeding in salt marsh. Try Island, a remnant of hardwood forest, provides a long view of salt marsh stretching toward the bay. In late summer Whimbrels feed on fiddler crabs scuttling around the boardwalks that cross the marsh, while uncommon Forster's Terns might forage along the beach. One evening at Goose Pond, I watched a Green Heron still-hunt until it stabbed a fish through its eye. Poised near it at pond's edge was a Yellow-Crowned Night-Heron—lankier, more nocturnal, and scarcer than a Black-Crowned. Overhead, some Fish Crows honked like American Crows with sinus issues. Steve could never resist the old birders' joke about their nasal, naysaying calls. "Are you an American Crow?" he would ask. *Uh uh*, a Fish Crow would answer. No.

Ever since Eugene O'Neill put on plays with the Provincetown Players over a century ago, the Outer Cape has drawn artists who know the birds on their patches. Cape poets conjure the rippling and rotting of salt marsh, catbirds mewing in thickets of dusty green beach plums, poverty grass crunching underfoot, or a hummingbird wheeling past a silvery pond. In Mary Oliver's "White Owl Flies into and out of the Field," a Snowy Owl strikes the ground and its prey "with a force that left the imprint of the tips of its wings—five feet apart—and the grabbing thrust of its feet, and the indentation of what had been running through the white valleys of the snow." Brendan Galvin's *Whirl Is King* (2008) is a whole book of bird poems. Jays call back and forth with "voices full of elbows." Towhees are painted black and reddish with Japanese brush strokes. In his "A Constant, A Mystery," the crows are both a constant, trapping a Merlin in a pine top or stutter-stepping as they glean beaches, and a mystery, self-reliant yet somehow "pulling together out of divided labors."

The sands rising along the highway by Pilgrim Lake signal visitors to the Outer Cape that they're nearing land's end. As early as 1800, through wind and human-abetted erosion, the dunes here had started to bury Provincetown. Beyond Pilgrim Lake, a lagoon now shut off from the sea, the sands creep up trees and encroach on the road. In "The Spiral" from *A Place Apart: A Cape Cod Reader* (2009), Cynthia Huntington describes living on a foothold of sand "beyond the last bedrock, past the crust of the glacial deposit." The dunes are the "ground the sea gave back, returned from every shore its storms have ripped or currents tugged or tides unraveled." Her foothold is constantly moving, the sand keeping its form "barely longer than water; only the most recent wave or the last footprint stays on its surface." Her shack rocks in the wind, the pilings gently lifting. "When the lamps are put out," she says, "we feel the whole place sway like a boat at anchor, and there is nothing fixed or steady, only these currents carrying us along in the dark."

At Race Point—the last stretch of Cape Cod National Seashore—there's a powerful sense that you've reached the end of the line. Here, wrote Thoreau, "there was nothing but that savage ocean between us and Europe." With the sea lurching toward him, each wave leaving "the sand all braided or woven, as it were, with a coarse woof and warp," he felt that primeval chaos still reigned on this shore. Along the beach he found "ceaseless activity" in storm or calm, "fugacious" terns crying out amid the breakers, shorebirds "keeping time with the elements," and the "tender young of the Piping Plover, like chickens just hatched, mere pinches of down on two legs, running in troops, with a faint peep, along the edge of the waves." The boldness of the gulls prompted him to expound on the derivation of "gull"—to fool, to take in. "Indeed," he concludes, "all gulls are foolishly bold and easy to be shot."

Race Point is actually the westernmost point of the Outer Cape—the wrist of a hand reaching back eastward. Stellwagen Bank is just a few miles north, and the water remains deep close to shore. Seabirds migrating south are intercepted by a land mass jutting into the ocean. Many rarities have been found here, like a Yellow-Billed Loon in 2016 (twice I trudged, twice I missed). In late summer and early fall it's the best place on land in our state to watch jaegers and shearwaters. The shearwaters are "tubenoses" with specialized nostril tubes that, in a vast, pathless ocean, enable them to track the chemical odors of plankton, which lead them to fish and squid. They use their sense of smell both to forage and to find their way back to their home territories. They're named for their long-winged, angling, shear-the-waves flight, a means of using surface winds to glide from updraft to updraft in a style that distinguishes them from other seabirds. In late August 2017, huge schools of "peanut bunker" (juvenile menhaden) drew thousands of four shearwater species—Greater, Cory's, Sooty, Manx—to feed for days in a frenzy close to shore. Off a stretch of beach that will one day be ocean floor again, the shearwaters, like Melville's seabirds on Rock Rodondo, seemed indifferent to any human activity. Birders waded into cold ankle-deep water to film the spectacle all around them. One observer counted eighteen thousand Greater Shearwaters in a day.

The Outer Cape is the edge of a continent, but you can find more seabirds if you keep going east, out to sea. On Cape Cod, like Cape Ann, birders often join whale watches to look for oceanic birds with the whales, and each year the BBC offers a schedule of "dedicated" (to birds) pelagic trips, including two-day outings from Hyannis that head beyond Nantucket Shoals and the Gulf of Maine to Hydrographer, Atlantis, and Veatch Canyons. Darwin, during his voyage on the *Beagle*, was amazed by the abundance of oceanic life he found along submarine canyons. Like many birders, I'm of two minds about pelagic trips. I've spent days on rough seas in a steady state of green-about-the-gills queasiness, and I've never been able to sleep on board, either with the engine noise and oil smell in the bunks below deck, or under the stars on the top deck, where the boat's ceaseless rocking has rolled me back and forth all night. Still, as we leave land behind, with the wind in our faces, I feel a pull, a mounting anticipation, for we never know when birds might appear between boat and horizon or what birds they might be. Seabirds are the world's great wanderers.

Canyon trips offer possibilities of birds rarely seen from land. Audubon's Shearwaters, the smallest of North American shearwaters, breed in the Caribbean and wander north into the warm waters of the Gulf Stream south of Cape Cod. Long-tailed Jaegers, sleek Arctic breeders, migrate far off our coasts toward their winter homes in the Southern Hemisphere. Red-Necked Phalaropes, spindly and needle billed, and their less common cousins, Red Phalaropes, are aquatic shorebirds that nest on Arctic tundra ponds and winter in small flocks along lines of "rockweed"—seaweed that surf has detached from coastal rocks. Birders from around the county come on

BBC trips for the chance to see White-faced Storm-petrels, which breed off the northwest coast of Africa. All storm-petrels "walk" on water—thus their name, after Saint Peter—but while the common, darker Wilson's Storm-Petrel tippy-toes and patters, the white-bellied, black-masked White-faced bounds and hopscotches, like a stone skipping itself across the Atlantic.

Pelagic birding presents identification challenges. Many storm-petrels and shearwater look much alike; they're ever on the move; and we're trying to identify them while bobbing and reeling with a boat. BBC trips have several experts on board to spot distant birds and make the tough calls. In 2007 we found a Little Shearwater, the first record ever in Massachusetts waters. I could tell that it was little, smaller than an Audubon's, and I noted its pale face and rounded head, but if I ever see another Little Shearwater, I'll need another expert to tell me so. A friend on one trip didn't realize we'd seen a rare Band-Rumped Storm-Petrel until he got home and scrutinized his hundreds of storm-petrel photos. Birders are primed to identify birds first and foremost, but I've learned to keep watching individuals after I know what they are: to discover their habits, to imprint on memory their styles of flight—Leach's Storm-Petrels tack and climb walls of water as if chased—or to take in the drama of a Common Tern dodging through a gauntlet of pirate jaegers. When a humpback whale breaches and whirls above the sea or bottlenose dolphins glide through air like Apollo's children or a whale shark butts the stern of the boat as if playing bumper cars, I might forget about birds altogether.

On the long ride back to port I'll chat with fellow birders, reliving birds we've seen and hoping for species we've yet to see—a skua, please—but after a while, as the birds thin out, my thoughts will drift like floating rockweed. I'm a watchman at the prow with Champlain scanning the horizon for landfall on a great crossing into the unknown. Or I'm with Thoreau at

Race Point, looking strangely west across the ocean as the sun sets over the "native hills" of Massachusetts. Or I'm stranded at sea, homeland gone, no future in sight. Before I started birding, I taught a family of Vietnamese refugees, all exceptional students, all determined to become self-reliant in America and grateful to their teachers, their "soul engineers." The youngest, a shy physics major, was quiet in class all semester until we discussed Stephen Crane's "The Open Boat," a story of four shipwrecked men, lost at sea, who curse Fate's cruelty and Nature's indifference. "This story is truth," he told his surprised classmates. "I was on an open boat. With my mother and sisters and brothers. For many days and many nights. We were scared. We didn't know what will become of us. We wished we could fly away like birds. I ask God: why must this happen to us? I curse, I beg."

On my last return from the canyons I thought of Steve Leonard when the captain announced that we were due east of Montauk at the tip of Long Island. When I last saw Steve he was looking for birds outside his eleventh-floor room at Beth Israel Hospital in Boston. Laura de la Flor, Susan Hedman, and I were there with his mother and two sisters—a warm family in which wit flowed easily. Steve turned from the window and said, "Once you become a birder, it's something you'll always have." After he died, from a brain tumor, his mother, Louise, told me, "Steve found himself through birding." He'd known some rough times, but through birds he'd found his passion and friends who shared his passion. Louise would sometimes go birding with his binoculars in "silent communion" with Steve. He'd chosen his own resting place—an aerie high on a bluff at Fort Hill in Montauk flanked by a Native American burial ground. Hawks hunt from the crags on the hill. Seabirds soar across Block Island Sound. Weathered boulders transported by glaciers mark the passage of time.

Chapter 18

RAVENS' HOME

West from My Patch

In satirical maps depicting the United States as seen by New Yorkers, like Saul Steinberg's 1976 *New Yorker* cover, New York City is huge and detailed, while the rest of the country is compressed, distorted, vague, or unwelcoming. Indian Territory is just west across the Hudson. The Gulf of Mexico, a few Great Lakes, and Japan lie on the city's outskirts. The South is the land of "Pig Humping and Religious Nuts." A vast blank area in the center is designated "High Fructose Corn Syrup." New England consists of "Fucking Red Sox Fans."

Bostonians, in the "hub of the universe," may not be quite that parochial, but our state too has always had an eastward slant. The name "Bay State" signifies our history of coastal orientation. Our State House, looking down on Boston Common, is far from the state's geographical center. A divide within our state was epitomized by construction of the Quabbin Reservoir in the 1920s, after expansion of a local water source into Wachusett Reservoir proved insufficient to provide enough water for metropolitan Boston. The Swift River Valley was ideally situated, a natural bowl that had to be damned only at the south end. The dams' foundations rested on the ledge of prehistoric riverbeds, and gravity would deliver water through aqueducts to lower-lying Boston. Engineers let the topography determine the reservoir's shape. Four towns—Dana, Enfield, Prescott, Greenwich—were flooded; 2,600 people were forced to relocate, 7,500 bodies relocated from local cemeteries to Quabbin Park Cemetery.

Throughout the state, unemployed workers hoped for tree-cutting jobs in clearing the valley, but Governor James Michael Curley let his cronies give the jobs to men in their eastern districts. Valley residents called these workers "woodpeckers" because many had never handled axes. Resentment was exacerbated by a plan, never realized, to divert the Connecticut River into the Quabbin. People in central Massachusetts complained that their resources were being used to subsidize the growth, waste, and poor planning of metropolitan Boston. Growth follows available fresh water. More water would bring more expansion; more expansion would bring demands for more water.

The history of our state's birding community also reflects a separation of east and west. The 1994 *A Birder's Guide to Eastern Massachusetts*, in the American Birding Association's series of state guides, stopped at the Quabbin. It wasn't until 2002 that westerners had their own *Bird Finding Guide to Western Massachusetts*. A popular Facebook photo-sharing page is called "Birding Eastern Mass," while the journal *Bird Observer* just dropped "Eastern Massachusetts" from its official title. Understandably, most bird reports come from the east, where birders are more concentrated, but while some shore and salt marsh birds rarely head inland, other species—Ruffed Grouse, Black Vultures, some breeding warblers—are far more likely outside eastern Massachusetts. I organized the Association of Massachusetts Bird Clubs, with clubs from around the state, in part to bring east and west together. We live in a small commonwealth. We want to see and protect the same birds. It would be a missed opportunity not to join forces.

Coming to Harvard from Illinois, I adopted the prevalent myopic view of Massachusetts. I hung out where students hung out, Harvard Square, the Back Bay, local schools with girls. Roxbury and South Boston might as well have been Dakar and South Dublin. The furthest I traveled was Wellesley, where high school friend Hillary Rodham, later Clinton, went to college. Gloucester, if I knew of it, was fuzzily north and fishy. Out west were boondocks, a few colleges, Tanglewood, cold winters, and runty mountains.

In my first years of birding, I rarely went far from home. There were birds around and great places on the North Shore to find them—the Great Marsh, Mass Audubon sanctuaries on the Ipswich River and Marblehead Neck. I learned to associate certain birds with certain locations, but I thought little about *why* they were in those locations. Birds' names were as likely to confuse as inform. Wood Thrushes liked woods, but so did "shorebird" woodcocks. Connecticut Warblers weren't any more likely in Connecticut. Only the Ipswich Sparrow, a subspecies, was named after any place in our state. I took note when birders showed surprise to find birds in peculiar spots—a Wild Turkey sixty feet up a tree on my first trip to Crooked Pond—but I wasn't sure where turkeys or other birds were supposed to be. Some birds had clearly strayed out of their element, like one Virginia Rail shopping in a convenience store, but it didn't seem so odd that American Tree Sparrows preferred bushes, or ground, to trees. They were birds; they could fly; they could go where they wanted. Wasn't that the point of being a bird?

It took me a surprising while to move from location—this bird can be found *here*—to the concept of habitat: this bird is here because this marsh or forest supplies what it needs to live and breed. A child of suburbia, I'd never considered the habitat needs of robins or jays. Like squirrels, these creatures were just there. In later travels, landscapes and seascapes remained mere scenery. That's an awesome mountain, that's a perfect stretch of beach. See how the light ripples on that woodland stream. If a pretty bird, big bear, or spindly moose flew, waddled, or splashed across the scene, well, great. It took the idea of habitat to make the world both more localized and more organized, more plausibly inhabited. Birds needed available food, safe nesting locations, water, places to hide, and a little or a lot of territory for each pair. If a habitat couldn't fill these needs, the birds weren't there. The sizes, bodies, colors, and behavior of birds were all connected to their habitats. On one trip to Peru I went out alone during lunch breaks and saw a few birds that mystified me. I didn't have a camera, but I carefully noted field marks and observed behavior. When I looked up the birds in my Peru book, they weren't there. I told our guide about my sightings and suggested possibilities, but he dismissed them out of hand. Vegetation too dense for one species, wrong altitude for another's habitat. I'd seen birds, but which birds he couldn't guess. I hadn't thought about habitat.

Most bird reports from across the state specify location without mention of habitat, but if the reports omitted birds altogether and instead described habitats within natural communities, you'd have clues to which birds you might find in these locations. A floodplain forest, for instance, is flat land covered by water when a river reaches its maximum height. Once common in our state, undisturbed floodplain forest communities now remain only in a few patches. One of my first westward destinations was Oxbow National Wildlife Refuge in Harvard—still east but outside the Route 495 corridor, a psychological border for birders from the coast. Much of the refuge is floodplain forest along the Nashua River, whose changing course has formed oxbow lakes. Many of our wetlands have disappeared or been degraded, and by 1970 the Nashua was counted among the country's ten most polluted rivers. The river is healthier now through conservation efforts, but this is hardly a pristine natural community, for the refuge borders Fort Devens Military Reservation. "Do not touch any unusual metallic objects you may discover," warns a brochure.

A disconcerting feature of birding here is the occasional sputtering of gunnery and whirring of helicopters.

At Oxbow I follow a loop route along the river, through wooded swamp, across a wetland with an active beaver colony, and down a woodland path that parallels railroad tracks. The changing course, height, and velocity of the river make this a dynamic community. Breeding birds are separated by habitat, with some overlap. Along the river bank I check for sprite-like Blue-Gray Gnatcatchers and, higher up, throat-flashing Yellow-Throated Vireos. Pine Warblers and Scarlet Tanagers sing in the swampy woodlands, where skunk cabbage and cardinal flowers live, often in heavy shade, amid red maple stands and yellow birches stilted on their root systems. One morning I heard a tanager singing very late in the season—a sign, Wayne Petersen has told me, that the bird might be a "Darwinian loser" who'd failed to mate or whose mate had died after eggs were hatched. Sedentary, sing-now-and-then Black-Billed and Yellow-Billed Cuckoos breed around forest edges and glades inhabited by colonies of sensitive and ostrich ferns. Wood Ducks nest in boxes and tree hollows along a boardwalk through sloughs with mud-loving water arum and arrowhead. In more open areas, Blue-Winged Warblers might *bee buzz* from low shrubs, while Indigo Buntings whistle from treetops. On a sunlit trail a row of garter snakes might slither off like a chorus line unfolding.

I investigate the local news, the caws of crows flying toward some source of excitement, or fresh scat along a trail. Like many birders, I can be too restless, but I've tried to learn to linger with the birds. Marie Read describes how photography taught her the patience and birdlike stillness to watch until birds ignore her: "You'll notice the subtle behavior cues birds give before doing something cool and dramatic—a duck performing its courtship display, an eagle taking flight, or a waxwing tossing back a berry." Painter Catherine Hamilton discovered that when she draws a bird, the bird draws her into its realm. Observation "encompasses not only what that bird is or what it is doing, but also what that bird might do." I usually pass by the monotonous, hard-to-spot Red-Eyed Vireos, but one morning, on a whim, I started counting a vireo's songs. I got to two hundred before I remembered that Canadian naturalist Louise de Kiriline Lawrence once reported a Red-Eyed singing 22,187 times in a day. I turned to a Brown Creeper, spiraling up one tree trunk after another, searching bark crevices for spiders, looking like bark itself, an object lesson in inconspicuousness. A female Black-Throated Blue Warbler baffled me until I noticed the diagnostic white "handkerchief" at the base of her primaries. She wasn't blue; her throat wasn't black. Like many females, she'd been stuck with her mate's name. At forest's edge I waited along with a female Sharp-Shinned Hawk, perched still and concealed, watching for that moment when some songbird failed to be watchful enough. Finally the hawk bulleted into a thicket, but its intended prey, maybe a Song Sparrow, eluded it. The hawk and its shadow disappeared.

I have one target species at Oxbow, the Ruffed Grouse, a bird I've seen twice here and heard on other visits. Grouse are also targeted by hunters, who, like birders, try to detect clues in habitat with an animal's steady vigilance. One day I came upon a young, camouflaged hunter returning disheartened from a failed grouse quest. Awkwardly aware of our conflicting interests, we chatted about grouse decline. I was glad he hadn't shot a grouse but discouraged about my own chances. Above us, a Blue Jay mocked a Red-Shouldered Hawk's *keer keer keer* to send a false alarm or just for the hell of it. Next, the jay might taunt us by drumming like a grouse. I've often missed grouse, along with other scarce birds reported here, like White-Eyed Vireo, but if you curse the birds you've missed on a given day in Massachusetts, you might as well curse the birds you didn't see that day in Key West or Madagascar. The should-have-seen lists that some birders keep can soon lead to regretful lists of desirable mates they should've hooked up with in high school, when they had the chance.

West of Oxbow, the Quabbin reservation is a vast area with varied habitats and trails to explore. The word "Quabbin" derives from the Nipmuck *qaben*, or "meeting of the waters." Most Nipmucks ("freshwater people") were killed or driven out of Massachusetts after they joined the Wampanoags in a raid on Brookfield during King Philip's War. A war marker in New Braintree commemorates Sarah Rowlandson, who died after a few days in captivity from wounds suffered during a raid on Lancaster. Her mother, Mary, wrote an often anthologized "Indian captivity narrative," a popular seventeenth-century genre, part adventure story, part testament of faith. To my knowledge no marker commemorates any of the Nipmucks who were captured or killed in raids of their homes.

Travel in most of the Quabbin reservation is restricted to foot. Fishing, dogs, and alcohol aren't allowed. Thomas Conuel titled his book about Quabbin *The Accidental Wilderness*, or wilderness as afterthought, brought about by limitations on access and restrictions to protect the water. We live in an age when wildlife habitats can "grow" in places no longer inhabited by humans. On the Colorado prairie, Rocky Mountain Arsenal has been called our nation's most ironic nature park. Used for chemical weapons manufacturing in World War II, then production of pesticides, the arsenal was one of our country's worst toxic dumps, designated a Superfund site. But once people were gone, it became a park and, after cleanup, a national wildlife refuge—a winter roost for Bald Eagles and home to Burrowing Owls, American White Pelicans, and bison. The demilitarized zone (DMZ) between North and

South Korea—a heavily mined strip 250 kilometers long and 4 kilometers wide—has been called a "de facto wildlife preserve" and "accidental paradise." The deserted wetlands have become winter homes for rare Black-Faced Spoonbills and Red-Crowned Cranes, which need big, open spaces. Ironically, DMZ birds would probably suffer as much from a lasting peace treaty as from resumption of all-out war. War would bring bombs and disruption. Reunification would pave the way for farms and factories and farms that would fragment and degrade the habitat. Wildlife may thrive in the DMZ only if it remains a no-man's land.

In Quabbin Park a birding tour often starts at Winsor Dam by the visitors' center on the reservoir's southern shore. Wild Turkeys roam the edges of grassy fields by the dam. Common Ravens have nested on the rock face near the bridge. Pairs at their nests defend territory from other ravens, head out to scavenge, and shelter their young, squawking to stay in contact. One day I was lucky enough to watch as a twosome rose in a courtship dance. They rolled through updrafts, lifted up, banked, and tumbled down like bungee-jumpers.

Past the bridge, near a memorial to engineer Frank Winsor, "warbler ridge" is a good spot for migrant warblers and breeding birds like Yellow-Bellied Sapsuckers and American Redstarts. With patient help from Steve Leonard, leading a BBC trip, I saw my first Cerulean Warbler here, a flash of blue moving high through the trees. Like Hermit Thrushes, Cerulean Warblers are absent from forests with tracts smaller than about 460 acres. Steve usually resisted club trips—"too damn many people"—but on the rare occasions when he led trips, he became as solicitous as a Mallard with ducklings. He couldn't rest easy until everyone had seen every bird.

BBC groups often picnic beneath the tower on Great Quabbin Mountain, five hundred feet above the floor of the Swift

River Valley, with a panorama of wooded hills along the wide horizon and former mountains that are now islands in the reservoir. In fields around the base of the tower hill we've found breeding Prairie Warblers and Field Sparrows. Nearby Enfield Lookout is a popular place to watch for Bald Eagles, once common Northeast breeders but then extirpated in Massachusetts through pesticides, pollution, and shooting. The state's first successful eagle restoration project began at the Quabbin in 1982. We scan the water's edges for eagles perched erect in tall pines. In winter, if the reservoir is frozen, they'll gather on the ice at a deer carcass that might also attract ravens, crows, and coyotes. Golden Eagles have been seen here, but they're rare and wary. In late spring you can hear the echoed cries of breeding Common Loons, also once extirpated in our state but making a comeback at Quabbin. Hurricanes have blown seabirds, like a Leach's Storm-Petrel and a rare White-Tailed Tropicbird, all the way from the ocean to the Quabbin's inviting waters.

Along the reservoir's west side is a highway named for Daniel Shays, a former Revolutionary War captain from Pelham who organized a rebellion against the national government over worthless currency and corruption. The rebels were defeated by militia in 1787 after they tried to capture the Springfield arsenal. Shays escaped to Vermont and was eventually pardoned. Old Pelham cemetery is the site of Warren Gibbs's notorious "poison epitaph" tombstone, inscribed by his brother William to accuse Warren's wife Mary of killing him with arsenic-laced oysters. Because of multiple thefts the current tombstone is a replica, and one local historical curator believes that the whole Gibbs story may be a hoax, old fake news. At West Quabbin the north birds meet the south birds. Breeders with more northernly ranges, like Yellow-Rumped Warblers and Blue-Headed Vireos, mingle with southernly breeders like

Yellow-Throated Vireos and Acadian Flycatchers. BBC groups walk along wooded ravines, past crumbling stone walls and old cellar holes, to look for the Acadians in deep forest as they "sing"—two abrupt, accented notes—from perches along the edges of dark, cool brooks.

Near the Swift River on the reservoir's east side is Gate 40. For decades Mark Lynch has led birding trips around Quabbin and around the state (and at museums to identify birds in works of art), and he's seen more varieties of animals along the trails here—turtles, snakes, flying squirrels, bobcats—than at any other place in Massachusetts. On my first hike here I looked up to find a plump porcupine eating buds off a stunted hemlock. I'm still hoping for an opossum, a relative newcomer to the region who's not crazy about our winters. I can still envision the scenes where BBC trip leaders pointed out my first Red-Shouldered Hawk crying *keer keer keer* over Pottapaug Pond, my first Alder Flycatcher rolling its notes from an exposed perch at Cotton Grass Marsh, and a startled Ruffed Grouse seeking cover near the old cellar foundations of Dana Common.

North of Quabbin, just below the New Hampshire border, is Royalston, a lovely little town I would never have discovered except for birding. A white church steeple rises above the town common and quiet roads lined with white picket fences. At Royalston Falls, a tributary of the Tully River plunges into a misty ancient gorge bordered by tall cinnamon ferns. At nearby Doane's Falls, rocky Lawrence Brook rushes under a stone arch bridge and cascades over granite ledges shaded by hemlocks and pines. I was brought to Royalston on BBC trips to look for winter finches, which breed further north but sometimes move south into our state searching for food in winter. At a feeder on the outskirts I saw my first Evening Grosbeaks—noisy, big-headed, big-billed uberfinches that roller-coaster through air like binged-out goldfinches that have been scorched by tropical yellow lightning. In town were my first Pine Grosbeaks, a bit bigger but more subdued in color and demeanor as they poked around crabapples and shuffled along the ground, tolerating our close presence. That day they were joined by a group of rare Bohemian Waxwings, equally tame as they fed on fruit. Like more common Cedar Waxwings, which breed in our state, Bohemians sometimes gorge on frozen berries until they have trouble getting airborne or, intoxicated on fermented berries, find themselves stumbling along. The positions of their crests tell whether they're relaxed or fearful. Like Northern Flickers, waxwings illustrate the "you are what you eat" principle, since their diet can affect plumage color. The waxy yellow tail bands for which they're named may turn orange if they eat too many honeysuckle berries.

One winter day, alone, I tracked a band of Golden-Crowned Kinglets as they foraged in yards around Royalston. High-metabolism birds, smaller than warblers, kinglets must eat all day long, feeding mostly on hibernating caterpillars, to avoid starving and freezing to death in winter. They face risks whether they migrate or stay north through winters with severe storms and icing. As they moved through town the kinglets kept calling to stay in contact. They need to stay cohesive until night, when they huddle together, fluffed out to conserve heat with heads and feet tucked into their feathers. In *Winter World* (2003) Bernd Heinrich celebrates kinglets for their toughness and adaptability: their defiance of the odds proves "the fabulous is possible." Their evolutionary history is linked to the Ice Ages: "Always it was those that could either stand the cold longest or that could fly the farthest that would collect the largest bounty in the spring."

At Skinner State Park, west of the Quabbin, a shaded road winds up Mount Holyoke, the westernmost peak in the

Holyoke Range. Rugged trails traverse the range's woodlands. The mountain was formed about two hundred million years ago when lava flowed from the valley floor, cooled, and was upended. Glaciers scoured the mountain and exposed bedrock. Forest fragmentation has driven songbirds from many of our woodlands, but the intact habitat here still draws breeding Hermit Thrushes and Cerulean Warblers. Blackburnian Warblers flare orange throats in the canopies. Drabber Worm-Eating Warblers trill insect-like on the slopes. Dark-Eyed Juncos, gone from lower elevations in spring, flash their tails. BBC trips here are often reunions of former presidents like Eddie Giles, Glenn d'Entremont, Linda Ferraresso, and Laura de la Flor—all regulars who come for the birds, the leisurely uphill hike, and the companionship of old friends. If I think I've heard a Cerulean, Glenn, our go-to guy for song identification, might remind me that the more common Black-Throated Blue can sound similar. Last year we tracked down an Acadian Flycatcher singing near Devil's Football, an oval glacial erratic in the woods.

At the summit, the site of an old lodge with a deck and rocking chair, we look out on the Connecticut River, an oxbow lake to the southwest, the farms of Pioneer Valley, hills on the western horizon, and on clear days a view of four states. About four hundred miles long from its headwaters near the Canadian border to its mouth on Long Island Sound, the Connecticut is New England's largest river. In the ancient valley here, alluvial fans were formed by broken bedrock washed off the mountains. Prehistoric tracks imprinted on the rocks were once thought to be those of large birds but were probably left by small early dinosaurs. The river didn't form until the last glacier melted, retreated, and left long, narrow Lake Hitchcock, which eventually emptied and left a river flowing through the lake bed. Now, raptors fly over the valley during the days, while citizen scientists come to the summit at night to listen for nocturnal flight calls.

Westover Air Force Base, near Chicopee, is among the best places in the state for grassland birds that need large territories to breed. In recent years the Hampshire Bird Club, Allen Bird Club, and BBC have teamed up to lead trips here to seek "area-dependent" Upland Sandpipers and Grasshopper Sparrows, which now breed in our state only at airports, large remnant hayfields, and conserved meadows. The changing status of these birds reflects our state's ecological history. After the last glaciation New England was repopulated by tundra plants—lichens, mosses, stunted birch and willow—then spruces with sedge, then northern hardwoods that still stretch across the Berkshires and oak and hickory further south. Settlers pushing inland deforested the land, first for firewood, timber for building, and the clearing of land for farming, later for iron smelting and wood-burning locomotives and steamboats. Bald Eagles and Ospreys grew scarce. Interior-forest-nesting songbirds declined. Most beavers were gone from our state as early as the American Revolution, until they were reintroduced in the 1920s in the Berkshires, where a few deer and bear remained.

Early nineteenth-century Massachusetts has been called Indiana-like, a land with few trees and many fields of disturbed ground with weeds like crabgrass and devil's paintbrush, often introduced species which farming had spread across Europe. As distributions of forest birds shrank, grassland birds proliferated, including Eastern Meadowlarks, Vesper and Grasshopper Sparrows, and Upland Sandpipers, leggy "shorebirds" with long, tapered tails. After settlers quit farming, the abandoned fields were eventually taken over by second-growth forests of white pines and red cedars indicative of former grasslands—distinct from the mature old-growth or "virgin" forests now rare in our state. Despite ongoing development, almost two-thirds of Massachusetts is now covered by secondary forest, a far cry from Thoreau's time, when nearly three-quarters of the state had been deforested. Some birds of prey, like Cooper's and Red-tailed Hawks, grew more common as farmland was converted to forest. Others, like Barn Owls and Northern Harriers, declined as the grasslands they needed were lost or fragmented. Upland Sandpipers—birds heard screaming by Thoreau on Cape Cod—diminished as well.

Ecologist Aldo Leopold once said that if we want to restore a land's ecological integrity, we need to know what the land was like to begin with. But where to begin can be problematic. Some ecologists now debate *when* these grassland birds colonized the Northeast. Regional declines of grassland species were once largely ignored by conservationists, who considered these birds non-natives from western prairies that had colonized our region's "neosavanna" only because Europeans had cleared the land. But in 1997 Robert Askins argued that many of these birds are in fact native to the region, since they'd probably colonized the Northeast soon after Native Americans started using fire to clear land for farming, about 2000 years ago. The debate raises difficult questions. In discussions of natural communities like savannahs or forest floodplains, the word "natural" is often used to mean "undisturbed by humans," but unless our own species is unnatural by definition, the natural forces that shape habitats include the behavior of people who can transform and even eliminate a community. If we're to preserve Upland Sandpipers, does it matter whether it was Native Americans or Europeans who inadvertently brought them to our state? How long does a bird species, or a human family for that matter, have to live somewhere before we call it a "native"?

In spring and fall the mountains of central and western Massachusetts are the best places in our state to watch migrations of raptors, a spectacle that draws hawk-lovers as devoted and single-minded as pilgrims. To see good numbers of hawks, says raptor expert Paul Roberts, you have to *look* for hawks, at the right time and place, rather than hope for hawks in the usual course of birding. In fall, ideal migration conditions often occur on the day of or after the arrival of a high-pressure system, when cold air riding over warm earth on a clear day forms "thermals," columns of rising warm air. Broad-Winged Hawks, migrating as far as five thousand miles, rely on thermals, and hawk assemblies often ride a thermal in concentrations called "kettles." With few wingbeats, the hawks soar hundreds or thousands of feet to the point where the thermal dissipates, use the altitude to glide, then peel off and descend until they find another thermal to ride. Their kettles, Robert says, "often seem to boil to the limits of vision."

Wachusett Mountain, a 2,004-foot monadnock with open views in all directions, is our state's best-known hawk-watch site, drawing both diehards and now-and-then birders wanting to watch multitudes of raptors stream across the sky. In September 1978 more than ten thousand Broad-Wings flew over Wachusett within three hours. Some experienced watchers, looking off elsewhere, were astonished when they turned to find, passing overhead, the largest raptor procession ever seen in our state. Migrating raptors aren't all "hawks." They include Turkey Vultures and falcons like kestrels, and they vary in size, shape, wing and tail lengths, flight styles, and peak migration times. Dedicated hawk-watchers have spent years learning to distinguish them quickly and often at great distance. Some species, like Sharp-shinned Hawks, tend to be "ridge fliers," hunting as they migrate and relying on "orographic lift" created by wind deflecting off slopes or ridges. Raptor-lovers from the Eastern Mass Hawk Watch count passing birds as exactly as possible and publish annual data.

To hawk-watch at Mount Watatic, in the Wapack Range, you need to hike a rather steep trail, along paper birches and hemlocks, to reach the bald, rocky summit, but along the way you might see a Yellow-Bellied Sapsucker tapping for sap or hear White-Throated Sparrows singing *Old Sam Peabody Peabody Peabody*. At the summit the thermal and ridge fliers ride the wind, tilt, straighten, and careen off. Their patterns in the sky leave invisible contrails across the blue. One day I hiked up Watatic to see a rare Gray Jay that had come down from the north. Notorious as a beggar and "camp-robber," the jay kept its distance as other hikers mulled around the summit, but once they were gone, it hopped over companionably to see if I'd share my lunch.

Southwest of Wachusett, in the Ware River watershed, is Barre Falls Dam. Lured by reports of Golden Eagles, I drove here one morning to join a small, friendly group of hawk-watch regulars. Hawk identification takes birding to what Roberts calls "the limits of conjecture"—a truth born out when, after two hours, one regular called out "Golden Eagle." Given the bird's distance, the identification seemed premature, if not absurd, but minutes later a Golden Eagle, massive and dark golden in sunlight, with a now obvious dihedral, soared directly above us.

Afterwards I tracked down the ravens I'd heard croaking around a spillway past a bridge. Forget about eagles, these ravens seemed to say, in their guttural, inflected voices. If you want impressive birds, check us out. Ornithologists have isolated around eighty distinct raven vocalizations, which vary in pitch, intensity, duration, sequence, and repetition rate. In ancient cultures ravens were honored and feared for a spiritual power derived from their humanlike attributes—their ability to communicate, their apparent capacity for evil design—but they could transcend human limits because they possessed what the Celts called "raven knowledge," the ability to see and know all about the living, the lost, and the dead. Ravens are improvisational problem-solvers that can work alone or in teams. Living in a complex social order, they can keep track of all the other players, and their suspicions of fellow ravens while food-caching suggest that they possess a key prerequisite for social intelligence, a "theory of mind"—the ability to grasp that other individuals have minds of their own, with their own desires and intentions. To find food and suitable territories, ravens must seek out and learn from new experiences, and they seem to have struck the perfect balance between curiosity and wariness, between risk-taking and prudence. In their book *In the Company of Crows and Ravens* (2005), John Marzluff and Tony Angell say that the Common Raven may be the world's most adaptable bird, for it's the only species that "inhabits deserts, forests, scrublands, grasslands, taiga, *and* arctic tundra." Ravens know how to adapt to us.

Many of my ventures west have been rarity chases. Birders need occasional quests, and rare birds anywhere in the state offer quest opportunities. Sometimes the bird is dramatic, like the Trumpeter Swan in a flooded field in Northampton. Its lithe, long-necked whiteness seemed to shape the whole field into a swan-focus, and when it vocalized it became the grand white honking swan of ponds in Yellowstone and Denali. It hardly mattered when the Massachusetts Avian Records Committee couldn't determine that the swan was "wild," rather than reintroduced, because of its unknown origin. Less dramatic, in a Montague field, was a Henslow's Sparrow. The sparrow is more hiccuper than singer, yet it was satisfying to see a hardy individual from a species that, before it lost vast areas of habitat, once commonly bred in Eastern grasslands. The "quest" for an Allen's Hummingbird at a Great Barrington feeder was memorable for the bird itself—green and orange, tail feathers like pins—and for an ultimately fatal transmission breakdown that forced me to drive back across the whole state without coming to a full stop. My twitch for a Yellow-Legged Gull in

Turner Falls is harder to explain to a non-birder, since I'd seen this gull well in Europe and had already twitched for a putative Yellow-Legged on the cape that was eventually judged to be a probable hybrid offspring of other gulls. I couldn't find yellow legs on any of the gulls parked on the ice in Barton Cove, and James Smith, the gull's finder, never submitted an official record because this gull was probably a hybrid too. But it was a pleasant drive across the state to a pretty town.

My guide to birding beyond eastern Massachusetts stops at the Connecticut River, still some distance from the New York border, but one day I'll explore the plateaus and valleys of western Massachusetts, head up October Mountain for breeding Mourning Warblers, or join the Hoffmann Bird Club for an excursion in the Berkshires. Or I'll drive to the Quabbin to bike-bird around the villages of New Salem and Petersham with their spacious commons, high-spired churches, old burial grounds, granite hitching posts, and a country store with Greek Revival columns. The Harvard Forest museum in Petersham features dioramas illustrating the evolution of New England forests since the seventeenth century. I might stop along the way to explore some forest or bog that catches my eye. "There is pleasure," wrote Byron, "in the pathless woods."

Chapter 19

CONVALESCENCE

I can't see the bird, but I feel it. It's pecking, no, *sucking* on my index finger, with pressure, like a lippy little mammal at a nipple. The bird is warbler-sized, but the bill doesn't feel right for a warbler. Can you ID a bird by the heft of its beak on your finger?

I slip in and out of druggy dreams. Sheets twist into knots. My legs can't find a happy position. "Everything went fine," the doctor warbled. "You're doing terrific," chirped the visiting nurse. But the pain pills won't tolerate sleep or logic. Thoughts wobble like vultures that never land to eat. Oh, to be a woodcock, brain upside down and eyes able to see all around and above my head. I'll dance the woodcock cha-cha, forward, back, booty bopping. Flight calls: I'll spiral into dusky sky and twitter the air.

The bird's at my finger again, under the blankets. It's wounded. It wants comfort. I quiet my body. New lists: birds in dreams, birds felt while on heavy Oxycodone dosage, birds identified from bed. I rely on Mary for reports of changes in my consciousness. I moaned all night, snored. I must've slept.

Between dreams I patrol the street on crutches, up and down. Each day I pick up the pace a bit. Last year, a fused ankle. This year, a new hip with a "revision" of an old hip replacement to follow. Parts of me need rewriting. I'm lacking cartilage, but I don't have cancer. Geezer logic: arthritis reminds us that we're lucky to have outlived whatever evolution had in mind for our bodies. I hear an Osprey's punctuated whistle. I scan but can't find the bird. I crutch my way down the street to get open sky. There it is, like a fierce, shaggy gull-hawk floating over our house. New yard bird, chased on four legs.

I like the naming of birds. I like knowing their names. Firewood-Gatherer, See-see Partridge, Oleaginous Hemispingus. In Alaska our guide, Dave Stejskal, called the Olive-Sided Flycatcher the All-Excited Flycatcher. The bird sightings in the *Boston Globe* used to be transcribed from Voice of Audubon recordings. The transcriber wasn't a birder:

City Shearwater
Abe Lincoln Sparrows
Parallel Warbler
Pair of Green Falcons
Blue-Gray Napcatcher

Something taps beside my head. This is no dream. Sunlight floods the bedroom. More tapping. I tap back, loud, a territorial warning. It's a Downy Woodpecker. "Go away! We feed you suet. We let dead trees stand so you have cavities to nest. Why must you attack our house?" Tapping resumes, across the room now. I can't guard every wall.

Under the blankets the bird is at my finger, snuggled, convalescing. The moment feels naked. I feel another bird, at another finger—the same species, I'm sure, but with a lighter touch to its beak. A fledgling? How did these birds get here? It must've been on the flight back from England. The birds were cold, wind broken, they needed help. I hid them nestled under my jacket. I think they're goldfinches. I would never cage birds. It changes their songs forever.

I hear rumbling, a grouse drumming deep inside the earth. I hear petals growing, a chipmunk's pulse. My ears are binoculars. If we could hear all the life around us, if we could feel every sensation, we couldn't bear it.

I'm birding with an orthopedic boot and cane at Mount Jacob Cemetery. A woman walking her dog comes up to me and asks: "Does your mother know you're here?"

"I don't know. Maybe." I'm rarely asked this question. My mother has been dead for thirty-five years. She'd be 117 now.

"What do you think the future holds?"

This question is too general for my taste. It seems conversationally unpromising. "I'm hoping the immediate future holds breeding Broad-Winged Hawks."

She offers me *The Watchtower*. "If I leave this, will you promise to read it?"

I answer mentally: "If hawks come, I will convert to your ways." I say "no, thank you" and wish her and her dog a nice walk. No hawks. This doesn't feel like a dream.

I'm on crutches, inside the screen door to the deck, about to embark on patrol. At my feet are two limp corpses, one brilliant yellow, the other washed out. American Goldfinches. I feel relapsed. But no, it can't be: there are no American Goldfinches in England. Then I realize: I haven't been to England in years. Thank goodness I didn't post a report. How embarrassing: to confuse the goldfinches of different hemispheres. Why do birds have to die in my dreams? I make up my own birds.

Least Bitter
Frig-It Bird
Digsizzle
Short-Built Dowager
Evening Grows-Bleak

I'm on my back, wide awake—an interlude between bouts of spinning into a sleepable spot. If I can't go birding, why torment myself? Why read the MassBird reports? Brown Booby in Provincetown, Brown Pelican in Chatham, a tropicbird blown across the state by a hurricane. I've seen all these birds but never in Massachusetts. It's annoying—I picked a bad time to need a new hip. Last year a woman reported a Brown Pelican from her hospital bed in South Boston. I chased the pelican but never found it. My hospital list: twelve House Sparrows, five American Crows, one Herring Gull. Oh, lists breed envy and regret. What, after all, is Massachusetts? Why am I always getting ready to live?

Inspiration! I'll write a romance, a bodice-ripper with Dickensian characters. Bird names. Anna, lovely, flighty as a hummingbird, seduced, abandoned, murdered. Her orphaned daughter Grace, my heroine, pure of heart, industrious, as fetching as a warbler. Ruddy Turnstone, a wandering dipsomaniac beachcomber who raises the orphaned girl. Sage Thrasher, a vagrant framed for the murder, now an escapee from his dungeon. Barnacle Gosling, the crusty, black-hearted judge at Thrasher's trial. Manx Shearwater, a sea captain shipwrecked off the Isle of Man, given up for dead but finds his way home twenty years later to reveal Gosling's evil secret. My hero? Dark, angular, mustached, mysterious, he solves the mystery and wins Grace's heart. Merlin. No, wait, a Merlin might eat a warbler.

Out again, in again. There are lucid moments. It was Peru, not England. Mary and I just came back from Peru. Astonishing birds we saw there. An Andean Potoo swooped screaming in the dark—uncanny sound—zoomed over our heads, and perched on a snag in a spotlight like a rigid ghost. But I don't dream about Peruvian birds. I hear local woodpeckers tap-tap-tapping. I dream finchy dreams. They're back, the goldfinches, a few last nibbles at my fingers, and they're healed. They flutter, fly, they're gone. Someone must have opened the window.

It's natural to make birds into metaphors. I'm my own fledgling. My heart hums like a hummingbird. In sleep I'm a hummingbird hibernating.

I'm at the screen door again, no corpses at my feet. Two weeks out of surgery and I'm off narcotics. Plain old Tylenol. I can walk, sort of. I can cha-cha. It's a miracle! With fledgling hesitancy I step on to the deck. Lovely day. A Downy Woodpecker batters the fascia beside a window. Go ahead, bird, what the hell, it's only a house. A Northern Flicker works on the gutter over our bedroom. His mate knows him by his red mustache.

At our thistle feeder, two, four, six goldfinches gather round, spacing themselves. They have their pecking order, their squabbles, but they're forbearing, willing to share. *Tristis*, their Latin name, means "sad song," but they don't sound sad. The Mourning Doves below them aren't mourning. They're not metaphors. Soon I'll be able to drive again. The booby's still in Provincetown. Wait, I'm getting ahead of myself. Walk before you run.

I hobble across the yard. A radio blares "love the one you're with" and drowns out the flicker. Stupid song, as if a love so easy could mean anything. But it might be true of birds. The music is turned down. The flicker resumes. He cackles at me. A flicker once drilled holes in the nose cone of a space shuttle. I make my way up the street. Behind me sweet goldfinches chirp at the feeder.

Chapter 20

FURTHER ADVENTURES IN FOUR-LEGGED BIRDING

The four legs are mine and my crutches', not those of a mythical or mutant bird or any combination of two birds. After two hip replacements, two knees, two ankle fusions, a hip revision and four dislocations, I know how to get around with ambulatory aids. I gain speed and endurance. Soon I'll be race-worthy for the Boston Marathon crutches division. I've seen some fine birds from crutches. An early Brown Thrasher was working on his latest mix on a stir-crazy morning when I walked Sierra across the Essex fields. One winter's day I crutched the full length of the granite slabs of Dog Bar Breakwater. Mary walked with me to make sure I didn't go over the edge. At the end we stood above 153 Purple Sandpipers, close enough to see why they're called purple. My doctor winces when I tell these stories. What was I thinking? "Birds," I answer.

Soon after I was revised, a rare Spotted Towhee was found in a yard in Rockport. Susan Hedman drove us to the spot. Herman d'Entremont, in his trusted fold-up chair, was there with his wife, Eva. Herman was an inspiration, a Methuselah undeterred by afflictions worse than mine and still birding after 157 years in the field. I propped myself up beside him. Another birder, tickled by the sight of two white-haired, disabled birders together, took photos of us.

Susan and I gave the towhee about an hour. Every birder knows the drill: the waiting, the patience, the impatience, the dwindling of hope, the yawning hole of boredom, the restless drifting away from the stake-out hub, the encouraging reports—seen this morning, you just missed it—that come to seem like cruel taunts, the growing conviction that, except for House Sparrows and crows, there isn't a single damn bird, much less a Spotted Towhee, within a quarter-mile radius. After failing to find some other good birds reported in the neighborhood—Dickcissel, Yellow-Breasted Chat—Susan and I returned twice to the towhee stake-out, with no luck. It wasn't the first time we'd chased in vain.

Weeks later the towhee was still being reported in the same spot. It bothered me, nagged at me, to miss a new state bird hanging around just a few miles away. I had to try again. Mary, just retired as a nurse, voiced misgivings as she drove me to the stake-out, but, wise to birders' ways, she didn't try to dissuade me. "I'll be fine, honey," I called as she waved and drove off. "I'm birding!"

For the first fifteen minutes, only crows were around. It's hard to ignore crows. My friend John Ronan says in his poem "Crows along Paradise Road" that it's because crows are like us: loud, angry, entitled, insatiate. Like us, they're curious; they've got to check everything out. On intelligence tests, says David Quammen in *Natural Acts*, "they have made other birds look doltish." Testing crows is tricky. A crow won't perform a task if it suspects that you want the task done.

Too smart for their own damn good, some would say. Wise guys, bandits, adult delinquents with too much time on their claws for mischief, career criminals proud of misusing their God-given intelligence. It's no accident that a gang of crows is called a "murder." They're not the neighborhood watch. They're the Mafia. They take care of their families, and, sure, they'll keep an eye out, but when you're not looking, they'll eat your young. They've got no respect for life or anything else.

The crows finally took off. Probably bored. Fortune smiled on me. The instant the crows were gone, the towhee appeared. Nice look, beautiful bird, like an Eastern Towhee with spots on its back—a Spotted Towhee. The two used to be considered the same species. The towhee came and went a few times, scratched through some leaf litter, and vocalized with no other birders around to hear it.

I crutched over to Loblolly Cove. Without a scope I couldn't ID some promising seabirds in the cove, so I moved on to the Dickcissel feeder and parked myself. This bird had flown from somewhere in South America, maybe the Venezuelan llanos, to keep bad company with 1,708 House Sparrows. The crows were back. One cawed as it flew low overhead. "So you saw the towhee, and now you think you'll get the Dickcissel? Fuhgeddaboudit." Crows think they're comedians. They like to mess with people. They'll find the eggs at your kid's Easter egg hunt. They'll steal your ball from the eighteenth green. They'll swipe jewelry they can't possibly use, just because they can. They play practical jokes on pets, think up con games to sucker credulous jays, subject owls to verbal abuse.

I gave up on the Dickcissel. The chat was still on my mind, but it had started drizzling. Better not test the limits of prudence. I crutched my way to a road to thumb a ride to the tile store where Mary sometimes worked. She'd doubted my hitchhiking plan. Passing motorists might view this birder-on-crutches persona as the ruse of a creative psychokiller. Indeed, forty drivers passed me by, smiling wanly or pretending to avert their eyes. It rained harder. A crow flew over. "Still hoping for a ride, pal? It's getting wet out." The couple in car 41 took a chance on me. The damp, sloppy dog in the back seat snarled at the intruding crutches and shifted its rump begrudgingly to make room. The couple delivered me to the tile store. They left with a story to tell about this crazy-ass hitchhiking birdwatcher on crutches who . . . what the hell bird was he looking for, dear?

Inside the store Mary was "working"—sipping coffee with her feet propped up and laughing with our friend Dennis, the handsome, highly ambulatory store owner. Dennis joked about the safe arrival of the "soaked handicapped husband" whose wife had abandoned him curbside so she could visit her boyfriend. Mary laughed, Dennis laughed, I laughed. All in good fun. A passing crow wanted me to take the bait, but I trust my wife, and anyway, I was feeling too good to be suckered by a squirrely little emotion like jealousy. I mean, I just saw a Spotted Towhee, didn't I? When I got on my computer at home, I saw that Herman and his buddy Oakes Spaulding had found the towhee just a short while before I did. Good karma all around. I'll never see all the birds Herman and Oakes have seen, but I'll try—on four legs, two, or one.

Chapter 21

GEEZER BIRDING

I once wrote an article, "Birding as a White Male," about the wonderful freedom of birding—the freedom of mind in nature, freedom from everyday hassles, the freedom to go forth alone wherever one might please. This freedom, I acknowledged, is not absolute. It's circumscribed by factors like concern for birds' welfare, property rights, and prudent regard for the elements and, in some places, dangerous animals.

But some birders, I claimed, are less free than others. I recalled places I'd birded alone. On a swampy back trail at Crooked Pond, at dusk, I was startled by a big, unleashed dog and a hulky man with a sheathed knife and a head-to-toe bugsuit that hid his face. On a winding dirt road in rural Virginia, where I'd looked for a Henslow's Sparrow, a surly woman with a shotgun halted me and demanded to know what business I had there. Had I been a woman at Crooked Pond or birding while black in Virginia, I would surely have felt more threatened—less free. One winter a rare Gyrfalcon spent a few weeks hunting gulls at the Black Falcon Terminal by the South Boston docks. Birders came with scopes and climbed to the roof of a parking garage for an open view of the buildings and Logan Airport across the water. The day I went, two cops interrogated two dark-skinned Indian American birders, a father and son from New York. A score of us white birders went unquestioned.

When I showed the article to female birding friends, I got a range of reactions. Some nodded and told me stories about places where they'd felt unsafe and the strategies they used to cope with this feeling—get a dog, bring pepper spray, check for escape routes, avoid certain spots altogether. A few were reluctant to talk about themselves as potential victims. One woman granted my point but considered it a minor illustration of the refined threat-consciousness that all women are forced to develop. One questioned my ability, or that of any man, to capture the mix of emotions women feel—anxiety, resentment, resolve, self-doubt—when calculating the risk of birding alone in a forest. Megan Crewe, a good friend and professional birding guide, assured me she'd never allowed her gender to limit where or when she'd go birding. I would've shown the article to my black birding friends if I'd had any at the time. I never did submit it. What authority did I have to speak for women or black men?

I don't have this problem with another topic: birding while old. And as a certified geezer birder, I know I have plenty of company. I need only scan the audience at a bird club meeting: lots of graybeards and baldheads, not many tattoos and nose rings. Or I can browse tour catalogs and find various cruises, train rides, and "easy and relaxed" trips designed for aging clients who, whatever their skills as birders, won't get far on foot. On our first birds tours I was usually around the middle of the age pack, a juvenile compared to the eighty-year-old Wisconsin farmer who hopped across Mexican streams or the ninety-five-year-old Brit, permanently hunched, who left the van only when informed that a good raptor was in the air above the Pyrenees. Now I'm entering the ranks of the senior seniors. In Guatemala our guide, Jesse Fagan, then thirty-four, was dismayed that people, younger people, had begun to address him as "sir." When he became a guide, did he know he was signing on for a career of parading wobbly geezers through jungles to see motmots and guans? At moments on our tour he might have been mistaken for an orderly who was shepherding nursing home residents on their weekly adventure.

The obvious drawback of being a geezer birder is physical deterioration: a fading ability to hear waxwing calls, a diminished capacity to spot skulking birds, and the ubiquitous arthritis, often compounded by other ills, that makes any outing less fun. By a certain age hardcore listers start making risk assessments, prioritizing birding destinations on the basis of declining physical capabilities. Well, the Bahamas sound inviting, but if I'm ever going to see a Black-Billed Capercaillie in Mongolia or a Colima Warbler at Big Bend, I'd better do it soon. The same concern applies locally. How many more times can I hack the South Beach trudge or climb the mountain in New Hampshire where I found my first Black-Backed Woodpecker? The possibility of memory loss becomes a good incentive to promptly record all birds you see.

While physical problems may shrink the geezer's world, it's the social problems that most irritate. For me the greatest is embarrassment. I know it's silly, but I can't help myself, and so I hear these pathetic stories leaping from my tongue—how I high-jumped in college, played football till fifty, ascended Mount Katahdin without a cane. It's the age-old cry of the old: please believe me, I wasn't always this way. I had hair, hippie hair. I was agile. I didn't need birders' Viagra to get up a mountain for a warbler. "Well, I done got old," sings bluesman Buddy Guy. "Can't do the things I used to do." Or as the Who put it on *Quadrophenia*: "I'm wet and I'm cold, but thank God I ain't old."

Hanging out with other geezers, birders or not, is hazardous too, mainly because of the inanity, the repetitiousness, the brain-numbing, energy-sapping, death-would-be-a-blessing tedium of hearing about the infirmities of your fellows. Thankfully, most birders are devout stoics, but there are always a few spoilers. On and on they go about time's assaults on their bodies, in graphic and gross detail. And you hardly know these people. Retaliate with a litany of your own physical indignities—I've got a supply—and they'll escalate. No, they insist, their pain can beat your pain, and they'd like to share it. Have mercy, you beg, change the subject, tell me about your flight delays, the wondrous talents of your grandchildren, talk to me about birds for God's sake, but no, the complaints go on. Only death will silence them.

There are advantages to being an aging birder, but the one most cited—the wisdom of experience—is not among them. Yes, I now have twenty years of birding experience under my belt, but if I'd started at twelve, not fifty-plus, I could have that experience and still be younger than Jesse Fagan. The real advantages are the more general benefits of retirement: leisure time, freedom to chase a bird at a moment's notice, and, for some, disposable income. That's why these often lengthy and expensive international bird tours are filled with elderly birders. Soon after I retired, a rare Magnificent Frigatebird was reported in Chatham. The next morning, a weekday, I was off early, arriving before eight o'clock. Two other cars pulled up, filled with my recently retired contemporaries. With smug grins we all shook hands. A fog rolled in. We kept smiling. Fogs lift. We headed off in opposite directions, scoured the coastline, and regrouped at noon. No frigatebird, nor much of anything else. No problem. It beat working, and we still had the rest of the day.

So, you might ask, how old is old? Well, that's not easy to judge. The glib like to say "you're as young as you feel," a vague, subjective standard. Some parts of me—my weakness for a good knock-knock joke—are still in preschool. My knees feel 139. Average the two and you approximate my actual age. Bertrand Russell reputedly said that he never felt like an old man but rather like a young man who had something not quite right with him. When self-pity intrudes, I remind myself that aging is relative. I've been lucky to have lived at a safe remove from the stresses of poverty and backbreaking labor that might have killed me long before my so-called appointed time. In Senegal and Bolivia I met ancient peasants—wrinkled, wizened, bent—who were at least ten years younger than I was. In Thailand some teenagers stared open-mouthed as our birding gang headed off on a jungle trail in the noonday heat. We were old, some of us, older than their grandmothers, older than great-grandmothers. Why weren't we napping at home with grandchildren tending to us? In the United States, apparently, old people aren't just rich. They're crazy. They don't know how old they are.

If you're not old now, you will be—an irrevocable fact that's foolish to bemoan. Old age, they say, ain't for sissies, but I'd rather be a geezer birder than the alternative. I'm ambulatory, out with the birds. And I'm heartened by birders well beyond my years, tough, gritty folks still out romping with binoculars and scopes. Herman d'Entremont and Oakes Spaulding have passed away, but they birded till the end. My friends Ida Giriunas and Mollie Taylor have slowed but still find pleasure in birds and camaraderie with other birders. They make the most of it without a whiff of whine. May I bird on with such endurance and grace.

Geezer birders ask: how long can I do this? But there's another question: who will bird when I'm gone? Birding has been called the country's fastest growing recreational activity, but membership data for bird clubs suggests that the core birding community is aging and may be dwindling. Birds' welfare depends on successive generations who care about birds enough to conserve them and their habitats. In pockets of our country, like Massachusetts, birding has become a cultural tradition, just as it was once a tradition to shoot birds on sight.

Traditions come and go. The freedom to bird won't mean much if there aren't birds to see.

Richard Louv's 2006 *Last Child in the Woods* tell us there's little ground for optimism. Our children or grandchildren suffer from "nature-deficit disorder." They don't know the names of birds or trees. Some haven't experienced any animals beyond pets, zoo residents, and animated movie characters. Baby Boomers, Louv warns, "may constitute the last generation of Americans to have an intimate, familial attachment to the land and water." How can we interest children in wildlife if they never venture into the wild?

Some old-timers have cautioned me that such pessimism is hardly new. Just as each generation of literary critics foresees the end of the novel, so each generation of birders warns of the death of birding as we know it. The same fear of estrangement from the natural world inspired the "back to nature" movement in the late nineteenth century. I know only that we all must help to cultivate young birders, whatever their gender or color. It's the best legacy we can leave: not a life list but a new generation that will love birds and strive to preserve them.

Chapter 22

OUR BIRDS

Mary and I spotted the bird on our first outing in Guatemala, by a pond. I knew it right away—a bird long admired for its beauty, warming blue above, clay-chested—but it took me aback. What the hell are *you* doing here? With recognition came the delight of finding an old friend in an unexpected place, in odd company with Social Flycatchers, a raucous clique of Band-Backed Wrens, and a distantly calling Ocellated Quail. The Eastern Bluebird wasn't a species I'd come here to see, and I wouldn't have grumbled if I'd missed it. I left it when Jesse, our guide, called out a Rufous-Collared Robin, a life bird for me. In a flurry with local sparrows and siskins were other birds I knew, Eastern Wood-Pewee, Magnolia Warbler, Ruby-Throated Hummingbird—all "our birds," common where we live in eastern North America. The bluebird and pewee didn't get their names because they hail from East Guatemala.

When I recognize familiar songbirds far from Massachusetts, I swell a bit with local pride. "That beauty is one of our birds!" Morning light catches the winter-yellow throat of a Blackburnian Warbler on a Venezuelan mountain. Two Wood Thrushes posture like street toughs and bicker over turf in our "yard" at Chan Chich Lodge in Belize. Their winter territories, guarded alone without mates, are small, and some thrushes fail to hold territories. I see these species at home every year. The thrushes raise young in my patch. Migrant warblers are the birds that foreign birders most crave when they visit New England in spring. But are they "our" birds? If home is where you spend most of your time, or the place to which you always return after long journeys, then home for these birds is tropical America, the Neotropics, among manakins and potoos exotic to a New Englander. They've got Spanish names too.

Meeting migrant birds abroad is like running into friends you've known only on the job. Some seem transformed. Eastern Kingbirds, so bossy on breeding territories at home, fighting rivals, scaring off crows, join crews of soft-spoken, fruit-seeking kingbird transients in western Amazonia. The kingbird's pugnacity, says Steven Hilty in *Birds of Tropical America* (1994), "is traded for docile subordination to virtually all its tropical relatives, and its territoriality is traded for a period of nomadic wandering." And that Hooded Warbler couple, so tight-knit at their nest in Massachusetts, now barely seem to know each other. They came down on separate flights, hang out in different clubs, and eat at different restaurants. Mates of some species act as if they've been legally separated. Females and males might even compete for territories. Some migrants seem surprisingly abundant, but they're packed into a space—suitable habitat in Central America—much smaller than their potential nesting area in the north. In the Guatemalan mountains, Wilson's Warbler and Townsend's Warbler became known to us as Mr. Wilson and Mr. Townsend, always around, always together.

But the on-the-job/off-the-job analogy won't hold up, just as it doesn't apply to many humans who work harder at home than at work. These birds aren't on vacation sipping umbrella drinks by the beach. They must work hard just to get to the tropics, much less thrive once they arrive. They make energy-sapping trips of thousands of miles, back and forth, often in miserable weather, without Google maps for navigation or travel insurance, and utterly self-propelled, with a self-reliance alien to most human leisure travelers. They're not grumbling about leg room or body scans.

In *Living on the Wind* (1999), his study of migratory birds, Scott Weidensaul calls the Gulf crossings of Neotropical migrants "one of the great crapshoots in bird migration." There are such opportunities for failure. Birds don't die of "old age." They undergo risks until the odds catch up with them. They can be weakened when they take off to migrate. Purple Martins feeding in deforested Brazilian fields—some roost on pipes at an oil refinery in Manaus—might be sick from pesticide exposure. Birds returning south might be debilitated from the demands of parental care in the ongoing struggle to balance reproductive success and their own health. Migrant birds must fly fast and on course, especially in spring when a late arrival can mean a meager breeding territory or no territory at all. If they meet strong headwinds or storms, they can die of exhaustion at sea or get thrown off course or grounded in lousy habitat without enough fuel to fly on. Once reliable stopover links, necessary for food, rest, and shelter in transit, might be degraded or gone. Especially on foggy nights, when they can't see the stars to navigate, disoriented migrants might stream toward city lights and collide with buildings and towers—a major cause of bird fatalities. During a convention at a glass-enveloped high-rise Dallas hotel, where clouds in sky drifted into a mirrored sky with clouds, I found about thirty corpses of Lincoln's Sparrows and Bewick's Wrens scattered on the patio next to oblivious conventioneers chatting with one another and on cell phones.

Through natural selection migratory breeding birds have evolved to migrate at a time that maximizes their chances for reproductive success. An internal calendar sensitive to changes in photoperiod—the amount of light and darkness in a twenty-four-hour period—seems to be the primary trigger for the precise timing of migration and eventual reproduction. Birds kept in laboratories or as pets may exhibit *Zugunruhe*, or "migratory restlessness," during migration season at night, when most songbirds and shorebirds migrate. Birds have also evolved to "prepare" for their journeys: they show a marked increase in appetite and increased efficiency in fat production and storage. The further they migrate, the fatter they must get. Blackpoll Warblers, flying nonstop for eighty to ninety hours from Brazil to northern Canada, double their weight before they leave and travel with extraordinary fuel efficiency. After winters of sexual dormancy, when reproductive organs shrink, the testes of migrant male birds increase dramatically in size and weight through renewed glandular activity. The neural mechanisms involved in song learning and production also may expand during the breeding season. Many birds must shift radically from being active exclusively in daytime to flying at night.

Humans have long tried to grasp how migrant birds stay oriented and navigate thousands of miles twice a year, year in and out, to the exact same places: what scientists call "site fidelity." In one experiment a Manx Shearwater from Stokholm Island in Wales was released at Logan Airport and returned to the island in under thirteen days, flying at least 3,100 miles. No single sense organ can explain birds' sense of direction. It was once believed that birds had some ill-defined sixth sense of homing, but recent research on homing pigeons and other birds has determined that navigation involves an array of factors, some far beyond ordinary human capabilities, including celestial navigation at night, the use of magnetic fields, echolocation, and sensitivity to sound frequency. Birds refine navigational skills in subsequent migrations. A migrant warbler will keep heading north whether over forest, grassland, desert, or the Gulf of Mexico.

When Neotropical migrants like Wood Thrushes reach their breeding grounds, their forests may have turned into fragmented "ecological traps"—places where nesting success is so low that populations dwindle. If and when migrants return to the tropics, "home" may have become pavement, houses, or land cultivated for coffee or soybeans. Whether back at last year's home or in a new neighborhood, fall migrants, however exhausted, have no time to rest. There are groceries to be gotten, a new set of predators to evade, and testy territorial neighbors, often specialists whose dominance of tropical niches may have driven the migrants to start migrating in the first place. Ruby-Throated Hummingbirds may have to contend with bigger, butt-in-line hummingbirds. Migrant birds need not compete for breeding territories in winter, but migrants generally, bird or human, are at a competitive disadvantage in making use of local resources. But the different habitats in the Neotropics off new opportunities as well as competition. Only a few northern birds, like Cedar Waxwings, subsist primarily on fruit year-round, but many northern insect-eaters, like Eastern Kingbirds, become tropical fruitarians in winter.

North American birders on their first trips to tropical America are often stunned by the sheer diversity of birds. Struggling to identify all the new birds on my first international tour, in Ecuador, I felt like a Little Leaguer up against Major League pitching. Populations of rain forest species are often smaller than those in temperate forests, but the species richness is amazing, especially in habitats with many layers of foliage. I've wondered if first-time bird migrants from New England are as astonished as I was. Who knew there were so many flycatchers? We've got flycatchers at home, like the kingbirds, gone by autumn, but in tropical America one of ten species is a flycatcher—from a family that, Hilty says, can "utilize every stratum of the vegetation." To migrant birds as well as birders, some residents might seem plain strange, without temperate-latitude counterparts: the ground-cuckoos following herds of wild peccaries; the sicklebills, hummingbirds with long, radically curved bills that look like miniature haying tools; or the scythebills, bark-probers like our woodpeckers at home but wielding fierce hooks that dwarf the sickles of sicklebills.

Many resident Neotropical birds have their own ways to make a living. Some antbirds are "professional ant followers," an occupation unavailable in Massachusetts. Hordes of roving army ants serve as beaters, and their followers, sometimes including migrant wood warblers, feed not on the nasty-biting ants but on insects flushed by ants. To migrant insect-eaters like vireos, always on the move, the resident fruit-eaters might seem like sluggards, feeding in bouts on stationary, easy-to-capture food, then relaxing with other fruitarians. Sit-and-wait foragers, like puffbirds, simply wait for insects to come to them rather than expend energy in searching.

About half the world's birds have both summer and winter homes. For large parts of their lives they're either preparing to migrate or migrating. Few places on earth, however forbidding—tiny oceanic islands, vast deserts, Arctic ice floes—haven't been visited by some migrating bird. Why do birds take the risks? What pressures or drives have evolved the urge to fatten and fly? Why migrate at all and why so far? Why does one species migrate when its closest relatives doesn't? In *The Homing Instinct* (2014) Bernd Heinrich asks, "What knowledge and what kind of urges does it take for some birds to fly nonstop for nearly ten thousand kilometers, spending all day and night on the wing, until their body weight halves as they not only burn up all of their body's food stores but even sacrifice muscle, digestive tract, and other entrails—almost everything except their brains?"

A winter visit to tropical America is also a trip back in time, recapitulating the dynamic course of avian life and history of migration in the Western Hemisphere. In *Diversity and the Tropical Rain Forest* (1992), ecologist John Terborgh sums up two basic theories of why birds migrate: the "retreat hypothesis," birds retreating from climate cooling and intensified seasonality, and the "advance hypothesis," birds on the fringes of the tropics seeking new breeding territories. "In either case," he says, "it requires that an advantageous tendency to wander be given a directional component by natural selection." The migratory patterns we see now evolved in response to long-term changes in climate and habitat. In heading south, some species, including many sparrows and shorebirds seen in Massachusetts, are not flying "home," for their ancient origins can be traced with some assurance to temperate or boreal regions in North America. When glaciers moved south, these birds went south too, forced to journey to regions where food could be found. When the glaciers retreated, the birds returned to their ancient breeding grounds, where food was again available. Many relive these prehistoric journeys south when the food supply grows leaner each fall.

Other migrants, including hummingbirds, wood warblers, and orioles, come from families that probably originated in the American tropics. In migrating south, these birds are indeed coming back to an ancestral home. Rudyard Kipling once divided men into two basic types, those who stay at home and those who don't, and the same might be said of birds. John Kricher, a tropical ecologist at Wheaton College and author of *A Neotropical Companion* (1997), says that Neotropical migrants "represent the relatively few that ventured northward into the temperate zone, extending their ranges, perhaps because the northern summer presents an abundance of proteinaceous insect resources for the rearing of young, longer days in which to feed, fewer predators, plus the availability of abundant nesting sites." Hilty calls these pioneers the "gamblers," though the birds themselves were not calculating their risks. Rather, the success and failure of their migrations were determined through natural selection. In their customary dispersal after the breeding season, some young birds traveled beyond their existing ranges. While many no doubt died, others survived, found mates to breed with, and thus extended the ranges of their species.

These northbound migrations were driven by both local competition and opportunity in the wind. In Central America various species compete intensely for nest sites while facing a high risk of nest predation by animals ranging from forest-falcons to kinkajous. North America offered a chance to exploit unfilled niches. New World warblers are a classic example of adaptive radiation, an evolutionary process through which organisms diversify from an ancestral species into a multitude of new forms, with expanding ranges, when resources have gone unused or environmental changes have opened up new resources. When food-seeking warblers and flycatchers return in winter, some fly farther south than seems necessary in order to avoid competition with closely related species. Some birds that usually winter in Central America, like Rose-Breasted Grosbeaks, may roam to the West Indies, which suggests, Terborgh says, that their "winter ranges are constantly being subjected to the test of natural selection."

If transcontinental migrants are gamblers, then the stay-at-home Neotropical residents are what Hilty calls "reproductive conservatives." Again, these birds aren't strategists weighing the potential rewards and risks of being homebodies. They aren't the Clash asking: "Should I stay or should I go?" As with mammals and reptiles, whole families of birds are endemic to one region despite their apparent potential to disperse and colonize a new region. Some stay-at-homes lack the flexibility to change their habits. Certain Amazonian birds can't adapt to the bright light outside tropical jungles. Other species are so agoraphobic that they won't cross any body of water, even a river, much less fly many hundreds of miles nonstop across the Gulf of Mexico. The Wren-Like Rushbird, a small marsh species more often heard than seen, never strays more than a few miles from the spot where it hatched. Unwillingness or inability to migrate can have fatal costs. Some species are called "the living dead" because, through road-building and clearing of forests, they've become trapped in degraded habitats without enough food to maintain populations. The habits of other residents remain mysterious, such as Andean hummingbirds known only from the slope of one mountain and seen feeding on only one flower, which blooms for just a month. "For the rest of the eleven months of the year," Hilty says, "we have not the faintest idea where they go or what becomes of them."

And some migrants seem to push their luck so far that it's hard to call it gambling at all. In a woodland in northern Chile our group was stopped short by the tail flash of an American Redstart, a warbler recorded only a few times in Chile. It raised questions we often ask of vagrant birds: Why did you come *here?* Did you feel wanderlust? If there are resources for you here, how could you know about them? Are you a pioneer, are you lost, or both? The redstart's behavior offered no obvious answers. Most wayward migrants are juvenile birds, and the mortality rates for juveniles are much higher than for adults. One recent study revealed that up to 80 percent of young Ospreys migrating from New England don't make it back, compared to only 15 percent of adults. Young birds can disperse a species and colonize new terrain, but a bird far off its usual migration route is more likely inexperienced, dazed and confused in an unfamiliar landscape, blown off course by a hurricane, or, for some neurological reason, "directionally challenged." Vagrants are the rare birds that birders most intensely seek, but the thrill of a chase comes with uneasy awareness that a misoriented bird probably won't re-find its breeding population or survive. We want to see the bird. We know it shouldn't be where it is. We might tell ourselves: I feel for this poor creature, but I'm just witnessing a natural phenomenon.

If the redstart, which breeds just a few miles from our house, is not one of "our" birds, which birds are? Well, the residents surely, the Downy Woodpeckers and White-Breasted Nuthatches at our feeders and the owls in our woods, Great Horned, Eastern Screech, our New England comrades who suck it up, tough it out, and don't dream of retiring to Florida at the faintest hint of cold. Our stay-at-homes can survive winter scarcity, though some, like Carolina Wrens, relative newcomers as New England breeders, might suffer great losses in winters with prolonged snow and ice cover.

But if we define "home" by duration of stay—one human definition of residency—we'd also have to include birds like Harlequin Ducks, Arctic breeders we call "winter visitors." Whether we say they're visiting or returning to a winter home, these ducks are as inseparable from coastal New England in winter, as well-fitted to the habitat, as the woodpeckers and nuthatches that spend their whole lives here. Watch the Harlequins forage in rough surf in their element on Cape Ann, and you'll see why they've been called North America's only "torrent" duck.

If there's pleasure in finding a local breeding bird in the tropics—a Wood Thrush hopping past our doorstep in Belize—there's a converse pleasure in seeing these winter neighbors on their Arctic breeding grounds. When I went to Alaska I wanted to see birds I'd never seen before—Rhinoceros Auklet, the legendary Bristle-Thighed Curlew—but I was just as enthralled by birds I thought I already knew. The Harlequins were far inland at a mountain stream—a stretch to call it a "torrent"—and acting as if they were American Dippers, walking the stream as they searched the rocks for prey. Other familiar species were now decked out in breeding plumage, the Lapland Longspurs now with bright yellow bills and stylish black ascots, and Red and Red-Breasted Phalaropes sporting the colors that gave them their names, not the drabber grays they wear when they migrate in fall off the coast of Massachusetts. A Long-Tailed Jaeger, a species I'd seen locally only far out to sea, was hundreds of miles from any ocean, hunting in boundless tundra below Denali. The Buff-Breasted Sandpipers, pretty but inconspicuous as uncommon fall migrants in Massachusetts, were going nuts. In courtship displays they jerked and raced about gaga, lifting their wings to flash their colorful armpits at seemingly blasé females. I realized I'd never known these birds at all. I'd glimpsed them. Their lives were strange, complex, and dramatic in ways I'd never imagined.

In truth, no birds are "our" birds. It's not just that we don't own them, though people may cage and name them as pets. Birds may evoke our sympathy, but the pace of their movements through time and extreme shifts in their routines give their life histories a dynamic shape radically different from even the most peripatetic of human lives. And there's so much about them we don't yet understand, though people have been trying to understand since Native American shamans looked to the passage of birds for clues about the mysteries of creation. My knowledge of many birds I've seen comes from books and a few moments of observation here and there. For many species the world of birds at night remains little known, though ornithologists have learned that their flight calls during nocturnal migrations are a means to keep flock members in contact and cohesive. In *Eye of the Albatross*, Carl Safina says, "Only the tiniest sliver of seabirds' lives—on land, when they breed—is accessible for detailed human observation. If seabirds studied us that way, they'd do all their research in our bedrooms." Since Safina wrote his book in 2002, scientists have used radio tracking to follow many seabirds' movements continuously over the course of a year or more, but there's still much to learn. We're one species. Birds are more than ten thousand species, and each species has its story.

"We are not either wanderers or settlers," Bernd Heinrich says about humans, in contradiction of Kipling. It's also just a convenient simplification to divide birds into gamblers versus stay-at-homes, or native northerners versus ancestral southerners. Natural selection is the test of birds' choices—to migrate or not—and for many species the choice is not either/or. Birds, says Terborgh, "exhibit every conceivable transition between strictly resident species and the opposite extreme." Some North American residents almost certainly originated in Eurasia. Some Neotropical migratory songbirds may actually have originated in North America. Some northern breeders on our continent probably established their migratory patterns long before the most recent glaciations. Within a given shorebird species, some individuals will migrate, while others don't. Arctic seafowl may migrate not south but east or west to find open water. Cattle Egrets, first reported in Massachusetts in 1952 and now found here annually, originated in Africa and have expanded their ranges to Asia, South America, and North America.

Wherever migrant bird species originated, whatever their destinations, the routes they take have long intrigued human observers. Some migration paths have been described as crooked, illogical, and needlessly long or roundabout. Blackpoll Warblers fly far offshore, catching trade winds over the Atlantic, from Canada to Brazil. How could such a route evolve? With many shorebirds, Terborgh says, "we have no clue as to the reason for their tremendous migration; we do not know what caused it, or whether it is of any necessity or advantage to the species biologically in modern times or not."

How did Arctic-breeding American Golden Plovers come to winter in Argentinian grasslands? And why do some plovers pass through Ghana, where our group saw a few along the Atlantic coast? Hudsonian Godwits, Arctic breeders now much diminished by market-hunting, were once so widespread on the Argentine pampas that some naturalists figured they must be a population of Antarctic breeders. Heinrich calls the godwits' northbound migrations "a mind-boggling demonstration of the epic importance of home," but why travel so far from home? At some point we can only marvel: at the knowledge that guides birds' flight paths, at their recognition of homes they've never seen, at their ability to overcome odds they can't calculate. "What do the bluebirds say?" asks poet Hayden Carruth in "Essay on Love." "They don't know why they wear that rare color, or why they gather now on that wire to fly tomorrow to Guatemala; they don't know, nor do I."

Yet in one important sense all birds *are* our birds, wherever they are, however they got there, and whether or not we ever see them. Chris Leahy, my Gloucester neighbor, has led Mass Audubon natural history tours around the world. He's said that all individuals on earth—every person, bird, organism—share a single ecosystem. This isn't just a figure of speech. When I travel to new lands I look for birds I won't see anywhere else, but I'm just as pleased to find my peregrinating neighbors, like Peregrine Falcons and Ruddy Turnstones (their Latin name *interpres* means "go-between"), both of which I've seen on six continents. The Saltmarsh Sparrows breeding in our Great Marsh might seem to inhabit a different world from the secretive Black-billed Capercaillies of Mongolian mountains, but they share neighbors, like Common Ravens and Northern Goshawks, and I could list another thirty species I've seen in both Mongolia and Massachusetts. Take any bird species, then take its neighbors, and you won't need six degrees of separation to connect all the birds in the world. Take away any species—pollinator, predator, prey—and its loss will cascade through the lives of many other bird species, animals, and plants.

Chris led his first Mongolia tour in 1982, and he now returns almost every year. The country draws him—its magnificent landscapes, wildlife, and people—and for more than a decade he's worked with a local company, Nomadic Expeditions, and an international team of naturalists to train guides, promote ecotourism, and build conservation programs. Through him I've learned that a Gloucester man can have more than one patch. Our Great Marsh, the Gobi Desert, the shores and mountains in between, they're all part of one ecosystem. The birds are all ours to the extent that we take a stake in them.

I've made only small migrations in my life—for opportunity, never out of necessity—and for almost half a century now I've been a stay-at-home, not sedentary but regular in my habits and comfortable on my territory. But in my travels to see birds I've found out things about myself I never learned at home. I'm lucky to still be alive. I'm lucky period: if you ever hear me whine about my circumstances, please slap me around. I might deny it, but I'm rich. If I weren't, as one Gambian guide reminded me, I couldn't afford to fly to Gambia and hire him.

When I think I'm self-reliant, I'm fooling myself. I've met people around the world—local bird guides, bus drivers, street merchants in Bolivia, women gathering thatch along a river in Botswana—whose everyday resourcefulness makes me realize how seldom my own resourcefulness is tested.

In Mongolia Mary and I became friends with the head of our Nomadic Journeys ground crew, Manalvaj, or Man, a lean, spry young man, calmly efficient and creative in the face of any contingency, wise and sardonically funny as we shared our stories. One day he asked how old I was. When I told him, he laughed and said, "That's a good age in Mongolia." He knows about the wildlife on a "patch" too huge for my little mind to encapsulate. I couldn't even find the pathways and signposts. Through a report from a contact in his network, Man led us down a forest path where, in twenty minutes, we found two male capercaillies, big, dark, grouse-like birds with bright red eyebrows. They were so cooperative that we made a movie of them—to the envy, no doubt, of other tour groups who've spent days climbing mountains and failing to find this rare species. Mary and I will probably never see Man again, but we stay connected on Facebook. It's a skimpy way to maintain friendship, but we like seeing the pictures of Man with his bride, then his baby, then with his sturdy new horse on a ridge overlooking an endless steppe where he's about to lead birders or horse trekkers on a journey across his country.

Mary and I hope to visit the Bahamas next winter. I'd like some new birds, like the Great Lizard Cuckoo, from a genus endemic to the West Indies, but I also hope to find old friends, like the Little Blue Herons from our local pond and the Pine Warbler that nests behind our house. It's unlikely that any birds I find will actually be individuals I know from Gloucester. Though some birds have been tracked electronically, birds' personal travel itineraries remain one of the great ornithological mysteries. When spring returns to New England, I'll look for these birds again, and the Common Terns common to Mongolia and Massachusetts, and those Guatemalan bluebirds. In winter I'll look again for Harlequin Ducks to take me back to Denali. These birds make me feel more rooted at home, yet connected to the places I've visited—marshes, forests, and steppes I won't see again—and the people who live with the birds there.

Chapter 23

TERRITORIES

I walk down our driveway to pick up the morning paper. Breeding birds sing on their territories: a persistent Chipping Sparrow by our shed, a House Wren with clockwork exuberance at its box next door, a Gray Catbird scribbling phrases near a crumbling rock wall that marks one boundary of our land. In *The Tuning of the World* (1977), a study of earth's soundscapes, Murray Schafer says, "Each territory of the earth will have its own bird symphony, providing a vernacular keynote as characteristic as the language of the men who live there." These singers are part of our local symphony, their acoustic definitions of space far more ancient than human property lines here.

This is our territory too, a plot of earth Mary and I legally own. Before we met I bought a little cottage here, what I could afford but exactly where I wanted a house—on a hilltop at the end of a dead-end street with an acre or so of woods and three sides without near human neighbors. After closing on the house, as I sat on the deck puffed out with the pride of first home ownership, it hit me that my feeling of possession was an illusion. Birds I couldn't identify then were singing territorial songs. Squirrels chased one another as if *they* owned the joint. Ants and spiders followed well-worn paths across the deck and up the shingles. And there were organisms in unimaginable numbers for which *I* was territory—an unsettling fact I'd just learned from Theodor Rosebury's *Life on Man* (1969), a study of the microbes that inhabit the human body.

Who owns the earth? In *A Country Year* (1986) Sue Hubbell is dizzied by the idea of censusing everything living on her land in Missouri. Indigo Buntings think they own the place, and she can't deny their claims. At Cross Creek in rural Florida, Marjorie Kinnan Rawlings, author of *The Yearling* (1938), came to feel that her right to the land, any human claim to territory, was tenuous: "But a long line of red-birds and whippoorwills and blue-jays and ground doves will descend from the present owners of nests in the orange trees, and their claim will be less subject to dispute than that of any human heirs." Emerson maintained in "Experience" that we're all transients on earth: "Fox and woodchuck, hawk and snipe and bittern, when nearly seen, have no more root in the deep world than man, and are just such superficial tenants of the globe."

A Pine Warbler is the earliest migrant breeder to stake a territory in our yard. In mid-April a male starts singing in a pine behind the house. I've seen a female, as well as drab offspring in late summer, but I've never seen a second adult male on our property. Science writer Robert Ardrey in his 1966 best seller *The Territorial Imperative* defines "territory" as "an area of space, whether of water or earth or air, which an animal or group of animals defends as an exclusive preserve." Possession of territories benefits birds in mating and maintaining pair bonds, knowing an area well enough to minimize trial and error in finding food, limiting competition, avoiding predators, and reducing the risk of spreading infection.

"Territoriality," a concept developed largely through bird studies, refers, Ardrey says, to "the inward compulsion in animate beings to possess and defend such a space." Different bird species defend spaces tremendously divergent in area: territory sizes range from one square meter for a Black-Headed Gull to as much as eight square kilometers for a Golden Eagle.

Some species don't defend territories at all. Some defend only a "mating station" or a small plot around a nest. Other species nest in colonies. Common Murres, which breed colonially on islands off Maine, may nest only a body width apart, with birds continually jabbing their beaks at intruders. Off Cape Ann in winter, a nonbreeding Glaucous Gull in a mixed gull flock might use its intimidating size and attitude to claim a small fishing boat as a temporary territory.

Bird territoriality varies with the seasons, availability of resources, and the costs in time and energy of territorial defense. In winter the Song Sparrows on my patch may stay on breeding territories with little sign of aggressiveness, but when breeding season comes, they'll set up "song posts" to mark territories. A female Song Sparrow holds no territory of her own but adopts her chosen mate's territory and helps to defend it. In many species males defend territory against males, females against females. Territory is usually defended against individuals of the same species, whether sexual rivals or competitors for resources. "One bush," says a Greek proverb, "does not shelter two robins." Through a principle of ecology called "competitive exclusion," two species won't continue to occupy the same niche because one will inevitably outcompete and displace the other. In a classic study from 1956 to 1957, ecologist Robert MacArthur discovered that breeding warblers in mature coniferous forests illustrate "niche partitioning." They minimize direct competition and coexist by seeking different insects in different zones of trees with varying vegetation. But a recent UCLA study determined that warblers may still direct territorial song at other warbler species that might compete for food. Owls partition niches with daytime birds of prey by hunting at night.

In late April I hear two towhees singing, one from a thicket beyond our shed, the other above the brush by our composter.

Later I'll see two males paired with mates and, eventually, females and males with offspring on the ground under our seed feeders. I've never seen the two males fight. I can't tell which one arrives first to claim a territory, and I don't know the territory size each towhee needs. They seem to have it worked out, as if they've negotiated a border, invisible to me, that they both respect.

"First come, first served" is a basic principle of bird territoriality. The early inhabitants soon occupy all desirable areas; latecomers may find likely territories saturated. Males that migrate south in winter usually try to reoccupy breeding territories when they return. In *Animal Species and Evolution* (1966), evolutionary biologist Ernst Mayr says that birds use their wings mainly to get back to territories they know. "The tactics for home ownership are often more sophisticated than random wandering," says biologist Bridget Stutchbury in *The Private Lives of Birds* (2010). "In some species, non-breeders harass owners of surplus real estate to relinquish the extra resources; in others, they wait in line politely to inherit a territory, and in still others, they get downright nasty and steal homes." Young female Tree Swallows figuratively knock on doors and may search widely for a vacant nest cavity. Competing females may fight inside a nest box. Colonial Purple Martins in the East once nested in crevices, cliffs, and tree cavities. Now their best chances for territory are gourds erected by people.

Migratory birds, says Stutchbury, don't "simply size up the forest for its nesting sites and food supply." A crucial factor is whether they can lead a "productive social life"—find a mate and breed. Birds wanting to breed may not respect property rights. Stutchbury characterizes the dense territories of Least Flycatchers as "hotbeds of sexual behavior." Their territories are so small and close together that both males and females can easily fly into adjacent territories, at some risk, for "extra-pair copulations" that improve their chances for reproductive success. A male might acquire and hold a territory, find a mate, copulate, and raise young but still fail to reproduce. Forest fragmentation harms all the flycatchers. Males may be unable to attract females to nest in undesirable territories, and both sexes lose chances for extra-pair copulations.

A towhee drops into a catbrier thicket. A catbird splashes, soaks, and preens in the little pond below our deck. Mary and I have tried to make our land hospitable to birds: excavated the pond, planted flowers for hummingbirds, and refrained from tearing out the catbrier—also called "hellfetter" or "blasphemy-vines," creepers with endless, thorny, tenacious tendrils hated by Mary the gardener but good cover for birds. We like to think that the towhee and catbird are the same individuals that chose our land last year, as if by choosing our home, they're choosing us. Biologist Jakob von Uexküll proposed the concept of *Umwelt*, or "self-centered world"—the idea that each animal species has its own subjective perception of space, its own ability to discriminate and evaluate, its own standard of desirable territory. The *Umwelt* of birds is a world we can't fully enter. Ornithologists have determined the habitat requirements of towhees, catbirds, and most other American birds. We know that, in comparing possible territories, songbirds discriminate on the basis of size, shape, height, and density of foliage as well as the distribution of light and shadow. Birds need places to perch, hide, and stay camouflaged. But we don't know exactly what tells a bird: "This is the territory for me!" American Robins, which have nested in our shrubs, may be more strongly bound to a site than they are to each other. Birds' attachment to territories usually increases with age and with each occupation of a nest site.

Many humans, individuals or paired, lack the resources to possess any territory. If they can afford to buy property, they make choices based on price, availability, safety, convenience, access to schools, and visions of an ideal home and location. Denis Dutton suggests in *The Art Instinct* (2009) that, as an inheritance from the Pleistocene Epoch, people regardless of culture gravitate toward a landscape with trees and open areas, human neighbors, and animals—a place to find security, community, and resources to exploit. When I was growing up, I never envisioned myself buying property, but in my dreams I'd be roaming outside a cabin in the woods with an overlook—a vision close to where we now live. Mary and I can't see the ocean from our land, but from the edge of our property we've got an expansive view of salt marsh and river. I don't think she mated with me because I possessed a desirable territory, but she's always loved it up here.

A male cardinal sings from the edge of our field. Another cardinal responds with what sounds like the exact same song. Male and female cardinals often duet, and without tracking the bird down, I can't tell whether the second singer is a female or a rival male. Among birds, as with other animals that communicate through sound, the listener is as important as the vocalizer. Through sexual selection the preferences of female birds shape the songs of males trying to attract them. In "Vocal Fighting and Flirting: The Functions of Birdsong," from *Nature's Music: The Science of Birdsong* (2004), Sarah Collins explains "sensory bias," an inclination in a female's perceptions that makes her prefer a trait reflective of male fitness: bright plumage (which may indicate fewer parasites), a hard-to-execute courtship display, or a song with "sexy syllables" that conveys information about a male's strength and ability to hold a territory. Females may prefer songs with energetic increases in intensity, a "structure that challenges the motor constraints on rate and frequency range," or a large repertoire of songs that correlates with longevity—evidence of the ability to endure, learn new songs, and raise offspring that survive. In one study of Song

Sparrows, song repertoire size correlated clearly with "territory tenure and reproductive success." A female may sing as well to maintain a pair bond, attract her mate or another partner, induce copulation, or defend territory.

A rival hears a different message in a song, not a courtship plea but a threat. While some animals use scent, birds claim and defend territory mostly by voice. A vocal threat may progress to threatening posture, pursuit, and even physical combat. Ethologist Konrad Lorenz says in *On Aggression* (1967) that a bird's song "indicates how strong and possibly how old the singer is, in other words, how much the listener has to fear him." Individual birds have distinctive voiceprints. For prospective mates and rivals alike, interpretation of a song depends on being able to recognize other birds both by species and as individuals. A bird on territory must be able to distinguish an intruder from a neighbor singing on his own territory. It must learn which other birds to tolerate, which to drive off. The internal command to defend a territory is innate, but the position and borders of a territory must be learned. Individuals have histories together; a bird's response to a rival's song requires gauging a threat based on past interactions. Stutchbury cites male nightingales that "assess the competitive ability of rivals based on a particular part of the song that is difficult to sing well." A nightingale might interrupt a rival with a song that has added "broadband trills" meant to intimidate.

Among those listening to territorial songs are "floaters"—birds defined by their lack of territory. Floaters are often described in picturesque language, as homeless vagabonds barely hanging on, as "skulkers" hiding silently in the undergrowth, or as "sneakers" waiting for territorial males to leave nests so they can slip in for a quick copulation. They're usually juveniles living at the edges of preferred habitats, unable to establish a territory—and often unable to mate—until a resident with a territory leaves or dies and a vacancy occurs. For raven floaters the wait can be long, since ravens rarely relinquish territories. "Breeding in ravens is a privilege of the select few," says Bernd Heinrich in *Mind of the Raven* (1999), "and that privilege is not easily acquired." In *The Homing Instinct* (2014), Heinrich describes Common Loons "scouting—making assessments of both the worthiness of the others' real estate and the defensive capabilities of the resident males—to gauge the possibility for future takeovers." Great Horned Owl floaters are usually young birds that dispersed after their birth and then became sedentary. They may maintain mental maps of keep-out areas as they hear other owls hooting on territories, since there's little evidence of owl floaters sneaking into established territories for copulations. But birds of many species, whether floaters, territory-holders, or mated females, often engage in extra-pair copulations. Stutchbury estimates that "a male Hooded Warbler who sneaks around on other birds' territories gets caught one out of every five trips, on average."

When I read studies of bird territories, I find myself thinking about sociological studies of college dorms or Edith Wharton novels about the conversational maneuverings at high-society balls. These birds aren't scheming and ostracizing like socialites, but their social dynamics can get complicated and tense. Observers of birds and humans alike have to learn the players. Who's vocalizing, when, and why? Who's paying attention, and how are they responding? Who's interrupting? Who's looking to move up in the world? Does the body language of the players offer clues? Donald Kroodsma, in studying birdsong, tries to listen to a group of birds until he can recognize each bird's "handle" or favorite song. Even mockingbirds have handles. "You never know," Kroodsma says, "which bird is going to tell you want you want to know." He's studied Marsh Wrens on tiny territories: "They were crammed in like city dwellers.

The debate over property rights was intense. This fierce competition in close proximity had apparently developed into a ritualistic countersinging, not to mention occasional outbreaks of violence when the wrens would destroy each other's eggs." If one wren's song overlaps another's, Sarah Collins says, that may signal "readiness to escalate contests."

A House Finch pair hogging our seed feeder shifts positions to push away a titmouse trying to join them on the feeding tray. Our regular male Ruby-Throated is perched above our hummingbird feeder. When a female flies in and lands on the feeder, he zips toward her and drives her off.

Territoriality has been called "site-dependent aggressiveness." Birds act aggressively to prevent access to mates on territories and to monopolize resources at specific sites, though aggression may also be triggered by predation on nestlings and thefts of eggs. The thieves, like jays and grackles, aggressively resist becoming victims of other thieves. When rivals fight over territory, the established holder of the territory almost always wins. The motivation to fight may be more important than an individual's weaponry or fighting skill. "Possession of a territory lends enhanced energy to the proprietor," Ardrey says. "The challenger is almost invariably defeated, the intruder expelled." Possession is nine-tenths of the law.

Bird aggression can also be misdirected or redirected. At our neighbor's house a male cardinal repeatedly thrusts its beak at another cardinal thrusting back from a shiny hubcap. The behavior is called "image-fighting"—an attack on a reflection in a window, mirror, or hubcap that's perceived as a rival. It's an instinctive response, not an acting out of cardinal self-hatred. Attacks are usually brief, but they can become obsessive, persisting for weeks against an enemy that just won't back down. Birds defeated by actual territorial rivals may redirect their aggression toward weaker birds.

Certain birds have long been celebrated by humans for their relentless aggression in battle. Huitzilopochtli, the Aztec war god, was often pictured as a hummingbird, and the Aztecs believed that dead warriors were reincarnated as hummingbirds. Uruguayan writer Eduardo Galeano describes a hummingbird as a Mayan warrior: "He glides over the camps of the enemy, assesses their strength, dive-bombs them, and kills their chief in his sleep." Male hummingbirds flash their bright metallic gorgets both to court females and evict male rivals. In most hummingbird species males don't build nests, incubate eggs, or feed offspring. They may use control of a food source to attract females, but after some quick mating they'll chase females off their territories.

But what's most striking about birds generally is not their willingness to fight at all costs but their avoidance of combat. They've evolved to become de facto pragmatists, avoiding battles when the costs in injuries might outweigh benefits. Birds on territory use songs, displays, and aggressive flight patterns to intimidate and repel competitors without actual fights. The repertoire of maneuvers used by birds and other animals in conflict has been labeled "agonistic behavior." The behavior is often ritualized and elaborate, as if choreographed like the gang rivalry dance in *West Side Story*. It can include threats, attacks, retreats, signals of submission, and withdrawals. Natural selection has usually worked to constrain aggression, not escalate it.

When birds do fight, it's rarely fatal, but in some cases, especially when territorial possession isn't clearly established, birds may indeed fight to the death or go at each other with enough determination to inflict lasting damage. In 2003 a young Peregrine Falcon named Louie challenged and eventually decapitated a rival male to take over the Gulf Tower in downtown Pittsburgh. Erie, Louie's sire, was also filmed in a twenty-minute, talon-locking, tumbling-in-the-air but non-lethal battle with a

Peregrine interloper on a fortieth-floor ledge of the Cathedral of Learning. Because Peregrine numbers had plummeted during the DDT era, conservationists viewed these fights as signs of a healthy population: the falcons had recovered and proliferated to the point where they were now competing for prized territories.

I'm watching a news report about the protest against the removal of a statue of Robert E. Lee in Charlottesville, Virginia. A racket of crows draws me out to the deck. The crows, six or seven of them, are mobbing and dive-bombing a Red-Tailed Hawk by our field. Crows will attack any invader suspected of preying on nestlings. A few crows keep on hounding the hawk in the air as if flies off, but eventually they disperse. I return to the news report. White supremacists are marching down a street with torches, chanting "Jews will not replace us." Some are hoping for an excuse to kill somebody. Some wouldn't mind a race war.

In *Law and Nature* (2003) law professor David Delaney calls human control of territory "the primary spatial form power takes." The Confederate monuments in the South were erected as symbols of territorial power. Daily these statues reminded black Americans that white people ruled this realm. Jim Crow laws kept specific territories off-limits to blacks: schools, beaches, lodgings, restaurants, bathrooms, and cemeteries. Territorial control was reinforced by the threat of violence. My mother grew up in Alabama. One of her earliest memories was witnessing a lynching when she was five years old. In the 1950s white supremacists in the South worried that the new United Nations Charter might interfere with segregation, but they were assured that the charter wouldn't jeopardize American sovereignty.

When life becomes too precarious in a territory, people leave for new territories that offer more safety or opportunity. In *The Warmth of Other Suns* (2010), Isabel Wilkerson tells the story of an epic migration in the first half of the twentieth century, when almost six million black Americans moved from the South to the North, where they often faced more territorial resistance. White Harlem residents banded together to fight what they called "an invasion of black hordes" and a "common enemy." Fear of lowered property values was used to rationalize the violent defense of some all-white territories. Between 1917 and 1921, fifty-eight houses on Chicago's South Shore were bombed to stop integration of white neighborhoods. In 1951 an anti-integration riot in Cicero, on the southwest border of Chicago, forced the governor to call in the Illinois National Guard.

Such violence seemed far removed from Park Ridge, the Chicago suburb where I grew up. Our town seemed the least territorial of places. I remember some rock fights with white Chicago kids who lived a block away, and I knew to stay clear of certain ornery neighbors, but my friends and I roamed the yards of our neighborhood without fear or much concern about property boundaries. There were no black people in Park Ridge. One summer, after we heard that Cubs shortstop Ernie Banks had moved into town with his family, a buddy and I searched on our bikes for weeks, but we couldn't find any sign of Ernie or anyone who might belong to him. In the 1960s, when race riots spread across the country, a high school classmate boasted to me that Park Ridge would never become a Cicero because the realtors in town, like his father, would never sell homes to black families.

What difference is there between crows mobbing a hawk and human mobs fighting off intruders of another color? Ardrey's *The Territorial Imperative* remains controversial fifty years later because he claims that human territorial aggressiveness is fundamentally the same as the territorial instincts of birds and other mammals. If we deny this shared inheritance, he argues, we question the very foundation of evolution. Ardrey calls territoriality the "the chief mechanism of natural morality." He sees no qualitative break between human morality and the "moral nature" of other animals. "If we defend the title to our land or the sovereignty of our country," he says, "we do it for reasons no different, no less innate, no less ineradicable, than do lower animals."

But many biologists question the existence of a simple territorial instinct. They believe that territoriality is not a single adaptation but a complex of adaptations evolved toward different ends in different animals with different needs and circumstances. In *Sociobiology* (1975) biologist Edward O. Wilson denies any universal aggressive instinct among animals. Rather, he views aggressiveness as a kind of contingency behavior that is displayed, suppressed, or redirected depending on animals' situations and social structures. Anthropologist Edward Hall in *The Silent Language* (1973) calls human territoriality an example of "infra-culture"—instinctive behavior that preceded human culture but, over great periods of time, has been modified and elaborated through culture into widely varying behavior. Even our physical sense of inviolate personal space—the invisible border between us and others that can't comfortably be crossed—varies among different cultures. People and birds alike may use territoriality to control resources, acquire mates, and achieve status within a group, but any more detailed analogy soon breaks down.

Ardrey also makes a huge leap from aggressiveness in individual animals, whether human or bird, to group territoriality in people, as in defense of the "sovereignty of our country." Bird territoriality is almost always individual or paired. Crows may briefly unite to drive off an intruder, but—it seems silly to say it—crows don't wage wars. They lack the organizational ability, weaponry, and, presumably, the motivation for a systematic, sustained, and massively lethal campaign against the

Red-Tailed nation. Birds don't become heroic defenders of avian Alamos or conscripts in militias to defend their homelands. People have sometimes launched so-called wars against birds that eat crops, but these campaigns aren't really "wars" because the birds have no means to counterattack. They can scatter and flee, or they may be too abundant to exterminate, but they can't carry out offensive military maneuvers.

Human territorial behavior, in contrast to birds, ranges from the personal to the international. "The history of man's past," says Hall, "is largely an account of his efforts to wrest space from others and to defend space from outsiders." Birds don't keep expanding their territories; only humans become imperialists and rationalize imperialism. But this doesn't mean that our species is innately aggressive or that human morality is based on territorial control. Ardrey resists any simple equation of human territoriality with innate belligerence, yet his belief that tribal or national territoriality is instinctive, ineradicable "natural morality" can all too easily become a biological justification of racism, xenophobia, and endless armed conflicts over possessions and boundaries.

Furthermore, territorial aggression in humans has been tempered through both natural selection and cultural evolution. Aggressiveness in animals, says Lorenz in *On Aggression*, is innate, healthy, and necessary, but hostile energies can be diverted from violence into either constructive or harmless ends. One focus of modern evolutionary biology has been the attempt to understand how individual aggressiveness in humans has evolved into coexistence, cooperation, and even altruism. In addition to the fight-or-flight response to threats, some biologists postulate a tend-and-befriend response evolved from the need to protect offspring and find a social group for mutual defense and sharing. There's no denying that human groups can be territorial—the Berlin Wall and Donald Trump's proposed border wall are obvious examples—but this territoriality is not a simple biological imperative. As for our "moral nature," biologists, anthropologists, and philosophers are still trying to puzzle out the evolution of human standards of morality.

In the nineteenth century, starting with the 1862 Homestead Act, our government launched one of history's great giveaways of territory to encourage settlement across the continent. Almost two million settlers were eventually granted about 10 percent of our country's total area in 160-acre parcels. The 1863 Emancipation Proclamation provided for 40,000 freedmen to receive 400,000 acres of abandoned Confederate land, while the Southern Homestead Act of 1866 was designed to allow landless black and white southerners to buy land at low prices. But President Andrew Johnson vetoed any proposal that provided land to former slaves, and the Southern Homestead Act was repealed in 1876. In the next century millions of black Americans would leave places in the South where they couldn't find or hold livable territories, while millions of settlers in the Dust Bowl were forced by drought and poverty to abandon land that could no longer sustain them.

Some birds prospered from the human expansion across the Promised Land. Many others lost terrain they had long claimed as territories. People who destroyed their habitats weren't aiming to wipe out birds; their decline in these places was an unintended byproduct of settlement. The natural soundscape of birdsong was gradually transformed and obscured by the sounds of locomotives, industrial machinery, and automobiles. Now, Kroodsma says, most birds and people live "smack in the middle of the auditory equivalent of a county dump." Our friends tell us how quiet it is on our hilltop, but even here the songs of towhees and robins mix with the sounds of steady traffic on the bridge over the Annisquam, the whir of our wind turbine, lawn mowers, chain saws. Wherever they are, in jungles or cities, birds must compete for acoustic signal space, and they must adjust their songs to the acoustical properties of their environments. Some birds have adapted to recognize songs degraded by competing noises on their territories. Others now struggle to determine the sources of songs and the distance between singer and listener.

Who owns the earth? Environmental historian William Cronon says that the natural world will always be "contested terrain." Property rights are a cultural concept that reflects power in a given historical stage. In early British law, private ownership of territory was effectively determined by the ability to stand one's ground, to occupy and hold, by force if necessary, a piece of land. Most early American colonists were landless people sometimes classified and demeaned as "surplus populations." Indentured servants were, by contract, disposable property. The Constitution of the new United States reflected the interests of the property owners who created it. Its definition of property encompassed people as well as animals and land. Through the Three-Fifths Compromise, a slave was defined both as property and as three-fifths of a person in determining legislative representation and taxation.

John Hay believed that birds "have as much right to the land as we do" because of their longevity on earth; they are "ancestral claimants, with a profound sense of direction and internal ties to their natal sites." The Nonhuman Rights Project is now trying to extend legal rights to other species. A judge in India, in a case involving five hundred caged birds in a market, argued that "it is the fundamental right of the bird to live freely in the open sky," though one Indian wildlife biologist responded: "If you free all the domesticated birds in India, it will be an ecological disaster." The Migratory Bird Treaty Act protects many birds from being killed, captured, possessed, transported, bought, or sold, but it doesn't grant birds the right to claim a territory.

The crows are back. I can't tell what they're up to, but one is staring at me as I restock our feeders. I imagine that, to most birds in our yard, I'm simply a large, animate, anonymous food-supplier, but the crows know who I am. I don't think I've done anything to piss them off, but if I have, they won't soon forget it. In Seattle experimenters used rubber masks to demonstrate that crows can remember the face of a threatening human years after the human frightened them at a roosting site. Why should only people hold grudges? Every few years, a large group of local crows moves to a new roosting site somewhere on Cape Ann, and they could eventually come here. Mary and I don't really want to sleep with hundreds of crows in our yard, but we're willing to share our territory.

Aldo Leopold, a pioneering American conservationist, wrote about the "great human impertinence" of anthropocentrism, the human belief that the world was created solely for human use and mastery. On his land in rural Kentucky, Wendell Berry realized that one of his ambitions was "to belong fully to this place, to belong as the thrushes and the herons and the muskrats belonged, to be altogether at home here." Mary and I have come to feel at home on our land. Do we belong to it, or does it belong to us? We can't will our property to the towhees and crows, but we've tried to make sure that our successors will respect their claims to territory here.

Chapter 24

THE BIRDS AFTER US

One morning I lay daydreaming about time-travel birding. I'd studied birds from many faraway places I'll probably never visit, like Ethiopia and Vietnam. Why not visit birds in the faraway past? I could write a travelogue. I'd take my readers back to see Eskimo Curlews and Heath Hens on Martha's Vineyard. We'd note the date when Eastern Meadowlarks first flew into Massachusetts. Or we could venture back much further, to about fifty million years ago, and check out the outrageous prehistoric birds of North America, like the gigantic, flightless Diatryma: a good six feet tall, heavy bodied, strong legged, small winged, with a massive neck and enormous hooked beak capable of shredding a pony. With a downloaded copy of Matthew Martyniuk's online *A Field Guide to Mesozoic Birds*, we could go back a hundred million years and beyond to trace the whole astonishing history of birds that adapted and evolved into Diatryma and ultimately into modern species.

As a fantasist I could wish away practicalities—what to eat, how not to get eaten, how to know where the hell I was—but I soon faced an obstacle that, even with a finely calibrated time machine, my imagination couldn't surmount. My illustrated field guide is extrapolated from fossils. Unless Diatryma were labeled by some deity, how would I distinguish it from a similar bird? I might be looking at the world's very first bird and mistake it for some birdlike dinosaur. If I spotted an ancient warbler and managed to recognize it as a warbler, it might or might not be the great ancestor of all the warblers that migrated successfully to North America. Paleontological taxonomy was beyond me. Sure, I'd see some cool birds, but they'd be curiosities, too distant to connect to the birds that share the earth I know. I terminated the fantasy.

Another time travel option might focus on birds of the future. Paleontologist Dougal Dixon's *After Man: A Zoology of the Future* (1981), set fifty million years from now, illustrates animals, including birds, that might evolve on earth after humans have become extinct and brought about the extinction of other wildlife. The book is organized by habitats—temperate grasslands, deserts, tropical forests—though the habitats don't include the concrete and steel ruins of human urban areas. The birds, clearly resembling existing birds, all have scientific and common names, though it's not clear who would be around to name them. They range from the fen-dwelling Angler Heron, which excavates shallow ponds and uses bait to attract beetles and flies, to a crow descendant named for its shaggy black feathers, the Bootie Bird, which feeds on lemming-like "meachings" on frozen tundra. Dixon's book is a creative "exploration of possibilities," not a prediction or a warning—our species' extinction is too distant to alarm anyone—and it could be seen as a hopeful illustration of life's ability to adapt and endure, but it's hard to feel kinship with birds that, however plausible, remain speculative.

After Man is predicated on a massive, irreversible extinction, but some scientists now think that extinctions need not be forever. Through genome manipulation they might achieve "de-extinction"—the re-creation of extinct species. A "genome-retooling method," says paleontologist Michael Archer, "could theoretically work on any species with a close living relative and a genome capable of being reconstructed." If we humans drove a species to extinction, Archer believes, we're morally obligated to resurrect it if we can. One scientist has proposed a plan whereby we could watch the Passenger Pigeon "rediscover itself." Well, thanks but no thanks. At best such schemes would misapply scientific expertise and human energy. I don't want to watch one Passenger Pigeon. I want to see millions darkening the sky, in a reconstructed ecosystem. If we're going to expiate our species' sins—a dubious ground for action—let's focus our energies on the birds we still have, before *they* are lost too.

If I could see future birds, I'd be content to fast-forward a century or so, and I'd start with my patch. Are whip-poor-wills singing? Are towhees breeding in our yard? For our state as a whole, Mass Audubon's recent State of the Birds reports provide the most reliable framework for trying to predict which birds might remain here after we're gone. These reports offer a comprehensive view of breeding birds and winter species based primarily on evidence from the two Breeding Bird Atlases, Christmas Bird Counts, and the continent-wide North American Breeding Bird Survey. In his foreword to the 2011 report, Edward O. Wilson says that it's based on "systematically gathered data that was tested for its accuracy using science-based analysis." It makes conservation recommendations where "problems are apparent and solutions seem possible."

The 2011 report designates various species as "winners" or "losers" as measured by the extent of breeding and overall population data in recent years. Of our state's breeding birds, 39 percent are declining. Breeding has generally increased in some habitats including intact forests and even urban areas where some species can adapt to dense human populations. Breeding has decreased, sometimes drastically, in habitats including freshwater marshes, grasslands, and shrublands. Each breeding species is given a conservation status, and the thirty-nine species designated "conservation action urgent" are concentrated in these habitats. Decline of bird life in a habitat usually reflects overall biological deterioration. Birds are often the most obvious indicators of environmental degradation through oil spills, pesticide contamination, and unsustainable forestry. The "most worrisome" birds, the report says, may be the "whisperers," common species like Northern Flickers, Eastern Phoebes, and Eastern Towhees that aren't immediately endangered but whose gradual decline "whispers" a warning about their prospects.

Mass Audubon's 2013 report focuses on case studies of "conservation action urgent" breeding birds. Each study tells a story of a species in trouble. Brown Thrashers, once common in backyards, are losing their shrublands habitat and suffer from continued pesticide exposure, as do declining birds like Killdeer, a representative "whisperer." Wood Thrushes have diminished through forest fragmentation and loss of habitat on wintering grounds, and they're threatened by the "Bambi plague"—overgrazing by deer that can restructure a forest ecosystem. Saltmarsh Sparrows have declined through mercury contamination and habitat degradation, in part through invasive plants. They're endangered by rising sea levels; flooding during the highest tides is already the primary cause of nesting failures. The decline of species is not uniform across any given habitat. Some forest-nesting birds seem to be thriving, but there's been a striking loss of "aerial forest insectivores" like whip-poor-wills, dependent on nocturnal flying insects which are declining through factors that include poor water quality, illumination in suburbs, and shifting emergence times for insects as a result of climate change.

The decline of Massachusetts breeding birds reflects more widespread threats to birds that have been well documented by the North American Breeding Bird Survey, a state of the birds report in the United Kingdom, and the International Union for the Conservation of Nature, the most widely accepted listing of globally endangered and threatened birds. The themes emerging from the case studies reflect a long list of threats worldwide including habitat destruction, birds' collisions with human-made structures, exposure to poisons, predations by roaming housecats and feral cats, and predation and degradation of environments by invasive animals and plants.

The overriding problem for about 80 percent of the world's threatened birds has been habitat loss and degradation through deforestation for logging and land-clearing for agricultural plantations, drainage of wetlands for residential and commercial development, and road-building, among other causes. Birds that lose habitat for breeding territories may have nowhere else to go, or they may be pushed into "forest islands" or "ecological sinks" where populations can't be sustained. Inability to find suitable nesting habitat has been a primary cause of bird extinctions.

Neotropical migrants like warblers and thrushes—"our birds" during breeding seasons—have been reduced here through loss of winter habitat thousands of miles away. Most migrant species have declined significantly in the past fifty years. "Their continued well-being," says ecologist John Terborgh in *Where Have All the Birds Gone?* (1989), "depends on the health of the environment over the entire Western Hemisphere." Bachman's Warbler is one clear example of a migrant extinguished through habitat destruction on its winter grounds. Most migrants winter in Mexico, Central America, and the Caribbean, all largely deforested for logging and industrial-scale agriculture. "The pace of tropical forest destruction," says Scott Weidensaul in *Living on the Wind* (1999), "has been unmatched in human history." Illegal logging in the world now surpasses legal logging. American demand for wood is a prime cause of tropical deforestation. Migrants that must compete with residents and one another on winter grounds struggle to secure territories. They might delay spring migration because they're not strong enough to make the long journey north. "Birds carry part of their winter habitat with them when they fly north," says Bridget Stutchbury in *Silence of the Songbirds* (2007), "not on their backs but deep inside their bodies." Late arrival on breeding grounds means later nesting and lower nesting success.

Mass Audubon's 2017 report focuses on birds' vulnerability to climate changes resulting from "the rapid increase in greenhouse gases caused by human activities." The report uses data on population trends in computerized models to predict climate change effects based on different emissions scenarios. Major effects include increases in average temperature, changes in rainfall, and rising sea levels, which cumulatively influence the timing of migration and breeding, habitat availability, and food availability. The report acknowledges the complexity and variability of climate change effects, as well as the uncertainties involved in making projections based on "future climate data," yet it demonstrates that climate change has already disrupted fundamental ecological processes, adding stress to already stressed environments. The earth is warming at more than ten times the average rate of global temperature change since the last Ice Age. Depending on how aggressively we reduce emissions, Massachusetts may eventually resemble South Carolina in heat index. Sea levels have been slowly rising for thousands of years, but the current rate of rising is rapid and accelerating. "There is no credible doubt," says Chris Leahy in the 2017 report's foreword, "that the earth's changing climate and its living inhabitants are now on a collision course."

The 2017 report refines the conservation status score for each breeding species to establish a Climate Change Vulnerability score and classes 43 percent of species as highly vulnerable. Birds that can adapt to warmer climates, like Eastern Kingbirds and American Robins, may well increase in our state. Other species will likely be unable to adapt or will struggle to adapt without sufficient refuges. Black-Capped Chickadees will probably head northward and disappear from Massachusetts. Coastal nesting birds are especially vulnerable to rising sea level and increasing frequency and intensity of storms. Rising sea level may submerge our coastal marshes until they look like the mud flats and open water of Plum Island Sound. Piping Plovers and Roseate Terns, already endangered, will find their habitats shrinking. Prime offshore roosting areas, like Kettle Island in Manchester-by-the-Sea, will be reduced or swamped. Seabirds will find less food in waters with warmer surface temperature, while ocean acidification, "climate change's evil twin," threatens many marine invertebrates and the birds that feed on them. As preferred prey like Atlantic herring have declined, Atlantic Puffins in Maine colonies are now forced to bring their chicks fish too big to eat. Puffins are flexible in their prey choices, but we don't know how flexible they are.

For Neotropical migrants, rising temperatures are drying out winter grounds and disrupting the synchronization between migration and food availability, between plants and pollinators. If increased temperature triggers earlier spring plant growth in New England, migrants may arrive too late to feed on emerging insects. Some forest breeders like Scarlet Tanagers, wintering in South America, are already failing to keep up with changes in insect abundance. Offspring are reduced, and birds may be exhausted by hurried breeding. Songbirds migrate primarily in response to changes in photoperiod: warblers wintering in Panama can't know that spring has come earlier to Massachusetts. Many North American breeding birds are now shifting their ranges to cooler climes northward or up mountains, where they have to compete with long-standing residents.

The Mass Audubon reports don't present doomsday scenarios, but the most vulnerable species could well be extirpated in our state through cumulative threats exacerbated by climate change. If they lack suitable habitat beyond our borders, some species are at risk of extinction. "Without a massive intervention," says the 2017 report, "it is likely that Saltmarsh Sparrows will be extinct within fifty years." Bicknell's Thrushes, former breeders in our state, may be pushed uphill until they run out of livable mountaintop habitat. BirdLife International, a global conservation coalition, designates one-eighth of the world's ten thousand species as threatened with extinction and more than two hundred of those as critically endangered. Extinction is a cumulative process that reaches a tipping point of fatal vulnerability. The birds most at risk are narrowly adapted species endemic to a limited area, like an island. Some "pseudoendemic" species once ranged more widely, but their ranges have shrunk through fragmentation caused by human activities. Through a "trophic cascade" the extinction of one species, whether animal or plant, can jeopardize other species. Since life on earth is so interdependent, says Jared Diamond, author of *Guns, Germs, and Steel* (1997), "the disappearance of one species is likely to produce cascading effects on abundance of species that use it as prey, pollinator, or fruit disperser."

Since life began on our planet, extinction has been the common fate of almost every organism. The "fittest" species are simply those that have endured for long periods through beneficial mutations, adaptability, and natural selection. But, as science writer Elizabeth Kolbert observes in *The Sixth Extinction* (2014), there has been an enormous leap from the "background extinction rate" to a "mass extinction," the current scale of extinctions brought about by humans' rapid, overwhelming transformation of the planet. Some scientists label our current geological epoch the Anthropocene, a period when humans dominate earth's ecosystems. Our species has restructured the natural world through massive clearcutting of forests, diversion of rivers, depletion and pollution of available water, destruction of oceanic reefs, accumulation of garbage, and concentration of carbon dioxide in the atmosphere. Birds and other wildlife are forced to move but prevented from moving by human barriers. There's no realm beyond human reach.

In the Anthropocene, an epoch of "unnatural selection," Darwinian fitness has been redefined. "How could a creature be adapted, either well or ill," Kolbert asks, "for conditions it has never before encountered in its entire evolutionary history?" Fitness now means the ability to adapt to us, and the pace of change is too fast for many species to adapt. Some "weedy" species can adapt to disrupted environments. Black-Capped Chickadees may manage to breed in urban environments only because of their great vocal flexibility. Other species lack that flexibility.

It's too late to let "nature take its course," as some people suggest. We've altered its course too radically. Edward O. Wilson has called conservation biology a "discipline with a deadline" and "the intensive care ward of ecology." Some birds have been designated "conservation reliant." They won't endure in the wild without direct, vigilant, continued human intervention. In Massachusetts Piping Plovers and Roseate Terns require legal protection, management of breeding grounds, and continual monitoring. Offshore, the Stellwagen Bank National Marine Sanctuary regularly monitors seabirds, as well as fish and mammals, in some of the world's three thousand ocean sites that are crucial as breeding grounds and migration routes. Few birds aren't conservation-reliant on some level. In *Half-Earth* (2016) Wilson advocates the establishment of global wildlife reserves as the best hope for threatened species. Humans, he says, have so violently changed the world that without deliberate intervention "the future holds only more and more loss."

Some threats to birds seem almost too daunting to address, but even in these cases, solutions are feasible if advocates for birds persist. It's estimated that, nationwide, at least one hundred million birds die each year by crashing into buildings (especially illuminated skyscrapers), communication towers, wires, and windows. Homeowners can take preventive measures like window decals, but we could reduce bird fatalities on a larger scale through building designs that reduce collisions, an end to unnecessary night lighting, and the use of glass coatings that are visible to birds but not to people. Toronto now requires all new buildings to consider bird-friendly designs and minimize lighting at night. Cities throughout Massachusetts and the United States should follow suit.

Birds in the Anthropocene are jeopardized even without factoring in climate change, but some "skeptics" would have us believe that climate change warnings are cry-wolf scaremongering. One common ploy to discredit environmentalists as alarmists is to claim that since the most extreme climate change models, mostly from forty years ago, predicted catastrophes that haven't come about, we can confidently disregard all other predictions, whatever their time frame, as overblown and unreliable. Often this claim comes from people like Alex Epstein, in *The Moral Case for Fossil Fuels* (2014), who have a vested interest in promoting consumption of fossil fuels. Mass Audubon's 2017 report concludes that urgent action is required, but it's not alarmist, and it doesn't pretend to certainty in projecting the likely effects of climate change. Rather, the report uses the best available scientific data and lays out the full set of climate variables used in computerized models. The Intergovernmental Panel on Climate Change has considered more than a thousand climate change scenarios. Virtually every model, even the most conservative, predicts eventual catastrophic consequences unless current carbon emissions are much reduced.

The word "alarmist" applies only when alarm is unwarranted by the evidence. When Rachel Carson published *Silent Spring* in 1962, her opponents waged a campaign to discredit her as an angry, hysterical alarmist. But the evidence was on her side. It was indeed alarming that Bald Eagles, Peregrine Falcons, and Ospreys had all been decimated by pesticide contamination. In 1967, when I worked on a steamship for U.S. Steel, our ship chugged down the Cuyahoga River in Cleveland—less a river than a murky flowing sewer layered with an endless, iridescent oil slick. It alarmed a lot of people when, two years later, the river caught fire—a scene out of Dante's *Inferno*. It was alarming, though not surprising, when Lake Erie, larger than all of Massachusetts, was declared a "dead lake" a year later. The decline in our country's pollution since 1970 has coincided precisely with the formation of the Environmental Protection Agency and the passage and enforcement of anti-pollution regulations. It alarms me now that, in the name of progress and the economic interests of campaign contributors, Donald Trump and his minions are censoring, suppressing, and denying scientific evidence of climate change, while gutting laws that have protected people, birds, and the earth itself and have required the generators of pollution to pay the real costs of doing business.

Industrial pollution, toxic water supplies, and exposure to contaminated waste all harm people as well as birds. Often the worst effects—birth defects, cancers, respiratory illnesses, higher mortality rates—are concentrated in urban areas that have sometimes been written off as "lost to nature." Activists in the environmental justice movement, advocating for the needs of people in these areas, believe that their communities are as endangered as any animal species. Unregulated pollution, like pesticides, threatens all life dependent on clean water, clean air, and uncontaminated food.

Unless we act to reduce emissions, rising sea levels will swamp marshes where sparrows breed and islands where ibises roost, and the people concentrated in densely populated coastal areas will be swamped too. A recent Great Marsh Coastal Adaptation Plan concludes that climate-driven threats are accelerating to the extent that contingency planning is now essential for any coastal community. On Cape Ann the sea level rise projected by 2030 would inundate our beaches, all of Bearskin Neck in downtown Rockport, all the lower portions of downtown Gloucester, and Gloucester High School. Our hilltop home would be safely above water, but the roads that lead here would be flooded. It's hard even to imagine what would become of Boston and Cape Cod.

The future of birds depends on our commitment to preserving them. Birds can't know they're endangered, and even if they could, they can't defend themselves against pollution and rising seas. They lack legal rights, but we humans can claim a future that still has wildlife and ecosystems that haven't been ruined for profit or convenience. Our species has been living in a fantasy world, says Stutchbury, "consuming resources on our planet with abandon and ignoring the realities of how ecosystems really function and support life and human society." In the Anthropocene we've reached an unprecedented point in our power to destroy wildlife, wildlife habitats, and our own communities. Right now, says Kolbert, "we are deciding, without quite meaning to, which evolutionary pathways will remain open and which will forever be closed. No other creature has ever managed this, and it will, unfortunately, be our most enduring legacy."

Human needs—and the strength of our economy—are invariably used to justify habitat destruction and dismantling of environmental protections. Conservationists are stereotyped as impeders of progress who care more about birds or wilderness than the welfare of people. But the birds vs. people dichotomy is a false choice. What's bad for birds will ultimately be bad for all of us. Commercial fisheries in Louisiana's wetlands provide close to a third of our country's seafood. The coastal ecosystem here has been devastated by oil spills, pollution from petrochemical plants, and grand technological solutions with disastrous results. In writing *Strangers in Their Own Land* (2006), a study of Louisiana bayou country, sociologist Arlie Hochschild met petrochemical plant workers who had once hunted and fished in wetlands now thoroughly polluted by these plants. Yet, afraid of losing jobs, these workers resist any warnings about climate change and any governmental regulation of the petrochemical industry. One woman tells Hochschild, "Pollution is the sacrifice we make for capitalism." After the 2010 BP oil spill, some residents complained that environmentalists cared more about Brown Pelicans than about people. Well, if we're going to have pelicans, somebody has to protect them from the damage humans cause. But the bigger point is that if Louisiana becomes so environmentally degraded that it can't sustain pelicans or egrets, it will have become a place that can't sustain either shellfishing or tourism, both of which employ far more people than oil companies. We may not turn all the planet's people into bird conservationists, but we can strive to make it possible for people everywhere to live sustainably without destroying their countries' natural resources, birds included.

The birders I know are a mixed lot when it comes to the politics of conservation. Some are activists committed to bird protection as well as educational opportunity, racial justice, and defense of children against gun violence. A few are lifelong birders who rarely say anything about bird conservation, dismiss climate change warnings as alarmist, and rant on Facebook about migrant invaders and activist agendas that supposedly threaten the continuation of Western civilization. Other birders would rather not talk politics at all. The "sorry truth," says Scott Weidensaul, is that "birders as a community have been woefully neglectful of the conservation side of the birding equation." In 1962 Roger Tory Peterson told a friend that birders had been "playing at conservation." People who didn't care about birds were aggressively destroying the country he loved. "We have got to be far more militant," Peterson said.

In Massachusetts and nationally, conservationists have achieved some great successes in the past century: the end of the plume trade, the passage of the Migratory Bird Treaty Act, the establishment of a wildlife refuge on Plum Island, laws to protect endangered species, and restrictions on beach access to protect Piping Plovers. These accomplishments all came about through years of determined effort by individuals and groups committed to a mission, often in the face of bitter opposition and entrenched economic interests. In other periods conservationists have been quiescent. Now, when the stakes are even higher, many of us seem overwhelmed and immobilized by the immensity and profusion of threats faced by both birds and people. In the 1970s and 1980s my students would sometimes ask: What happened to the idealism of the 1960s? What went wrong with the generation that fought for civil rights, an end to the war in Vietnam, and the formation of the EPA? I've never held myself accountable for the behavior of an entire generation—Donald Trump is a man of my generation. I could come up with a host of explanations for my students, but they all add up to one answer. Too many of us failed to persist. The question remains open: will outrage lead to committed, constructive action? "We should impart our courage," Thoreau said, "and not our despair."

I've puzzled over how to end this book. People don't rouse easily. We've heard it all before, doomsday warnings, guilt trips. There's no point in getting self-righteous because we all have failed to live up to our righteous ideals, whether we own mutual funds invested in companies we'd prefer not to know about or react to Trump's latest outrage with little more than anger emojis on Facebook. I'll save any guilt for myself. I know only that if I have deathbed regrets, they won't be about the birds I never saw but what I could have done for people and birds yet failed to do. If I'm preaching to the choir, that's all right. Choirs keep coming together each week to sing as a community and resolve to do better as individuals.

"Nature is not a place to visit," says the poet Gary Snyder. "It is home." Our physical and psychic health is inseparable from the health of our home. If our home becomes degraded, if we lose marshes and meadows, whip-poor-wills and towhees, we lose something vital to being human. In Robert Frost's "The Oven Bird" a warbler sings about the end of spring abundance and the coming of fall: "The question that he frames in all but words / Is what to make of a diminished thing." Our home has been diminished, but nature keeps trying to adapt, revealing mysteries and new realms to explore. There's a story that on his deathbed, Thoreau was asked by a friend if he could glimpse the hereafter. "One world at a time," he answered. "One world at a time."

References

CHAPTER 1

The quotations from Ernst Mayr and poet David Wright come from Jeremy Mynott's *Birdscapes: Birds in Our Imagination and Experience* (2009). Xavi Bou's photography is featured in the January 2018 *National Geographic.*

CHAPTER 2

The quotations from Ted Steinberg and John Winthrop on the epidemic come from Steinberg's *Down to Earth: Nature's Role in American History* (2009). Elizabeth Waugh's *The First People of Cape Ann* (2003) provides details about the lives and artifacts of indigenous peoples. Joseph Garland's *The Gloucester Guide* (1973) contains his description of the Squam River and the story of Peter Coffin. Thomas Merton describes meadowlarks in *When the Trees Say Nothing* (2003). Mark Barrow's *A Passion for Birds: American Ornithology after Audubon* (1998) discusses the significance of Margaret Morse Nice's work in the development of American ornithology.

CHAPTER 3

Amy Clampitt's "A Whippoorwill in the Woods" is in *The Collected Poems* (1997). "Barn Burning" can be found in *Collected Stories of William Faulkner* (1950).

CHAPTER 4

The story of Saint Brendan is told in Samuel Eliot Morison's *The European Discovery of America: The Northern Voyages* (1971). Roger Tory Peterson describes Columbus's encounters with birds in *All Things Reconsidered: My Birding Adventures* (2006). Cartier is quoted in Peter Farb's *Face of North America* (1963). Champlain's encounters with American birds are narrated in *Voyages of Samuel de Champlain, 1604–1618* (1967 reprint). The references to John Smith all come from the Library of America's *Writings with Other Narratives of Roanoke, Jamestown, and the First English Settlement of America* (2007). Henry Kittredge is quoted in Paul Schneider's *The Enduring Shore: A History of Cape Cod, Martha's Vineyard, and Nantucket* (2000). John Lawson describes hummingbirds in *Lawson's History of North Carolina* (1952 reprint). The story of David Ingram is told by John Bakeless in *The Eyes of Discovery: America as Seen by Its First Explorers* (1989 reprint). Jonathan Edwards's characterizations of birds come from *Images or Shadows of Divine Things* (1948 reprint) and *A Jonathan Edwards Reader* (1995). Peter Matthiessen's 1959 *Wildlife in America* is the source for his characterization of Spaniards and Cotton Mather's "useful" quotation. The de Crevecoeur quotations all come from the 1986 Penguin Classics reprint.

CHAPTER 5

The gull descriptions come from John Kieran's *Footnotes on Nature* (1947), "Torn from Glory Daily" and "Gull" in *The Complete Poems: Anne Sexton* (1999), "May 20, 1959" and "Pentecost" from *The Collected Poems of Charles Olson* (1987), "Maximus: Earthly Paradise" from *A Charles Olson Reader* (2005), and Niko Tinbergen's *The Herring Gull's World* (1961 reprint). Olson celebrates Smith in *Collected Prose* (1997). The quotations from Eliot's poems come from *Collected Poems, 1909–1962*. Details about Emerson's visits to Cape Ann, including the quotation from Holmes, come from David Mikics's *The Annotated Emerson* (2012). John McPhee's 1983 *In Suspect Terrain* is the source for Longfellow's comment about Emerson. Emerson's descriptions of Thoreau and their outings together can be found in his *Selected Journals, 1841–1877* (2010). Norman Foerster discusses Emerson's bird poems in *Nature in American Literature* (1958). Forbush's description of the Ivory Gull is in *Birds of Massachusetts and Other New England States* (1925–29).

CHAPTER 6

Grackle descriptions come from "The Voice of the Grackle" in Marge Piercy's *The Hunger Moon: New and Selected Poems* (2011), "The Grackles" in Brendan Galvin's *Whirl Is King: Poems from a Life List* (2008), and Lisa Williams's "Grackles" from the anthology *Bright Wings: An Illustrated Anthology* (2010), edited by Billy Collins.

CHAPTER 11

Melville's review "Hawthorne and His Mosses" appeared in 1850 in the *New York Literary World*. Schiller's "The Choice of Innocence: Hilda in *The Marble Faun*" is in the Winter 1994 issue of *Studies in the Novel*. William Cullen Bryant and Parke Godwin are quoted in the introduction to Gilbert Muller's *William Cullen Bryant: Author of America* (2008). Bryant's poems are collected in *The Poetical Works of William Cullen Bryant* (1969 reprint). The quotations about John Greenleaf Whittier come from Hyatt Waggoner's introduction to *The Poetical Works of Whittier* (1975), the source of the quoted poems. Higginson's bird essay is in *The Magnificent Activist: The Writings of Thomas Wentworth Higginson* (2000). The source for Longfellow's poems is *The Complete Poetical Works of Henry Wadsworth Longfellow* (1993). The quotations from Dickinson's letters come from her *Selected Letters* (1958). Quotations from her poems come from *The Complete Poems of Emily Dickinson* (1961), edited by Thomas Johnson. Susan Dickinson's eulogy is quoted in *A Spicing of Birds: Poems by Emily Dickinson* (2010).

CHAPTER 12

The unattributed quotations in this chapter come from the Brookline Bird Club bulletins. The Brookline Public Library maintains a file on the club that includes a near complete set of bulletins from 1913 to the present, all issues of *Bird News for the Schools* from 1933 through 1943, and newspaper clippings from the club's first three decades. The author has copies of Larry Jodrey's anniversary speeches from 1963 and 1988. John Bakeless's *The Eyes of Discovery: America as Seen by the First Explorers* (1989 reprint) is the source for quotations from Frank Chapman and Nell Harrison. Chris Leahy discusses the plume trade in *The Birdwatcher's Companion to North American Birdlife* (2004). Celia Thaxter is quoted in Joseph Kastner's *A World of Watchers* (1986). Charles Eliot is quoted in Peter Schmitt's *Back to Nature: The Arcadian Myth in Urban America* (1969). Roger Tory Peterson discusses birdwatching servicemen in *A Birdwatcher's Anthology* (1957).

CHAPTER 13

Félix Fénéon's "novels" are collected in *Novels in Three Lines* (2007), a New York Review Books Classic.

CHAPTER 14

Nathan Pieplow's "Why I Love Spectrograms" and Sophie Webb's "Why I Love to Draw Birds" are in the anthology *Good Birders Still Don't Wear White: Passionate Birders Share the Joys of Watching Birds* (2017), edited by Lisa White and Jeffrey Gordon. Amy Clampitt's "Shorebird-Watching" is in *The Collected Poems* (1997). John Updike's

"Seagulls" is in the collection *Hugging the Shore: Essays and Criticism* (1994). Thomas Jefferson is quoted in Jennifer Ackerman's *The Genius of Birds* (2016). The Elliott Coues quotation comes from Wilfred Stearns's *New England Bird Life, Part II* (1883), revised and edited by Coues. Chris Leahy's "A River of Thrushes" appeared in the October 2003 *Sanctuary* magazine.

CHAPTER 15

The quotations from Harriet Martineau, Louis Masur, Henry David Thoreau, Ralph Waldo Emerson, Emily Dickinson, Dorothea Dix, Margaret Fuller, Joseph Story, and Henry Wadsworth Longfellow all come from Stephen Kendrick's history, *The Lively Place: Mount Auburn, America's First Garden Cemetery, and Its Revolutionary and Literary Residents* (2016). Doug Chickering's "Birds and Stones," Paul Roberts's "Preying in Mt. Auburn: The Cemetery and Raptors," and Wayne Petersen's "The Yellow-Rumped Warbler: An Old and Familiar Friend" are in the anthology *Dead in Good Company: A Celebration of Mount Auburn* (2015), edited by John Harrison and Kim Nagy. William Brewster's description of Mount Auburn's hills is in Wayne Hanley's *Natural History in America from Mark Catesby to Rachel Carson* (1977).

CHAPTER 16

Iris Murdock is quoted in Jeremy Mynott's *Birdscapes: Birds in Our Imagination and Experience* (2009). C. S. Lewis is quoted from *A Grief Observed* (1961). Edna St. Vincent Millay's poem is in *Collected Poems* (1956). The quotations from Joseph Severn and John Keats's letters come from Walter Jackson Bate's *John Keats* (1964). The David Bottoms poem is in the anthology *Birds in the Hand: Fiction and Poetry about Birds* (2004), edited by Dylan and Kent Nelson. Mary Oliver's "The Return" is in *What Do We Know: Poems and Prose Poems* (2003).

CHAPTER 17

Mary Oliver's heron and owl poems are in *Owls and Other Fantasies: Poems and Essays* (2003).

CHAPTER 18

Marie Read's "Why I Love Being a Bird Photographer" and Catherine Hamilton's "*Color y Calor*" are in the collection *Good Birders Still Don't Wear White: Passionate Birders Share the Joys of Watching Birds*

(2017). Paul Roberts's "Fall Hawkwatching" guide is in the August 2011 issue of *Bird Observer*. The quotation from Lord Byron comes from *Childe Harold's Pilgrimage* (1812).

CHAPTER 19

Robert Campbell catalogues unprecedented sightings in the *Boston Globe* in "First Galactic Records" in the October 1997 issue of *Bird Observer*.

CHAPTER 22

James Fisher and Roger Tory tells the story of shearwater site fidelity in *The World of Birds* (1964). Hayden Carruth's "Essay on Love" is in his *Collected Shorter Poems, 1946–1991* (1992).

CHAPTER 23

Marjorie Rawlings's quotation comes from *Cross Creek* (1944). Emerson is quoted from his 1844 essay "Experience" in *Selections from Ralph Waldo Emerson* (1957). Donald Kroodsma's discussion of birdsong is in *The Singing Life of Birds: The Art and Science of Listening to Birdsong* (2005). Eduardo Galeano is quoted in Gary Paul Nabhan's *Cultures of Habitat: On Nature, Culture, and Story* (1997). William Cronon discusses contested terrain in the introduction to *Uncommon Ground: Rethinking the Human Place in Nature* (1996), edited by Cronon. The John Hay quotation comes from *The Way to the Salt Marsh: A John Hay Reader* (1998). The ruling on caged birds in India is discussed in the March–April 2016 *Audubon* magazine. The Aldo Leopold quotation comes from *The River of the Mother of God and Other Essays* (1991), the Wendell Berry quotation from *The Long-Legged House* (1969).

CHAPTER 24

The discussion of de-extinction comes from Carl Zimmer's "Bringing Them Back to Life" in *National Geographic*, April 2013. Mass Audubon's State of the Birds reports are available online at www.massaudubon.org. Jared Diamond is quoted in David Quammen's *The Song of the Dodo: Island Biogeography in an Age of Extinctions* (1997). Edward O. Wilson is quoted from a note on the All Species Foundation in the March–April 2003 *Harvard Magazine*. Scott Weidensaul discusses birders as conservationists in *Of a Feather: A Brief History of American Birding* (2007). Roger Tory Peterson is quoted in Val Shushkewich's *More than Birds: Adventurous Lives of North American Naturalists* (2012). Thoreau's comment on courage is from his 1854 "Economy" in *The Selected Essays of Henry David Thoreau* (2013). Gary Snyder's essay on nature, "The Etiquette of Freedom," is included in *The Practice of the Wild* (1990). Robert Frost's "The Oven Bird" is in *Collected Poems* (1995). Thoreau's deathbed words are quoted by Jonathan Rosen in *The Life of the Skies: Birding at the End of Nature* (2008).

Recommended Reading List

Ackerman, Jennifer. *The Genius of Birds.* New York: Penguin, 2016.

Baker, J. A. *The Peregrine.* New York: Harper and Row, 1967.

Benfey, Christopher. *A Summer of Hummingbirds.* New York: Penguin, 2008.

Beston, Henry. *The Outermost House: A Year of Life on the Great Beach of Cape Cod.* New York: Ballantine, 1971.

Birkhead, Tim. *Bird Sense: What It's Like to Be a Bird.* New York: Walker, 2012.

Bryant, William Cullen. *The Poetical Works of William Cullen Bryant.* New York: AMS Press, 1969.

Cocker, Mark, and David Tipling. *Birds and People.* London: Jonathan Cape, 2013.

Conuel, Thomas. *Quabbin: The Accidental Wilderness.* Amherst: University of Massachusetts Press, 1990.

Cronon, William. *Changes in the Land: Indians, Colonists, and the Ecology of New England.* New York: Farrar, Straus and Giroux, 1993.

Dickinson, Emily. *The Complete Poems of Emily Dickinson.* Edited by Thomas H. Johnson. Boston: Little, Brown, 1961.

Dunne, Pete. *Pete Dunne's Essential Field Guide Companion: A Comprehensive Resource for Identifying North American Birds.* Boston: Houghton Mifflin, 2006.

Eliot, T. S. *Collected Poems, 1909–1962.* New York: Harcourt Brace Jovanovich, 1963.

Emerson, Ralph Waldo. *The Annotated Emerson.* Edited by David Mikics. Cambridge: Belknap Press, 2012.

Finch, Robert, ed. *A Place Apart: A Cape Cod Reader.* New York: Countryman Press, 2009.

Forbush, Edward Howe. *Birds of Massachusetts and Other New England States.* 3 vols. Boston: Massachusetts Department of Agriculture, 1925–29.

Galvin, Brendan. *Whirl Is King: Poems from a Life List.* Baton Rouge: Louisiana State University Press, 2008.

Gessner, David. *Return of the Osprey: A Season of Flight and Wonder.* Chapel Hill, NC: Algonquin, 2001.

Griscom, Ludlow, and Dorothy E. Snyder. *The Birds of Massachusetts: An Annotated and Revised Checklist.* Salem, MA: Peabody Museum, 1955.

Harrison, John, and Kim Nagy, eds. *Dead in Good Company: A Celebration of Mount Auburn Cemetery.* Boston: Ziggy Owl Press, 2015.

Hawthorne, Nathaniel. *Mosses from an Old Manse.* New York: Modern Library, 2003.

Hay, John. *Spirit of Survival: A Natural and Personal History of Terns.* New York: Dutton, 1974.

Heinrich, Bernd. *The Homing Instinct: Meaning and Mystery in Animal Migration.* Boston: Houghton Mifflin, 2014.

———. *Mind of the Raven: Investigations and Adventures with Wolf-Birds.* New York: HarperCollins, 2002.

Hill, Jen, ed. *An Exhilaration of Wings: The Literature of Birdwatching.* New York: Penguin, 2001.

Kendrick, Stephen. *The Lively Place: Mount Auburn America's First Garden Cemetery, and Its Revolutionary and Literary Residents.* Boston: Beacon, 2016.

Kolbert, Elizabeth. *The Sixth Extinction: An Unnatural History.* New York: Henry Holt, 2014.

Krause, Bernie. *The Great Animal Orchestra: Finding the Origins of Music in the World's Wild Places.* New York: Little, Brown, 2012.

Krech, Shepherd. *Spirits of the Air: Birds and American Indians in the South.* Athens: University of Georgia Press, 2009.

Kricher, John. *The New Neotropical Companion.* Princeton, NJ: Princeton University Press, 2017.

Kroodsma, Donald. *The Singing Life of Birds: The Art and Science of Listening to Birdsong.* Boston: Houghton Mifflin, 2005.

Leahy, Christopher. *The Birdwatcher's Companion to North American Birdlife.* Princeton, NJ: Princeton University Press, 2004.

Leahy, Christopher, John Hanson Mitchell, and Thomas Conuel. *The Nature of Massachusetts.* Boston: Addison-Wesley, 1996.

Marler, Peter, and Hans Slabbekoorn, eds. *Nature's Music: The Science of Birdsong.* London: Elsevier, 2004.

Marzluff, John, and Tony Angell. *In the Company of Crows and Ravens.* New Haven, CT: Yale University Press, 2005.

Melville, Herman. *Moby-Dick.* New York: Norton, 2002.

Mynott, Jeremy. *Birdscapes: Birds in Our Imagination and Experience.* Princeton, NJ: Princeton University Press, 2009.

Nice, Margaret Morse. *The Watcher at the Nest.* New York: Dover, 1967.

Oliver, Mary. *Owls and Other Fantasies.* Boston: Beacon Press, 2003.

Peterson, Roger Tory. *All Things Reconsidered: My Birding Adventures.* Edited by Bill Thompson III. Boston: Houghton Mifflin, 2006.

Sibley, David. *The Sibley Guide to Bird Life and Behavior.* New York: Alfred A. Knopf, 2001.

———. *The Sibley Guide to Birds.* 2nd ed. New York: Alfred A. Knopf, 2014.

Strom, Deborah, ed. *Birdwatching with American Women: A Selection of Nature Writings.* New York: W. W. Norton, 1986.

Stutchbury, Bridget. *Silence of the Songbirds: How We Are Losing the World's Songbirds and What We Can Do to Save Them.* New York: Walker, 2007.

———. *The Private Lives of Birds: A Scientist Reveals the Intricacies of Avian Social Life.* New York: Walker, 2010.

Teal, John, and Mildred Teal. *Life and Death of the Salt Marsh.* New York: Ballantine, 1969.

Terborgh, John. *Where Have All the Birds Gone? Essays on the Biology and Conservation of Birds That Migrate to the American Tropics.* Princeton, NJ: Princeton University Press, 1989.

Thoreau, Henry David. *Selected Journals.* Edited by Carl Bode. New York: New American Library, 1967.

———. *A Week on the Concord and Merrimack Rivers, Walden, The Maine Woods, Cape Cod.* New York: Library of America, 1985.

Veit, Richard, and Wayne Petersen. *Birds of Massachusetts.* Lincoln: Massachusetts Audubon Society, 1993.

Weidensaul, Scott. *Living on the Wind: Across the Hemisphere with Migratory Birds.* New York: North Point Press, 1999.

Index

JOHN R. NELSON has written extensively about birds in literary and birding magazines. His essay "Funny Bird Sex," from the *Antioch Review,* was awarded a 2018 Pushcart Prize, and in 2012 Shenandoah awarded the Carter Prize to his essay on birds and dance, "Brolga the Dancing Crane Girl." In 2016 he founded the Association of Massachusetts Bird Clubs to promote bird conservation and alliances within the birding community. He serves as a director and field trip leader for the Brookline Bird Club and Essex County Ornithological Club, and as a director of the New England journal *Bird Observer.* A graduate of Harvard University and the University of Illinois, Nelson is professor emeritus at North Shore Community College and author of the book *Cultivating Judgment: Teaching Critical Thinking across the Curriculum.* He lives with his wife, Mary, in a hilltop woodland above salt marsh in Gloucester, Massachusetts.